THE EVERYDAY WORLD AS PROBLEMATIC

DOROTHY E. SMITH

The Everyday World As Problematic

A Feminist Sociology

*For Julie – a pleasure to
meet & talk with you*

Dorothy Smith

Northeastern University Press / Boston

Northeastern University Press 1987

Library of Congress Cataloging-in-Publication Data
Smith, Dorothy E., 1926–
    The everyday world as problematic.
    (Northeastern series in feminist theory)
    Bibliography: p.
    Includes index.
    1. Sociology. 2. Feminism. I. Title. II. Series.
HM51.S638   1987   301   87-15295
ISBN 1-55553-015-X
ISBN 1-55553-036-2 (pbk)

Composed in New Baskerville by Graphic Composition, Athens, Georgia.

MANUFACTURED IN THE UNITED STATES OF AMERICA
04   03   10   9   8   7

CONTENTS

THE EVERYDAY WORLD AS PROBLEMATIC

Introduction

I The Project: A Sociology for Women

The papers that make up the chapters of this book represent a line of thinking that I have been developing over a period of years. They address the problem of a sociology written from the standpoint of men located in the relations of ruling our societies. They propose and formulate a sociology from the standpoint of women and follow through its implications for research.

The papers originate in the women's movement's discovery that as women we had been living in an intellectual, cultural, and political world, from whose making we had been almost entirely excluded and in which we had been recognized as no more than marginal voices. When we started the critical work of which this line of thinking forms part, we did not realize how far and deep it would go. The first chapter in this book, "A Peculiar Eclipsing," is based upon my part in an interdisciplinary women's studies course I gave with three other women, Helga Jacobson, Meredith Kimball, and Annette Kolodny, at the University of British Columbia in the very early seventies. When we started there was very, very little material we could give our students to read. Partly for this reason, a central theme in the course was our feminist critique of that condition. Where I have gone since then in a critique of sociology and the proposal for a feminist alternative has been in the context of discussions among feminists both within sociology and outside. Every development I have made in my own work has been in the context of and has depended upon developments in the intellectual, cultural, and political powers of the women's movement and of women.

The chapters in this book were written over a period of ten years or so, for the most part as papers that I never thought would appear together in public. They have had, however, a coherent course of development. Each built upon the previous. Each took up the themes, problems, hints, and opportunities created by the previous papers and sought to go further. That there are repetitions here and there is a result of this step-by-step working forward from bases established in earlier papers.[1]

In writing a feminist critique and an alternative to standard sociology, I am doing more than a work for specialists. A sociology is a systematically developed consciousness of society and social relations. The "established" sociology that has been built up over a period of some fifty to eighty years in North America (depending on when you choose to date its beginnings) gives us a consciousness that looks at society, social relations, and people's lives as if we could stand outside them, ignoring the particular local places in the everyday in which we live our lives. It claims objectivity not on the basis of its capacity to speak truthfully, but in terms of its specific capacity to exclude the presence and experience of particular subjectivities. Nonetheless, of course, they are there and must be.

II Sociology and the Relations of Ruling

I will argue here that there is a singular coincidence between the standpoint of men implicit in the relevances, interests, and perspectives objectified in sociology, and a standpoint in the relations of ruling with which sociology's objectified forms of social consciousness coordinates. Established sociology has objectified a consciousness of society and social relations that "knows" them from the standpoint of their ruling and from the standpoint of men who do that ruling. To learn how to know society from sociology—as indeed many of us do whether we are sociologists or not, for sociological concepts and thinking constantly leak into the general currency of thinking about society—is to look at it from those standpoints. It is to take on the view of ruling and to view society and social relations in terms of the perspectives, interests, and relevances of men active in relations of ruling. It is to know ourselves thus.[2]

My use of the terms "relations of ruling" and, occasionally, "ruling apparatus" needs some explanation. Though I may make occasional use of the terms "state" and "class," my exploration of a sociology from the standpoint of women has insisted on a term that brings into view the intersection of the institutions organizing and regulating society with their gender subtext and their basis in a gender division of labor. "Relations of ruling" is a concept that grasps power, organization, direction, and regulation as more pervasively structured than can be expressed in traditional concepts provided by the discourses of power. I have come to see a specific interrelation between the dynamic advance of the distinctive forms of organizing and ruling contemporary capitalist society and the patriarchal forms of our contemporary experience.[3]

When I write of "ruling" in this context I am identifying a complex of organized practices, including government, law, business and financial management, professional organization, and educational institutions as well as the discourses in texts that interpenetrate the multiple sites of power. A mode of ruling has become dominant that involves a continual transcription of the local and particular actualities of our lives into abstracted and generalized forms. It is an *extralocal* mode of ruling. Its characteristic modes of consciousness are objectified and impersonal; its relations are governed by organizational logics and exigencies. We are not ruled by powers that are essentially implicated in particularized ties of kinship, family, and household and anchored in relationships to particular patches of ground. We are ruled by forms of organization vested in and mediated by texts and documents, and constituted externally to particular individuals and their personal and familial relationships. The practice of ruling involves the ongoing representation of the local actualities of our worlds in the standardized and general forms of knowledge that enter them into the relations of ruling. It involves the construction of the world as texts, whether on paper or in computer, and the creation of a world in texts as a site of action. Forms of consciousness are created that are properties of organization or discourse rather than of individual subjects.

III   *The Gender Subtext of the Ruling Relations*

The relations of ruling are rationally organized. They are objectified, impersonal, claiming universality. Their gender subtext has been invisible.

For the most part our thinking in the women's movement has addressed the visible predominance of men in such structures of power as a deviation from principles of universality and neutrality resulting from bias and discrimination. We had thought that women would be treated equally in law, in business, in jobs, and so on, were it not for distortions of rational process created by men's sexism. But the deeper our analysis, the better our knowledge of history, the longer our experience of the sources and modes of resistance to change, the more visible also is the gender subtext of the rational and impersonal.

Where there is society, there is gender, and the gender division of labor is pervasive.[4] Gender roles and relations are not tucked away in those zones called sexuality, the family, interpersonal relations, and the like, which are defined residually by the organization of paid work and the institutions of ruling. Gender is socially constructed in precisely the relations that de Beauvoir first identified as those wherein men could claim to represent at once the masculine and neutral principles. Women were confined to the subjective.[5] The patriarchy of our time has this form. Leading feminist thinkers such as Kate Millett and Zillah Eisenstein attend to this intersection of gender and the relations of ruling in their conceptions of contemporary patriarchy. While Millett focuses on the forms of dominance in sexual relations between women and men, she also locates patriarchy in the institutions of government, business, the military, and the media—in short, what I am describing as relations of ruling.[6] Eisenstein identifies patriarchy with hierarchical structures of power.[7] Both indict the fundamentally patriarchal character of ruling. We are looking at a gender organization of the apparently neutral and impersonal rationality of the ruling apparatus. The male subtext concealed beneath its apparently impersonal forms is integral not accidental. Women were excluded from the practices of power within these textually mediated relations of ruling.

IV Capitalism and the Relations of Ruling

This is the condition we confronted at the beginning of this new active phase of the long struggle of women for emancipation. The forms that the power of men over women have taken are located in relations coinciding with relations organizing the rule of dominant classes. Historically the organization of these relations and their dynamic expansion are intimately linked to the dynamic progress of capital. Capitalism creates a wholly new terrain of social relations external to the local terrain and the particularities of personally mediated economic and social relations. It creates an extralocal medium of action constituted by a market process in which a multiplicity of anonymous buyers and sellers interrelate and by an expanding arena of political activity. These extralocal, impersonal, universalized forms of action became the exclusive terrain of men, while women became correspondingly confined to a reduced local sphere of action organized by particularistic relationships. Alice Clark formulates the shift in this way as it appears in the theories of seventeenth-century political thinkers:

> For them the line is sharply drawn between the spheres of men and women; women are confined within the circle of their domestic responsibilities, while men should explore the ever widening regions of the State. The really significant aspect of this changed orientation of social ideas, is the separation which it introduces between the lives of women and those of men, because hitherto men as well as women lived in the Home.[8]

The differentiation of public and private which we have come to take for granted is structured in this progressively massive shift. Formerly common to both women and men, the domestic became a discrete and lesser sphere confining and confined to women and on which the domain arrogated by men has continually encroached. There has been a dialectical interchange between the narrowing local sphere assigned to women and the enlarging terrain appropriated by men of certain classes and ethnic origin and dominated by them. Skills and knowledge embedded in relations among particular persons have been displaced by externalized forms of formal organization or discourse mediated by texts. The functions of knowledge, judgment, and will are transferred progressively from individuals to the governing processes of capitalist enterprise,[9] to the practices of bureaucratic administration, to the extended social relations of textually mediated discourse, and to the productive and market processes of capitalism that incorporate what was formerly the exercise of skill into the use-value of the product. As the externalized terrain of social relations expands, that of the local and particular diminishes. The latter is increasingly regulated, penetrated, and organized by the former.[10] The extralocal forms of organization and discourse progressively absorb the organizing functions originally embedded in localized relationships. The functions organizing work and relationships are progressively leached out[11] of local settings.

V   A Bifurcated Consciousness

The course of thinking developed in this book is engaged with these relations of ruling and with their gender substructure, not, however, to objectify them, but to take them up as an organization of a lived world in which we are active and in which we find and make ourselves as subjects. I learned these relations and sketched their preliminary character in thinking about my own experience when I combined work as an academic at the University of California at Berkeley with the single mothering of two small children. When I went into the university or did my academic work at home, I entered a world organized textually (though I would not have seen it that way at that time) and organized to create a world of activity independent of the local and particular. Entering that world, I was located as subject in a conceptually ordered world in which the doings of administration, of organizations, of government, of psychiatric institutions and all the various subject matters of the sociological enterprise existed, occurred, appeared in just the same way, in the same mode, as the methods of thinking and investigation we used to investigate them. To propose, as ethnomethodology did, to call the ordinary reality of those institutions into question was to threaten the foundations of sociology.

But I went home or put down my books and papers to enter a different mode of being. I cleaned up after, fed, bedded down, played with, enjoyed, and got mad at two small children. I inhabited a local and particular world—the parks we would go to, the friends they had, my neighbors, the fire station across the road, the continual problems of arranging child care, the children's sicknesses, visits to doctor and dentist, their school or preschool schedules, our walks down the road to look out over the bay and the three bridges from the place we called the end of the world. The telling of this world is a potentially endless detailing of particulars. It was an absorbing world. Apart from the tensions and stresses created by having to coordinate the scheduling of my own passage from one to the other with the school and child-care

single / academic Mom

shift from one to another ↓ work academic ↓ single mom ↓ gender boundary

schedules of my children, and the like, it was also a refuge, a relief, from the abstracted practices of sociology. I liked coming down to earth.

This and later similar experiences were organized by the general relations I have sketched above. I could see, of course, the merits of being able to be totally absorbed in the relations of ruling. I could see that for men, that is how these matters had been arranged, for of course my practical problems, panics, and pleasures in this double life came from operating in both worlds across a gender divide that was at that time very marked. These were two modes of consciousness that could not coexist with one another. In practice of course they "existed" in the same person, often in the same places, and certainly they often competed with one another for time. But moving from one to the other was a real shift, involving a different organization of memory, attention, relevances and objectives, and indeed different presences. The strains and anxieties involved in putting and holding together work sites, schedules, and modes of consciousness that were not coordinated marked the separations institutionalized in a gender division of labor. Movement between a consciousness organized within the relations of ruling and a consciousness implicated in the local particularities of home and family transgressed a gender boundary. In the Department of Sociology at the time I taught there, there were more than forty men; the one or two transitory women were on temporary appointments. It was a male world in its assumptions, its language, its patterns of relating. The intellectual world spread out before me appeared, indeed I experienced it, as genderless. But its apparent lack of center was indeed centered. It was structured by its gender subtext. Interests, perspectives, relevances leaked from communities of male experience into the externalized and objectified forms of discourse. Within the discourses embedded in the relations of ruling, women were the Other.[12]

Seeing these experiences as embedded in relations of ruling has been the outcome of the explorations published in this book as well as of others. Our struggles as women to know our world in a new way have had their effect. My own efforts have transformed how I think. At the outset of the enterprise, we confronted the absence of a language, an analysis, a method of thinking. That has been radically changed. Those changes are the context as well as the theme of this work. They are present in the sequence of papers itself. Indeed from the first, "A Peculiar Eclipsing," to the last chapter, we cross a bridge from the forms of exclusion addressed in the former to new issues and questions arising as a discourse among women has established itself on the terrain of public discourse. I can remember for each paper the disquiets its formulations generated, for as each succeeded in moving forward the conceptual enterprise, it also caught up the unanswered and contradictory and lodged them in the overall project as presences standing on the margins, like the Eumenides waiting outside the domesticated circle of the living room in T. S. Eliot's drama *The Cocktail Party*.

The shadowy yet powerful contradictions evoked by chapter 1 are ones I now know better how to see. For I came to understand as I wrote, and because I wrote, that the critique claiming to be from a category of women in general had its own class and racial subtexts. The subtexts of class I have addressed in various ways in this book, particularly in chapter 3, "The Everyday World as Problematic," though I am not yet satisfied.[13] And although the methods of thinking sociologically, that are developed here are intended to create a site within which any woman (perhaps indeed any man) can speak from and of her experience and do not commit us to a particular set of feminist relevances, I have not yet understood fully the intersection of racial oppression with the gender organization of the relations of ruling. Hence the contradictions of class and racial oppression are still unsatisfied and are insistent presences speaking from beyond the text but not yet in it.

The enterprise represented by and explicated in these chapters proposes to make a sociology from the standpoint of women.[14] The sociology I learned and that organized the cognitive domain of my work at the university defined and interpreted the world of home and family, but there was no talking back. I have wanted to make an account and analysis of society and social relations that are not only *about* women but that make it possible for us to look at any or all aspects of a society from where we are actually located, embodied, in the local historicity and particularities of our lived worlds. In the sociology I knew how to think when I had finished my graduate training, I could look at the everyday world, at home and family, from a standpoint within the gendered relations of ruling, in which women were other or object. I could reflect on and interpret what I was doing as mother in categories and concepts that decentered my experience. I have wanted to make a sociology that will look back and talk back. This is the enterprise this book lays out. It asks the reader to try another method of thinking than those with which we are familiar, one I have learned to practice in the course of developing this work. Of course this method does not come from nowhere. It has both its visible and invisible preceptors from whom, in the long course of trying to find a different way of thinking sociologically, I have learned. The most important among them have been George Herbert Mead, Maurice Merleau-Ponty, Karl

Marx, and Harold Garfinkel, though there have been many others. I have not hesitated to learn from men; I could not imagine beginning all over again, and I learned, quite unscrupulously, from anyone whose work was of use to me in discovering an alternative to the methods of thinking I had been stuck with. But I am not a symbolic interactionist, nor a phenomenological sociologist, nor a Marxist sociologist, nor an ethnomethodologist. The sociological strategy I have developed does not belong to or subject itself to the interpretive procedures of any particular school of sociology. It is constrained by the project of creating a way of seeing, from where we actually live, into the powers, processes, and relations that organize and determine the everyday context of that seeing.

VI The Order of the Book

The approach I have tried to develop is above all conscious that we are not doing a science that can be treated in abstraction from the rest of society (indeed the possibility of such a science is a myth). Our intellectual work and the ways in which we can make a society conscious of itself are very much a part of that society and situated in institutional contexts we did not make, though we are working to be part of their remaking.

Chapter 1, "A Peculiar Eclipsing," creates a context within which the more specifically sociological orientation of what follows is to be read, addressing the issue of women's silencing in the relations mediated by writing and print in which men have dominated. It is the first in the series to formulate the problem of an intellectual world that claims universality, but is in actuality centered among men. It focuses upon the historical silencing of women, and how it appears in the everyday contexts of our speaking with men. In making visible the ways in which we were and are confined by the authority of the male voice, it also proposes to seize authority for our own voices so that we can both speak and be heard among women.

The second and third parts of the book are concerned more directly with sociology. The second, "Finding and Writing a Sociology for Women," contains two long chapters. In the first of those, "A Sociology for Women," sociology is examined as a constituent of patriarchal relations of ruling. In its texts, women appear as objects. An alternative standpoint of women is developed with which to inscribe women as subjects within the texts of sociological inquiry. I am looking for a *sociology*, not just topics within sociology, and therefore for a standpoint that will look out at the world at large and not just at those pieces of it of immediate relevance to women. In this chapter I propose the problematic with which I have worked since then, the problematic of the everyday world. It is a simple idea and wholly concurrent with our experience. It points to the fact that the everyday world as the matrix of our experience is organized by relations tying it into larger processes in the world as well as by locally organized practices. A feminist mode of inquiry might then begin with women's experience from women's standpoint and explore how it is shaped in the extended relations of larger social and political relations. The ontological and political grounding of such an enterprise in our relations with those of and from whose experience we might speak is further developed in chapter 3, "The Everyday World as Problematic."

The third part, "Research Strategies for a Sociology for Women," also contains two chapters, "Institutional Ethnography" and "Researching the Everyday World as Problematic." They convert the general ideas of the previous chapters into specific research practices. Of course this can be done in more than one way. But in my time as a sociologist, I have seen many bold critiques of sociology that have abandoned their project at the point of spelling out a research practice flowing from the proposal. I wanted to track through on the lines of thinking I had been doing to a research approach that would realize them. The chapter titled "Institutional Ethnography" is a general proposal for a method of work; following it is a more specific account of a research strategy used in a research project on which I have been working.

The final part returns us to the "Textual Politics" of feminism with which the book opened, to reflect on the implications for the women's movement of this critique of and proposed alternative to the patriarchal forms in which we have been and are made conscious of our society. Here I try to bring into focus some of the ambiguities and contradictions created for the development of our discourses by the institutional contexts of ruling. I want to keep in mind for myself and others that a radical critique and rewriting of sociology can be institutionally contained, to remain, in the old and telling phrase, "merely academic."

I have emphasized that the chapters of the book originated as a sequence of papers. Ideas laid out in one paper are reworked further down the line. Some repetitions have been eliminated, but in other cases the repetitions coexist like a palimpsest. It is as if the next attempt at formulation is written over the previous one. Such problems are indeed a necessary effect of the method the book recommends. Taking a standpoint outside the textually mediated discourses of social science has meant renouncing theoretical projects that seek full development and coherence prior to an encounter with the world. The method of inquiry recommended here adopts an inverse strategy. It works its way forward through an interplay between what the sociologist already knows how to think and an engagement with the world that teaches her to rework her formulations if they are to explicate actual relations and organization. So I have worked my way forward by moving from the actualities I could begin to see, to formulations intended to explicate them, and back again. So there are real shifts in how some topics are conceptualized at different stages in the sequence. Repetitions, apart from those retained for purposes of continuity within a chapter, are likely to represent some modifications of how the same topic had previously been addressed.

VII Appreciations

The working out of this line of thinking has not been done in solitude. My thoughts have benefited from my ongoing dialogue with the women's movement. I have talked with women about these ideas and have learned from them; I have also always been in subterranean dialogue with women. This book enters and speaks to the women's movement. Within it as general context, I owe a special debt to those I have already mentioned above, with whom I worked on the first women's studies course at the University of British Columbia. I owe a debt to those members of a seminar on my own work that I taught as Kreeger-Wolf Professor at Northwestern University in 1983 and to my longtime friend Arlene Kaplan Daniels, who sustained me in more senses than one. I owe another and special kind of debt to those who have been my companions in dialogue during the time I have been working on these papers—Himani Bannerji, Marie Campbell, Marguerite Cassin, Marj DeVault, Tim Diamond, Alison Griffith, Nancy Jackson, Adele Mueller, Roxana Ng, Marilee Reimer, George Smith, and Yoko Ueda. Nancy Jackson contributed specifically to this book by reading and commenting on parts of it in progress, and I thank her for her careful reading and valuable comments. I have also appreciated greatly the tactful and insightful editorial work of Nancy Waring and the gains in clarity brought to the text by Kathryn Gohl's careful copy-editing.

Notes

1. It may be helpful to know approximately when different parts of the book were written. The first chapter, "A Peculiar Eclipsing," was originally formulated in the early seventies; chapter 2, "A Sociology for Women," was written in 1977; chapter 4, "Institutional Ethnography," in 1983; chapter 3, "The Everyday World as Problematic," in its present form (it exists in an earlier sketch dating from 1981), chapter 5, "Researching the Everyday World as Problematic," and chapter 6, "Beyond Methodology: Institutionalization and Its Subversion," were all written in the nine months preceding the delivery of the final manuscript to the publisher.
2. Edward W. Said's *Orientalism* (New York: Vintage Books, 1979) is valuable reading for feminists. It analyzes the historical development and character of a body of *systematic* knowledge (as well as poetry and art) in the West that, from the standpoint of a Western imperium, constitutes the Orient and the oriental as other.
3. This collection of papers runs alongside, and is in many ways in dialogue with, a similar series of papers exploring the textually mediated relations of ruling as a social organization of knowledge.
4. Sandra Harding, "Why has the sex/gender system become visible only now?" in Sandra Harding and Merrill Hintikka, eds., *Discovering Reality: Feminist Perspectives on Epistemology, Metaphysics, Methodology, and Philosophy of Science* (Dordrecht, Holland: D. Reidel Publishing, 1983).
5. Simone de Beauvoir, *The Second Sex* (New York: Bantam Books, 1961), p. xv.
6. Kate Millett, *Sexual Politics* (New York: Avon Books, 1971).
7. Zillah R. Eisenstein, "Developing a theory of capitalist patriarchy," in Zillah R. Eisenstein, ed., *Capitalist Patriarchy and the Case for Socialist Feminism* (New York: Monthly Review Press, 1979), pp. 5–40.
8. Alice Clark, *The Working Life of Women in the Seventeenth Century* (London: George Routledge and Sons, 1919), p. 303.
9. Karl Marx, *Capital: A Theory of Political Economy* (New York: Vintage Books, 1977), 1:482.
10. These are the worlds of *Gemeinschaft* and *Gesellschaft* (Ferdinand Tonnies, *Community and Association* [London: Routledge and Kegan Paul, 1955]), the contrast between relationships oriented toward particular individuals and the impersonal, competitive, calculative relationships of the market viewed as in a dynamic interaction in which the latter progressively encroaches upon the former.
11. A process of removing soluble matter out of some material by making liquid percolate through it. The coffee we drink is (in some processes) leached out of the ground coffee beans, leaving the grounds behind. If you like dictionaries, there are some political puns embedded in this metaphor.
12. The otherness of women as an essential structurer of (male) discourse has been explored in contemporary French thinking as well as in the work of thinkers such as Derrida. Alice A. Jardine, in *Gynesis: Configurations of Woman and Modernity* (Ithaca: Cornell University Press, 1985), has made a brilliant analysis of the necessary otherness of women in the "configurations" of modernity.

13. I have also addressed the issue of women, class, and family in a lengthy paper of that title in Varda Burstyn and Dorothy E. Smith, *Women, Class, Family and State* (Toronto: Garamond Press, 1985).
14. A number of feminist thinkers, apparently independently of one another, have adopted the device of a feminist or women's standpoint to address epistemological issues raised by feminism. They include Jane Flax, "Political philosophy and the patriarchal unconscious: A psychoanalytic perspective on epistemology and metaphysics," in Sandra Harding and Merrill B. Hintikka, eds., *Discovering Reality: Feminist Perspectives on Epistemology, Metaphysics, Methodology, and Philosophy of Science* (Dordrecht, Holland: D. Reidel Publishing Co., 1983), pp. 245–81; Nancy Fraser, whose position in a forthcoming publication has been discussed by Terry Winant in "The feminist standpoint: A matter of language," in *Hypatia: A Journal of Feminist Philosophy* 2, no. 1 (Winter 1987): pp. 123–48; Nancy Hartsock, "The Feminist standpoint: Developing the ground for a specifically feminist historial materialism," in Harding and Hintikka, eds., op.cit., pp. 283–310. My own conception was developed before I had read the work of other feminists who have made use of the same concept. My conception differs from others in locating women's standpoint outside discourse-in-texts. Allison Jaggar in *Feminist Politics and Human Nature* (Totowa, N.J.: Rowman and Allanheld, and Brighton, England: The Harvester Press, 1983), pp. 369–89, Sandra Harding, *The Science Question in Feminism* (Ithaca: Cornell University Press, 1986), and Terry Winant, op.cit., provide important critical treatments of the concept of a feminist or women's standpoint in its various versions.

PART ONE

Opening a Space for Our Speech

Chapter 1, "A Peculiar Eclipsing: Women's Exclusion from Man's Culture," was developed from my introductory lecture to the sociological section of an interdisciplinary course in women's studies at the University of British Columbia around 1972. It has been through a number of manifestations in a number of forms since that time, a first version being published in International Women's Year (1975) by the *Canadian Journal of Sociology and Anthropology.*[1] This version was published in 1978 by the *Women's Studies International Quarterly.*[2] Politically it has been one of the most effective pieces of writing I have done. I cannot number the speeches I have given based on it, in many, many contexts. I have spoken on these topics in academic settings and, suitably modified, in other settings as well—to women in trade unions, women teachers, women in the rural interior of British Columbia and in many other sites. The topic was always relevant, showing less the significance of the paper than the ubiquity of the effects I was describing. When I first spoke to trade union women, I spent some time at their conference to get examples typical of trade union settings rather than academic settings. I had no difficulty in doing so.

This chapter speaks now from an earlier phase of the women's movement, before we were as aware as we are now of the practices, our own and men's, that depreciate what we say and write both for men and for ourselves and each other. Nonetheless, it situates these experiences in the more general context of the practices of our exclusion as women from the textually mediated organization of power that has come to predominate in our kind of society. It addresses the intellectual and cultural exclusions that are one aspect of the gender subtext of the relations of ruling, of which I've written in a prefatory fashion in the introduction to this book. It shows the formation of an intellectual and cultural world centered on men from which women have been consciously excluded. It shows the formation of thought containing this deep bias yet representing itself as universal and objective. Some of these defects have been remedied by the great renaissance of feminist scholarship of which this work is part. I have made some reference in footnotes to this new wealth of feminist thinking and research, though I have not, of course, attempted a comprehensive treatment, which would necessarily go way outside the intention of this book and the capacity of its author.

The fifth section of this chapter, "The Authority of the Male Voice," also illustrates a method I have made a central feature of the sociology worked out in the chapters that follow. For while the history and contemporary institutional forms of women's exclusion are addressed at a general level, they are also addressed at the level of the everyday and immediate where the greater authority of men as speakers for one another and for women and the practices through which they arrogate control of the topics of conversation ensure the perpetuation of that state of affairs. To break out of our own complicity in such practices, and out of the ways in which we have joined in silencing ourselves through denying authority to our own voices as well as to those of other women, is the first and essential step to the making of an intellectual and cultural discourse in which we are subjects and speak for ourselves. Thus this chapter establishes the first step toward giving that proposal practical effect in a sociological discourse developing a systematic consciousness of society and social relations from the standpoint of women.

Notes

1. It was published under the title "Ideological structures and how women are excluded," *Canadian Review of Sociology and Anthropology,* November 1975.
2. "A peculiar eclipsing: Women's exclusion from man's culture," *Women's Studies International Quarterly* 1 (1978): 281–95. Thanks to Pergamon Press, New York, for their permission to reprint this paper. The phrase "a peculiar eclipsing" is Tillie Olsen's. See her "One out of twelve: Women who are writers in our century," in Tillie Olsen, *Silences* (New York: Delacorte Press/Seymour Lawrence, 1978), pp. 22–46, 40.

A Peculiar Eclipsing:
Women's Exclusion from Man's Culture

1

I Texts, Talk, and Power: Women's Exclusion

The relations of ruling in our kind of society are mediated by texts, by words, numbers, and images on paper, in computers, or on TV and movie screens. Texts are the primary medium (though not the substance) of power. The work of administration, of management, of government is a communicative work. Organizational and political processes are forms of action coordinated textually and getting done in words. It is an ideologically structured mode of action—images, vocabularies, concepts, abstract terms of knowledge are integral to the practice of power, to getting things done. Further, the ways in which we think about ourselves and one another and about our society—our images of how we should look, our homes, our lives, even our inner worlds—are given shape and distributed by the specialized work of people in universities and schools, in television, radio and newspapers, in advertising agencies, in book publishing and other organizations forming the "ideological apparatuses" of the society.[1]

Being excluded, as women have been, from the making of ideology, of knowledge, and of culture means that our experience, our interests, our ways of knowing the world have not been represented in the organization of our ruling nor in the systematically developed knowledge that has entered into it. We explore in this chapter the history of this exclusion as a conscious and often a cruel practice; we look at aspects of its contemporary reproduction in the way women are distributed in an educational system that both produces and disseminates knowledge, culture, and ideology; we examine how these larger structures construct an authority for the writing and speech of individual men, which in the ordinary settings of our lives gives weight and influence to men and re-creates the circles in which men attend to what men have to say and carry forward the interests and perspectives of men. But we have assented to this authority and can withdraw our assent. Indeed this is essential to the making of knowledge, culture, and ideology based on the experiences and relevances of women.

This way of organizing society began to develop in western Europe some four hundred or five hundred years ago. It is an integral aspect of the development of a capitalist mode of production. Women have been at work in its making as much as men, though their work has been of a different kind and location. But women have been largely excluded from the work of producing the forms of thought and the images and symbols in which thought is expressed and ordered. We can imagine women's exclusion organized by the formation of a circle among men who attend to and treat as significant only what men say. The circle of men whose writing and talk was significant to each other extends backward as far as our records reach. What men were doing was relevant to men, was written by men about men for men. Men listened and listened to what one another said.

This is how a tradition is formed. A way of thinking develops in this discourse through the medium of the written and printed word as well as in speech. It has questions, solutions, themes, styles, standards, ways of looking at the world. These are formed as the circle of those present builds on the work of the past. From these circles women have been excluded or admitted only by a special license granted to a woman as an individual and never as a representative of her sex. Throughout this period in which ideologies become of increasing importance, first as a mode of thinking, legitimating and sanctioning a social order, and then as integral in the organization of society, women have been deprived of the means to participate in creating forms of thought relevant or adequate to express their own experience or to define and raise social consciousness about their situation and concerns. They have never controlled the material or social means to the making of a tradition among themselves or to acting as equals in the ongoing discourse of intellectuals. They have had no economic status independent of men. They have not had, until very recently, access to the educational skills necessary to develop, sustain, and participate in the making of a common culture.

Women, have, of course, had access to and used the limited and largely domestic zone of women's magazines, television programs, women's novels, poetry, soap operas, and the like. But this is a limited zone. It follows the contours of their restricted role in the society. The universe of ideas, images, and themes—the symbolic modes that are the general currency of thought—have been either produced by men or controlled by them. In so far as women's work and experience have been entered into it, it has been on terms decided by men and because it has been approved by men.

This is why women have had no written history until very recently, no share in making religious thoughts, no political philosophy, no representation of society from their view, no poetic tradition, no tradition in art.

II Men's Standpoint Is Represented as Universal

It is important to recognize that in this kind of society most people do not participate in the making of culture. The forms of thought and images we use do not arise directly or spontaneously out of people's everyday lived relationships. Rather, they are the product of the work of specialists occupying influential positions in the ideological apparatus (the educational system, communications, etc.). Our culture does not arise spontaneously; it is "manufactured."

The ideological apparatuses are part of the larger relations of ruling the society, the relations that put it together, coordinate its work, manage its economic processes, generally keep it running, and regulate and control it. The making and dissemination of the forms of thought we make use of to think about ourselves and our society are part of the relations of ruling and hence originate in positions of power. These positions of power are occupied by men almost exclusively, which means that our forms of thought put together a view of the world from a place women do not occupy. The means women have had available to them to think, image, and make actionable their experience have been made for us and not by us. It means that our experience has not been represented in the making of our culture. There is a gap between where we are and the means we have to express and act. It means that the concerns, interests, and experiences forming "our" culture are those of men in positions of dominance whose perspectives are built on the silence of women (and of others).

As a result the perspectives, concerns, interests of only one sex and one class are represented as general. Only one sex and class are directly and actively involved in producing, debating, and developing its ideas, in creating its art, in forming its medical and psychological conceptions, in framing its laws, its political principles, its educational values and objectives. Thus a one-sided standpoint comes to be seen as natural, obvious, and general, and a one-sided set of interests preoccupy intellectual and creative work. Simone de Beauvoir describes the effect for women in this way:

> *A man never begins by presenting himself as an individual of a certain sex; it goes without saying that he is a man. The terms masculine and feminine are used symmetrically only as a matter of form, as on legal paper. In actuality the relation of the two sexes is not quite like that of two electrical poles, for man represents both the positive and the neutral, as is indicated by the common use of man to designate human beings in general; whereas woman represents only the negative, defined by limiting criteria, without reciprocity.*[2]

Issues such as the use of male pronouns to represent the general are not trivial after all. They address exactly this relation.

Let us be clear that we are not talking about prejudice or sexism as a particular bias against women or a negative stereotype of women. We are talking about the consequences of women's exclusion from a full share in the making of what becomes treated as our culture. We are talking about the consequences of a silence, an absence, a nonpresence. What is there—spoken, sung, written, made emblematic in art—and treated as general, universal, unrelated to a particular position or a particular sex as its source and standpoint, is in fact partial, limited, located in a particular position, and permeated by special interests and concerns.

For example, I heard on the radio excerpts of a musical made from a book of women's and men's reminiscences of the depression years. But the musical as it was described and excerpted on the radio had the voices only of men. Hence only men's viewpoint and experience of that time were there for all or any of us to hear. Women's experience and viewpoint were altogether missing. Or again, a radio program concerning violence between husbands and wives spent most of the time discussing violence of wives against husbands, though violence of husbands against wives constitutes by far the most frequent and most serious form of violence between husbands and wives.

The biases of beginning from the experience of men enter in all kinds of ways into our thinking. Take for example the Freudian conception of sexuality. It is clearly based on the man's experience of his body and his sexuality. Hence we have a conception of sexuality based on male genital sexuality and of woman's body as deviating from this sexuality so that her psychosexual development must be thought of somehow as an attempt to do away with this fundamental defect. Her child, particularly her male child, is represented as a substitute for a missing penis. How extraordinary this is if we do not treat a man's body as normative. Think for a moment what it might be like to account for our psychosexual being using women's experience of our bodies and sexuality as a norm. How odd that would be if it were imposed upon men as normative. And how is it that we could not have an account that begins indeed from the actualities of our experience and recognizes the difference as just that, or perhaps indeed as complementary, rather than treating the sexuality of one sex as deviant vis-à-vis that of the other?

The enormous literature on the relation of family socialization and educational attainment, in which the role of the mother takes on such a prominent part, can be seen also to have its distinctive biases. The treatment of mothering in this literature is in various ways evaluative, critical, or instructive with respect to the practices and relations conducive to educational attainment or to the psychosocial well-being of children.[3] Virtually the whole of this literature presupposes a one-way relation between school and family whereby family practices, organization, and, in particular, mothering practices are seen as consequential for the child's behavior at school. The phenomenon of school phobia as it is vulgarly described is one notorious example, whereby the protectiveness of mother is understood as creating a dependence in the child and hence the child's fearfulness at school.[4] Or take the psychiatric literature on the family and mental illness in which the mother is continually the focus of an inescapable indictment.[5]

Who has thought to take up the issue of these relations from the standpoint of women? Might we not then have studies concerned with the consequences of the school and the educational process for how the child matures in the family and for the family itself? Where are those studies showing the disastrous consequences of the school for the families of immigrants, particularly non-English-speaking immigrants? Where are the studies suggesting that mothers' protectiveness of children who are terrified of school arises as a natural response to what is perceived as a source of damage and harm to the child? Where are the studies telling us anything about the consequences for family organization of societal processes that "subcontract" educational responsibilities for homework and so forth to the family and in particular to the mother? What effects does this odd role—lacking authority and over-burdened with responsibility for outcomes over which in fact she has little control—have on women? What are the implications of this role for family relations, particularly for relations between mothers and children?[6]

In the field of education research itself, our assumptions are those of a world seen from men's position in it. Turn to that classic of our times, Philippe Ariès's *Centuries of Childhood*.[7] Interrogate it seriously from the standpoint of women. Ask, should this book not be retitled *Centuries of the Childhood of Men*? Or take Christopher Jencks's influential book entitled *Inequality*.[8] Should this not be described as an examination of the educational system with respect to its implications for inequality among men.[9] The very terms in which inequality is conceived are based on men's occupations, men's typical patterns of career and advancement. Women's experience of work in this kind of society is located in standstill jobs lacking career structure and in a status system in which their position is derived from that of men. A work examining the educational system with respect to the inequality of women would be focused quite differently. It would, among other matters, be concerned with the educational system as systematically producing a differential of competence among women and men in almost every education dimension, including that of physical development. It would focus on inequality between the sexes as a systematically organized product of the educational process.

These examples only illustrate the outcomes of women's absence. We cannot inventory them fully. The problem is not a special, unfortunate, and accidental omission of this or that field, but a general organizational feature of our kind of society.

III   The Brutal History of Women's Silencing

The exclusion of women from the making of our culture is not the product of a biological deficiency or a biological configuration of some kind. As we learn more of our women's history we discover that a powerful intellectual and artistic current moves like an underground stream through the history of the last few centuries. It appears sometimes merely as a missing potentiality, as in the stories of women mathematicians whose biographies show in almost every case the effect of a general deprivation of education. In almost every case they have discovered mathematics by accident—sharing a brother's lessons, the interest of a family friend, the paper covered with calculus used to paper a child's room—some special incident or relation that introduced them to the territory of their art.[10] Lacking such an accident, there was no provision, no systematic training, no opening of an intellectual universe. Or we find that the intellectual or artistic practice itself was appropriated by a man, as Caroline Herschel's major work in astronomy, done in association with her brother William Herschel, is treated as his. We learn of the subordination of genius to the discipline of service in the home and in relation to children, and of the fragmentary realization of extraordinary powers of mind and dedication, as in the lives of Charlotte and Emily Brontë, of Emily Dickinson, and in our time, of Tillie Olsen—among others, known and unknown.

We can see also the submerged folk tradition of a true art sustained and perpetuated by women when the emergence of a high art excluded them and surely excluded distinctively womanly materials. Thus the artists of quilting have used forms, materials, and practices quite different from those that, until recently, have been identified with "art." Though if you see the quilts and read the accounts, you are clearly in the presence of artists of high technical excellence and design quality who were not treated or recognized as artists until the women's movement. A quilt was made to be used. It was integrated into particularistic relations—the piece of her grandmother's dress, her daughter's pinafore—and was sometimes made by a group of women working together. The making itself and the friendships were built into the design, the collection of fabrics, the stitching. A quilt was not a piece of art, therefore, to be seen in isolation from its history and the social relations of its making. It was not made to be set in the high walls of a gallery or museum. It was always a moment in the moving skein of family and tradition, raising suspicion against time and its powers of separation.

We have evidence now also of a submerged and repressed political and spiritual intelligentsia dating at least from that moment when in Europe the translation of the Bible into the vernacular made the authorities' book available to anyone who could read, among them women.[11] We have as yet fragmentary intuitions of an emerging female intelligentsia and the repressions to which they were subject; we hear for example of women such as Joan Boughton and her daughter Lady Yonge, who were burned at the stake in the late fifteenth century because they held fast to their right to direct interpretation of the Scriptures and to speak and express their own understanding of the Bible rather than on the authority of the clergy.[12] We can see a similar phenomenon in the reign of Henry VIII, when the Reformation enlivened the intellectual possibilities for women as well as for men, and women such as Sara Ann Askew were tortured and martyred for heresy. In the founding and organization of the Quaker sect, Margaret Fell (later to be Margaret Fox) played a leading and important role. Her influence was such that the Quaker sect was one of the few to grant a position of equality to women in religious matters. She herself, imprisoned many times for her beliefs, wrote in the seventeenth century a powerful pamphlet arguing the scriptural justification for the right of women to preach and teach.[13] Those however who actually took up such responsibility, as many women have in many forms, were not always received as leaders, as was Margaret Fell. In seventeenth-century North America, Anne Hutchinson was banished from the Massachusetts Bay Colony because she chose to preach and teach religion and claimed the right to do so as a woman.[14] The same struggle emerged again from its underground existence during the French Revolution when women were active in women's revolutionary organizations. Again it was repressed. The clubs were proscribed and at least two of their leaders, Olympes de Gouges and Manon Roland, were guillotined as an example to other women of what happens to those who step so far out of their place as to claim wisdom, learning, and political leadership.[15] Sojourner Truth's power of thought and rhetoric was heard against militant efforts to prevent her speaking in the conventions on women's rights in mid-nineteenth-century United States.[16] The underground movement of women surfaced again in Mrs. Packard's struggle against her Calvinist husband, who had committed her (as under the law of that time he could) to the Illinois Insane Asylum on grounds not only that she held religious opinions different from his, but that she insisted on her right to do so.[17] Closer to our own time, as women in the 1960s began actively to take up women's issues in the civil rights movement, they encountered ridicule, vilification, and an opposition from men that exhibited to them for the first time how they were despised.[18]

Let us be clear that what we are hearing in these brief biographical moments is the emergence into our view, into the view of a history written largely by men and with men's concerns in mind, of a continuing and active struggle renewed continually in different times and places by women who often had no knowledge of their predecessors and sometimes not even of their contemporary sisterhood.

The repression of the continuing underground sources of intellectual power and assertion among women shows us the rough stuff. There is an actively enforced barrier that we were unaware of until we looked at these kinds of examples. But studies accumulate, telling us of our history and breaking the silence of our past, we can see that other forces were at work, more conventional, seemingly more rational, but no less powerful and effective in ensuring the silence of women.

For example, we now have well-documented history of midwives in both England and the United States, showing how over a period of two hundred years they were reduced to an ancillary role in childbirth, or eliminated altogether, in a struggle fought consciously and deliberately by the medical profession. It was a struggle concerned to eliminate the competition not only of women, but of a continuing native tradition of learning that was at odds with the technical apparatus and technical knowledge of the emerging profession of gynecology. In the suppression of that art or the bringing of English midwives into a subordinate relation to the medical profession, the traditions perpetuated by the older art have been lost (we cannot now of course evaluate their possible importance). Further direct access to women's own knowledge of their sexual and procreative functions was cut off.[19]

We now know also that women were systematically and consciously excluded from the growing profession of medicine in the United States, where their admission to medical school was restricted to a very small number. Those who were trained found that the kinds of jobs open to them were largely in public health or institutional medicine. Again we find an organizational process that by excluding women also excludes their knowledge, experience, interests, and perspectives and prevents their becoming part of the systematic knowledge and techniques of a profession. This process has of course been of fundamental significance in the formation of practice and knowledge in gynecology. Its current practices are distinctively marked by the silence of women in its making.[20]

These are some of the forms in which silencing and exclusion of women have been practiced. Some have arisen inadvertently as a concomitant of women's location in the world; some have been a process of active repression or strong social disapproval of the exercise by women of a role of intellectual or political leadership; others have been the product of an organizational process. It is this last form of exclusion I shall focus on now, for in our society we see less of the rough stuff (though do not assume that it is not there) and more of a steady institutional process, equally effective and much less visible in its exclusionary force.

IV Contemporary Institutional Forms of Women's Exclusion: Women's Place in the Hierarchies of Education

The exclusion of women from participating in creating the culture of the society is in this day largely organized by the ordinary social processes of socialization, education, work, and communication. These perform a routine, generalized, and effective repression. The educational system is an important aspect of this repression. It trains people in skills they need to participate at various levels in the ideological structuring of the society (they must be able to read at least); it teaches them the ideas, the vocabularies, images, beliefs; it trains them to recognize and approve ideologically sanctioned forms of relations and how to identify authoritative ideological sources (what kinds of books, newspapers, etc. to credit, what to discredit; who are the authoritative writers or speakers and who are not). This repression is part of the system that distributes ideas and ensures the dissemination of new ideological forms as these are produced by the intelligentsia. It is also active itself in producing ideology, both in the forms of knowledge in the social sciences, psychology, and education, and in the forms of critical ideas and theories in philosophy and literature.

Prior to the late nineteenth century, women were almost completely denied access to any form of higher education beyond the skills of reading and writing. In one of the first major feminist works, *A Vindication of the Rights of Women*,[21] Mary Wollstonecraft places women's right to education at the center of her argument. She is responding specifically to Rousseau's prescriptions for educating women, aimed at training them for dependency, for permanent childishness, and for permanent incapacity for the autonomous exercise of mind.[22] During the latter part of the nineteenth century, in both Europe and North America, opportunities for women in higher education were a major focus of women's struggle. Though women's participation in the educational process at all levels has increased in this century, this participation remains within marked boundaries. Among the most important of these boundaries, I would argue, is that which reserves to men control of the policy-making and decision-making apparatus in the educational system.

When we look at where women are in the educational system, our focus should go beyond issues of social justice. Equality of opportunity is only one aspect of the problem. I want rather to draw attention to the significance of the inequalities we find for how women are located in the processes of setting standards, producing social knowledge, acting as "gatekeepers" over what is admitted into the system of distribu-

TABLE 1.1 Percentage of Women at Different Levels of the Canadian
Educational System, Various Years, 1969–73

Level	% Women	Years
Elementary teachers (ex. Quebec)	78%	1972–73
Secondary teachers (ex. Quebec)	37%	1972–73
Community College teaching staff (ex. Quebec)	19.5%	1970–71
University (all ranks)	15%	1969–70

Source: Canadian Teachers' Federation Status of Women, *The Declining Majority* (Ottawa: Canadian Teachers' Federation, 1978).

tion, innovating in thought or knowledge or values, and in other ways participating as authorities in the ideological work done in the educational process.

We can look at the statistics from two points of view—education itself has a status structure organizing its internal relations so far as sources of knowledge and academic standards are concerned. Though there are of course other socially significant aspects of schools and community colleges that are not related to the university, the university is important as a source of intellectual leadership vis-à-vis the rest of the educational system. Second, these differing levels of the educational system are related to the age structure of the educational process. Generally, more advanced training for older students has a higher status than education for younger and less advanced students. This status structure has little to do with the skills required or the social importance of the work itself and a great deal to do with control over the standards and substance of education.

As we go up the Canadian educational hierarchy from elementary to secondary school to community college to university we find a lower proportion of women teachers at each step (see table 1.1). At each level upward in the hierarchy of control and influence over the education process, the proportion of women declines. At the elementary level, women are the majority (although the proportion had declined to 74 percent in 1975–76),[23] but at the secondary school level they are already a minority, and their share of the educational process is lowest at the university level.

Further, within each level, we find women markedly unrepresented in administrative positions of professional leadership. In elementary and secondary schools women's relative share of administrative positions is much lower than their share of teaching positions. At each next position upward in the hierarchy we generally see the same pattern of

TABLE 1.2 Percentage of Women in Positions in Canadian Elementary and Secondary Schools (ex. Quebec), 1972–73

Position	Elementary	Secondary
Teachers	78%	37%
Department head	42%	21%
Vice-principal	20%	7%
Principal	20%	4%

Source: See table 1.1.

TABLE 1.3 Percentage of Women Educational Staff in Canadian Community Colleges by Position (ex. Quebec), 1970–71

Position	% Women
Teaching staff	19.5%
Academic administrative staff	11.9%

Source: Women's Bureau, *Women in the Labour Force: Facts and Figures, 1973* (Ottawa: Labour Canada, 1974), table 7.

TABLE 1.4 Percentage of Women in Canadian Academic Positions, All Ranks, 1969–70

Position	% Women
Lecturers and instructors	31%
Assistant professors	14%
Associate professors	8%
Full professors	3%

Source: Jill McCalla Vickers and June Adam, *But Can You Type? Canadian Universities and the Status of Women* (Toronto: Clarke Irwin/Canadian Association of University Teachers, 1977)

decline as we have seen in the overall educational structure (see table 1.2). A similar pattern shows in the figures for community colleges (table 1.3). Within the university the same pattern is repeated (table 1.4).

The inverse relation between status level and proportion of women is obvious at every level. Women are most heavily concentrated in the positions of lecturer and instructor, which are not part of the promotional system leading to professional rank (the so-called ladder positions) and are usually held on only a one-year contract. There is an appreciable drop even to the next level of junior positions, the assistant professors—the first step on the promotion ladder. Women form a very small proportion of full professors.[24]

It is important to keep in mind that we are looking at rather powerful structures of professional control. It is through this structure of ranks and the procedures by which people are advanced from one to another that the professions maintain control over the nature and quality of work that is done and the kinds of people who are admitted to its ranks and to influential positions within it. Two points are of special importance: first, the concentration of women in the relatively temporary nonladder positions. This concentration means that women are largely restricted to teaching, that their work is subject to continual review, and that reappointment is conditional upon conformity. The second point to note is the market break in the proportion of women between tenured and nontenured positions.

The tenured faculty to a large extent controls who shall be admitted to its ranks and what shall be recognized as properly scholarly work. This minimal "voting power" of women helps us understand why women in more senior positions in the university do not ordinarily represent women's perspectives. They are those who have passed through this very rigorous filter. They are those whose work and style of work and conduct have met the approval of judges who are usually men. And, in any case, they are very few.

In sum, the statistics show a highly inequitable distribution of women throughout the educational system. Though women are more than half of all teachers, they are very under-represented in the ranks of principals; there are very, very few women superintendents. In the educational bureaucracies, women appear almost exclusively in secretarial and clerical roles. In universities and community colleges, women are very markedly under-represented in the academic staff. They are clustered in the lower ranks with the greatest turnover and in a very limited range of subjects (think of who taught you and who taught what subjects). The officers of organizations representing educators are also predominantly men. We find in general that the closer positions come to policy-making or innovation in the ideological forms, the smaller the proportion of women. Power and authority in the educational process are the prerogatives of men.

V The Authority of the Male Voice

Men have authority in the world of thought as members of a social category and not as individuals. Authority is a form of power that is a distinctive capacity to get things done in words. What is said or written merely means what the words mean, until and unless it is given force by the authority attributed to its "author." When we speak of authority, we are speaking of what makes what one person says count. Men are invested with authority as individuals, not because they have as individuals special competencies or expertise, but because as men they appear as representative of the power and authority of the institutionalized structures that govern the society. Their authority as individuals in actual situations of action is generated by a social organization. They do not appear as themselves alone. They are those whose words count, both for each other and for those who are not members of this category. The circle I spoke of earlier is formed of those whose words count for one another. It excludes those whose words do not count, whose speakers have no authority.

We have by now and in various forms a good deal of evidence of the ways in which this social effect works. It is one Mary Ellman has described as a distinction between women and men in intellectual matters, which is both obvious and unnoticed. A man's body gives credibility to his utterance, whereas a woman's body takes it away from hers.[25] A study done by Philip Goldberg, which was concerned with finding out whether women were prejudiced against women, demonstrates this effect very clearly.[26] Here is Jo Freeman's description:

> *He gave college girls sets of booklets containing six identical professional articles in traditional male, female and neutral fields. The articles were identical, but the names of the authors were not. For example, an article in one set would bear the name John T. McKay and in another set the same article would be authored by Joan T. McKay. Each booklet contained three articles by "women" and three by "men". Questions at the end of each article asked the students to rate the articles on value, persuasiveness and profundity; and the authors on writing style and competence. The male authors fared better in every field, even in such "feminine" areas as Art History and Dietetics.*[27]

There seems to be something like a plus factor that adds force and persuasiveness to what men say and a minus factor that depreciates and weakens what women say.

The way in which the sex of the speaker modifies the authority of the message has been observed in other ideological fields. Lucy Komisar points out that in advertising it is men who give instructions to women on how to do their housework. Men tell women why one detergent or soap powder or floor polish is better than another. The reason, according to a leading advertising agency executive, is that the male voice is the voice of authority.[28]

Phyllis Chesler's study of preferences among psychotherapists and their patients shows that the majority of women patients prefer male therapists and that the majority of male psychotherapists prefer women patients. The reasons women give for preferring male psychotherapists are that they generally feel more comfortable with them and that they have more respect for and confidence in a man's competence and authority. Chesler reports that both men and women in her sample said they trusted and respected men as people and as authorities more than they did women.[29]

A study done by L. S. Fidell on sex discrimination in university hiring practices in psychology shows the intersection of this effect with the educational system of controls described in the preceding section. She used an approach very similar to Goldberg's, constructing two sets of fictional descriptions of academic background and qualifications (including the Ph.D.). Identical descriptions in one set had a woman's name attached and in the other a man's. The sets of descriptions were sent to chairpersons of all colleges and universities in the United States offering graduate degrees in psychology. They were asked to estimate the chance of the described individuals' getting an offer of a position and at what level, and so forth. Her findings supported the hypothesis of discrimination on the basis of sex. Men were likely to be suggested for higher levels of appointment. They received more regular academic positions of the kind leading to promotion and tenure, and only men were offered full professorships.[30] It seems as though the attribution of authority which increases the value of men's work constitutes something like a special title to the positions of control and influence and hence to full active membership in the intelligentsia.

It seems that women as a social category lack proper title to membership in the circle of those who count for one another in the making of ideological forms. To identify a woman novelist as a woman novelist is to place her in a special class outside that of novelists in general. Doris Lessing is described as one of the greatest women novelists of this century, rather than just one of the greatest novelists. Among the professional problems confronted by women writers, Tillie Olsen cites the following:

> *Devaluation: Still in our century, women's books of great worth suffer the death of being unknown, or at best a peculiar eclipsing, far outnumbering the similar fate of the few such books by men. I think of Kate Chopin, Mary Austin, Dorothy Richardson, Henry Handel Richardson (Ultima Thule), Jean Rhys, Storm Jameson, Christina Stead, Elizabeth Madox Roberts (The Time of Man), Janet Lewis, May Sarton, Harriette Arnouw (The Dollmaker), Agnes Smedley (Daughter of Earth), Djuna Barnes (Nightwood), Kay Boyle—every*

one of whom is rewarding, and some with the stamp of enduring. Considering their stature, how comparatively unread, untaught are Glasgow, Glaspell, Bowen, Parker, Stein, Mansfield—even Cather and Porter.[31]

And she points out further how work by women is treated quite differently from that by men. She describes "the injurious reaction to a book not for its quality or content, but on the basis of its having been written by a woman, with consequent misreading, mistreatment."[32] These effects are not confined to literature written by women. They are rather special instances of a general social organization of relations among women and men when the medium is communicative. Men have title of entry to the circle of those who count for one another. Women do not. The minus factor attached to what women say, write, or image is another way of seeing how what they say, write, or image is not a "natural" part of the discourse.

The examples so far given have been mainly of the written word. But the metaphor of a game points to our experience in actual everyday interactional settings.[33] We can and have observed these patterns ourselves, which serve to fill out our description of how male control over the topics and themes of discourse is maintained in actual situations of interactions. For example, F. I. Strodtbeck and R. D. Mann in their study of jury deliberations report that men talked considerably more than women. These differences, however, were more than quantitative. They also describe what seems to be a general pattern of interaction between women and men. Men's talk was more directed toward the group task while women reacted with agreement, passive acceptance, and understanding.[34] The pattern I have observed also involves women becoming virtually an audience, facilitating with support or comments, but not carrying the talk or directing remarks toward one another.

It is like a game in which there are more presences than players. Some are engaged in tossing a ball between them; the others are consigned to the roles of audience and supporter, who pick the ball up if it is dropped and pass it back to the players. They support, facilitate, encourage but their action does not become part of the play. In ordinary situations of meeting and working together we can find these same patterns. What women have to say may simply remain unsaid. Or it is treated as a byplay—not really integral to the game. If it comes into play at all it is because a male player has picked it up and brought it into play as his.

Characteristically, women talking with men use styles of talk that throw the control to others, as for example by interspersing their words with interjections that reassign the responsibility for its meaning to others, by saying "you know" or failing to name objects or things or to complete sentences. Expectations of how much and for how long men and women should talk have an effect on how much and how long they are seen to talk. William Caudill describes a supervisor of nurses as an assertive person, willing to express her opinion in unequivocal terms. Yet his data show that in meetings she spoke less on the average than the hospital administrative and psychiatric personnel, including a resident described as "passive and withdrawn."[35]

Candace West has made a study of differences between single-sex and mixed-sex conversations which focuses upon men's and women's different rights to speak. She observed a variety of "devices" used by men, apparently with women's consent, that serve to maintain male control of the topics of conversation. For example, men tended to complete women's sentences, to give minimal responses to topics initiated and carried by women, and to interrupt without being sanctioned. Her study describes how men control conversation through the use of interruption and by withdrawing active participation when women are developing their topics.[36]

In professional conversations we can also identify a collection of devices that may be used to restrict women's control of the development of topics. Among them are the devices used to recognize or enter what women have said into the discourse under male sanction. For example, a suggestion or point contributed by a woman may be ignored at its point of origin. When it is reintroduced at a later point by a man, it is then "recognized" and becomes part of the topic. Or if it is recognized at the time, it is reattributed by the responder to another male (in the minutes of the meeting, it will appear as having been said by someone else). Or the next speaker after the woman may use a device such as, "What Dorothy really means is . . ." Or the woman's turn is followed by a pause, after which the topic is picked up at the previous speaker's turn as if she had not spoken.

Celia Gilbert makes a vivid symbolic presence of this circle and the practices that exclude women in her poem "On Refusing Your Invitation to Come to Dinner." The dinner table reflects (both metaphorically and actually) the unspoken presence of women. Gilbert looks back on it from the standpoint of one who has already learned another practice of her being. She writes:

> But I am forgetting the language,
> sitting has become difficult,
> and the speaking, intolerable,

> to say, "how interesting"
> makes me weep.
> I can no longer bear to hear
> the men around the table laugh,
> argue, agree,
> then pause, politely
> while we speak,
> their breath held in, exhaled
> when we've finished,
> politely,
> then turn to the real conversation,
> the unspoken expectation of applause.[37]

The interpersonal order symbolizes and is the local expression of the circle of men across time and space whose discourse has excluded women. But it is also the actual practice of the circle. It is a practice we can and probably have experienced in our working and our personal lives. At the interpersonal level it is not a conspiracy among men that they impose on women. It is a complementary social process between women and men. Women are complicit in the social practices of their silence.

The practices extend to women's participation in art, music, literature, science, the health sciences, education. The figures showing us where women are in education represent an organization of social relations of a deeper level, extending throughout the educational structure and its articulation to the society it both serves and structures. In the education system at all levels and in all aspects, women have access and participate so that they may be present as subordinates, as marginal. Their training and education ensure that at every level of competence and leadership there will be a place for them that is inferior and subordinate to the positions of men.

●

VI   Grasping Our Own Authority to Speak

It is important to recognize that the deprivation of authority and the ways in which women have been trained to practice the complement of male-controlled "topic development"[38] have the effect of making it difficult for women to treat one another as relevant figures. We have difficulty asserting authority for ourselves. We have difficulty grasping authority for women's voices and for what we have to say. We are thus deprived of the essential basis for developing among ourselves the forms of thought and images that express the situations we share and make it possible to begin to work together. Women have taken for granted that our thinking is to be authorized by an external source of authority. Anya Bostock tells us that this is because we live in a world dominated intellectually by men. As a consequence women's opinions tend to conform to the approved standards, and these in the last analysis are men's. In consequence women's opinions are sharply separated from their lived experience. As they begin to develop their own opinions, they have to check them against their collective experience as women rather than merely their personal experience.[39] But it has not been easy for women to find their own voices convincing. It is hard for us to listen to each other. The voice of our own experience is equally defective.

Lack of authority, then, is lack of authority for ourselves and for other women. We have become familiar in the women's movement with the importance of women learning to relate to one another. We need also to learn how to treat what other women say as a source and basis for our own work and thinking. We need to learn to treat one another as the authoritative speakers of our experience and concerns.

It is only when as women we can treat one another, and ourselves, as those who count for one another that we can break out of our silence—to make ourselves heard; to protest against the violence done to women (and there is violence done); to organize politically for justice and equality in law; to work together to become more effective in the organizations representing us; to work together to resist the unloading of economic crisis onto women; and, as educators, to advance, develop, and pass on to our children (our daughters *and* our sons) a knowledge of women's history and experience, of our poetry, our art, our political skills, and our confidence. This is the road to full and equal membership in our society for women.

The institutionalized practices of excluding women from the ideological work of society are the reason we have a history constructed largely from the perspective of men, and largely about men. This is why we have so few women poets and why the records of those who survived the hazards of attempting poetry are so imperfect.[40] This is why we know so little of women visionaries, thinkers, and political organizers.[41] This is why we have an anthropology that tells us about other societies from the perspective of men and hence has so distorted the cross-cultural record that it may now be impossible to learn what we might have known about how women lived in other forms of society. This is why we have a sociology that is written from the perspective of positions in a male-dominated ruling class and is set up in terms of the relevances of the institutional power structures that constitute those positions.[42] This is why in English literature there is a corner called "women in literature" or "women novelists" and an overall critical approach to literature that assumes it is written by men and perhaps even largely for men. This is why the assumptions of psychological research[43] and of educational research and philosophy take for granted male experience, orientation, and concerns and treat as normative masculine modes of being.

The ideological practices of our society provide women with forms of thought and knowledge that constrain us to treat ourselves as objects. We have learned to set aside as irrelevant, to deny, or to obliterate our own subjectivity and experience. We have learned to live inside a discourse that is not ours and that expresses and describes a landscape in which we are alienated and that preserves that alienation as integral to its practice. In a short story, Doris Lessing describes a girl growing up in Africa whose consciousness has been wholly formed within traditional British literary culture. Her landscape, her cosmology, her moral relations, her botany are those of the English novels and fairy tales. Her own landscape, its forms of life, her immediate everyday world do not fully penetrate and occupy her consciousness. They are not named.[44] Lessing's story is a paradigm of the situation of women in our society. Its general culture is not ours.[45]

Clearly the issue is more than bias. It is more than simply an omission of certain kinds of topics. It involves taking up the standpoint of women as an experience of being, of society, of social and personal process that must be given form and expression in the culture, whether as knowledge, as art, or as literature or political action. This is the work we see now in progress in many forms in the women's movement and beyond. When we speak of "women's studies," we are identifying a broad range of work that develops and makes way for research, philosophic and theological thinking, poetry, literature, the study of art, history, sociology, law, and other fields giving expression to and building essential knowledge of this whole range of seeing the world from women's place in it. Women's studies identifies space in universities, colleges, and schools, making room for these developments and opening a conduit into the educational system for the astonishing work that is now being done by women in art, philosophy, poetry, scholarship, and political and social theory.

Notes

1. The concept of an "ideological apparatus" is taken from Althusser's conception of "ideological state apparatus." Although I have not used it here with any theoretical rigor, I use it to identify in general the same social forms to which his conception of "ideological state apparatuses" is applied. See Louis Althusser, "Ideology and ideological state apparatuses," in *Lenin and Philosophy and Other Essays* (New York: Monthly Review Press, 1971), pp. 127–86.
2. Simone de Beauvoir, *The Second Sex* (New York: Bantam Books, 1961), p. xv.
3. In much of this literature, women are not directly mentioned. It is the family that is represented as the operative social unit in a child's school achievement. But in practice it has been mothers who actually do the work of child raising, supervision of homework, management of school schedule, and the like in relation to children's schooling. The literature focusing on family and school achievement is largely concerned with what kinds of family organization and practices are most conducive to children's success in school. For example, see the studies in Maurice Craft, ed., *Family, Class and Education: A Reader* (London: Longmans, 1970).
4. J. Kahn and J. Nurstein, *Unwillingly to School* (London: Pergamon Press, 1964), pp. 13–15.
5. Elinor King, "How the psychiatric profession views women," in Dorothy E. Smith and Sara David, eds., *Women Look at Psychiatry* (Vancouver: Press Gang, 1975).
6. Though the feminist thinking and rethinking of "the family" is substantial and various, there is still a curious absence of thinking and investigation that takes up women's work as mothers in relation to their children's schooling from the standpoint of women. The latter has been provided with broad theoretical shelter by AnnMarie Wolpe, "Education and the sexual division of labour," in Annette Kuhn and AnnMarie Wolpe, eds., *Feminism and Materialism* (London: Routledge and Kegan Paul, 1978), but has yet to be established as integral to feminist thinking on mothering and family organization. Nancy Jackson has provided a valuable analysis of these relations at a general level in "Stress on schools + stress on families = distress for children" (Canadian Teachers' Federation, Ottawa, 1982). My own work with Alison Griffith in this area, touched on later in this book (chap. 5), explores this area.
7. Philippe Ariès, *Centuries of Childhood* (Harmondsworth, England: Penguin Books, 1975).
8. Christopher Jencks with Marshall Smith, Henry Acland, Mary Jo Bane, David Cohen, Herbert Gintis, Barbara Heyns, and Stephan Michelson, *Inequality: A Reassessment of the Effect of Family and Schooling in America* (New York: Basic Books, 1972).
9. Curiously, although there is now a considerable literature showing how the educational system produces gender inequalities, this tends not to be conceived as a general property of the educational system, as is "inequality" as Jencks conceives it or as the role of the educational system

in producing inequalities of class. "Inequality" in the educational context *means* class inequality. See for example the introduction to R. W. Connell, D. J. Ashenden, S. Kessler, and G. W. Dowsett, *Making the Difference: Schools, Families and Social Division* (Sydney: Allen and Unwin Australia, 1982), which is otherwise more successful than most in integrating gender into its description and analysis. Again, Marxist theories have been significant in remedying this deficiency. See Wolpe, "Education and the sexual division of labour"; Michele Barrett, "The educational system: Gender and class," in Michele Barrett, *Women's Oppression Today: Problems in Marxist-Feminist Analysis* (London: Virago, 1980); and Madeleine MacDonald, "Schooling and the reproduction of class and gender relations," in Roger Dale, Geoff Esland, Ross Fergusson, and Madeleine MacDonald, eds., *Education and the State*, vol. 2, *Politics, Patriarchy and Practice* (Basingstoke, England: Falmer Press, 1981), pp. 167–77.

10. See for example Lynn M. Osen, *Women in Mathematics* (Cambridge, Mass.: MIT Press, 1974).

11. These repressions have now, of course, been documented in many studies. Dale Spender's resurrection of the suppressed political thinking of women writing in the English language since the seventeenth century is a valuable introduction to this subterranean tradition: Dale Spender, *Women of Ideas and What Men Have Done to Them: From Aphra Behn to Adrienne Rich* (London: Routledge and Kegan Paul, 1982).

12. Sylvia L. Thrupp, *The Merchant Class of Mediaeval London, 1300–1500* (Ann Arbor: University of Michigan Press, 1962).

13. Margaret Fox, "Women's speaking justified, proved, and allowed by the Scriptures, all such as speak by the spirit and power of the Lord Jesus," in *A Brief Collection of Remarkable Passages and Occurrences* (London: J. Sowle, 1710), pp. 331–50.

14. Sheila Rowbotham, *Women, Resistance and Revolution* (Harmondsworth, England: Penguin Books, 1973).

15. Smache des Jacques, "Women in the French Revolution: The thirteenth brumaire of Olympe de Gouges, with notes on French amazon battalions," in Ann Forfreedom, ed., *Women Out of History: A Herstory* (Culver City, Calif.: Peace Press, 1972), pp. 131–40.

16. Angela Y. Davis, *Women, Race and Class* (New York: Random House, 1981), pp. 60–64.

17. Thomas Szasz, ed., *The Age of Madness: The History of Involuntary Hospitalization Presented in Selected Texts* (Garden City, N.Y.: Doubleday/Anchor, 1973).

18. Juliet Mitchell, *Women's Estate* (Harmondsworth, England: Penguin Books), 1972.

19. Jean Donnison, *Midwives and Medical Men: A History of Inter-Professional Rivalries and Women's Rights* (London: Heinemann, 1977).

20. Mary Roth Walsh, *Doctors Wanted, No Women Need Apply: Sexual Barriers in the Medical Profession, 1835–1975* (New Haven: Yale University Press, 1977).

21. Mary Wollstonecraft, *A Vindication of the Rights of Women* (New York: W. W. Norton, 1967).

22. Jane Martin has given us a brilliant analysis of Rousseau's prescriptions for educating Sophie as Emile's proper mate. Jane Roland Martin,

Reclaiming a Conversation: The Ideal of the Educated Woman (New Haven: Yale University Press, 1985).

23. With Jane Haddad and Yoko Ueda, I recently updated a study of the effects of declining enrollments for teachers in the public school system in Ontario, Canada. We found that in 1983–84, women were 13.2 percent of principals and vice-principals in elementary schools, and 9.2 percent of principals and vice-principals in secondary schools (Dorothy E. Smith, Jane Haddad, and Yoko Ueda, "Teaching as an internally segregated profession: Women and men teachers in the public schools of Ontario," typescript, Department of Sociology in Education, Ontario Institute for Studies in Education, January 1987). The larger figure for Canada in general in the early years is most probably due to the larger proportion of rural schools in other provinces. The Ontario records indicate a drop in the proportion of women principals when the smaller rural schools were amalgamated into larger units.

24. The contemporary figures cannot be intimately compared with the earlier ones because the bases are in some cases different. Though in general the overall patterns of male dominance persist, there do appear to be changes in the direction of greater equality, particularly among university academic staff. The situation of public school teachers, however, seems to have changed very little. Here is an update:

Note Table 1.1 Percentage of Women at Different Levels of the Canadian Educational System, Various Years, 1980–84

Level	% Women	Years
Elementary teachers	71.7%	(1980–81)
Secondary teachers (ex. Quebec)	33.8%	(1980–81)
Community college teaching staff (ex. Quebec)	30.5%	(1983–84)
University (all ranks)	16.3%	(1983–84)

Note Table 1.2 Percentage of Women in Positions in Canadian Elementary and Secondary Schools, 1980–81

Position	Elementary	Secondary
Teachers	71.7%	33.8%
Department head	33.5%	20.7%
Vice-principal	21.4%	7.6%
Principal	14.8%	3.9%

Source: Statistics Canada, *Educational Staff of Public Schools,* Cat. 81–202, Ottawa: Minister of Supply and Services, February 1982, table 1, "Number of Educators by Teaching Level, Staff Position and Sex, 1980–81."

Note Table 1.3 Percentage of Women Educational Staff in Canadian
Community Colleges by Position, 1983–84

Position	%Women
Teaching staff	30.5%
Academic administrative staff	24.9%

Source: Statistics Canada, *Educational Staff of Community Colleges and Vocational Schools*,
Cat. 81–241, Ottawa: Minister of Supply and Services, September 1985, table 1,
"Number of Full-time University Teachers by Rank, Sex and Region, Selected Years,
1960–61 to 1983–84."

Note Table 1.4 Percentage of Women in Canadian Academic Positions,
All Ranks, 1983–84

Position	%Women
Nonladder positions	37.0%
Assistant professors	26.7%
Associate professors	14.3%
Full professors	5.3%

Source: Statistics Canada, *Teachers in Universities 1983–84*, Cat. 81–254, Ottawa: Minister
of Supply and Services, January 1986, table 2, "Full-time staff by Province, Type of
Institution, Staff Position and Sex, 1983–84."

25. Máry Ellman, *Thinking about Women* (New York: Harcourt Brace
   Jovanovich, 1968).
26. Philip Goldberg, "Are women prejudiced against women?" *Transaction*,
   April 1969, pp. 28–30.
27. Jo Freeman, "The social construction of the second sex," in Michele
   Hoffnung Garskoff, ed., *Roles Women Play: Readings towards Women's
   Liberation* (Belmont, Calif.: Brooks/Cole Publishing, 1971), pp. 123–41.
28. Lucy Komisar, "The image of women in advertising," in Vivian Gornick
   and Barbara Moran, eds., *Women in Sexist Society: Studies in Power and
   Powerlessness* (New York: Signet Books, 1972), pp. 304–17.
29. Phyllis Chesler, "Patient and patriarch: Women in the psychotherapeutic
   relationship," in Gornick and Moran, *Women in Sexist Society*, pp. 362–92.
   Since her study, the situation has been radically transformed by the
   development of feminist therapeutic approaches. Editing a book on
   women and psychiatry and working with a feminist therapist in
   describing her experiments with a feminist strategy has given me some
   understanding. See Alison Griffith, "Feminist counselling: A perspective,"
   Rita MacDonald and Dorothy E. Smith, "A feminist therapy session," and
   Sara J. David, "Becoming a non-sexist therapist," in Dorothy E. Smith
   and Sara J. David, eds., *Women Look at Psychiatry* (Vancouver: Press Gang,
   1975). Feminist therapy has made very considerable strides since those
   early days, but Miriam Greenspan's *A New Approach to Women and Therapy:
   Why Current Therapies Fail Women—And What Women and Therapists Can Do*

about It! (New York: McGraw-Hill, 1983) indicates that there is still much to be done. Judith Antrobus's view is pessimistic.

> *The community of professional therapists committed to feminist therapy is extremely small. In the New York area virtually all therapists train at one of the psychoanalytic institutes after obtaining their advanced degrees. The institutes are conventional and traditional, and reflect a pervasive male bias. A few institutes offer a token course on the psychology of women or on psychotherapy with women. What impact will one course have alongside years of psychoanalytic training? Yet women as well as men flock to these institutes. When asked why, they say they need additional training or they need sources of referral later, or whatever. The point cannot be made often enough that most patients are women and most therapists are men who know little or nothing about the context of women's lives or the psychological development of women.*

(Judith Antrobus, "In the final analysis," review of Hannah Lerman, *A Mote in Freud's Eye: From Psychoanalysis to the Psychology of Women, Women's Review of Books* 4, no. 5 [February 1987].)

30. L. S. Fidell, "Empirical verification of sex discrimination in hiring practices in psychology," *American Psychologist* 25, no. 12 (1970): 1094–97.
31. Tillie Olsen, "One out of twelve: Writers who are women in our century," in Tillie Olsen, *Silences* (New York: Delacorte Press/Seymour Lawrence, 1978), p. 40.
32. Ibid.
33. See Jessie Bernard, "Talk, conversation, listening, silence," in *The Sex Game* (New York: Atheneum, 1972), chap. 6, pp. 135–64, for a general characterization of these patterns.
34. F. I. Strodtbeck and R. D. Mann, "Sex role differentiation in jury deliberations," *Sociometry* 19 (March 1956): 3–11.
35. William Caudill, *The Psychiatric Hospital as a Small Society* (Cambridge, Mass.: Harvard University Press, 1958), p. 249.
36. Candace West, "Sexism and conversation: Everything you always wanted to know about Sachs (but were afraid to ask)," M.A. thesis, Department of Sociology, University of California, Santa Barbara, California. More recent work substantiating and further specifying the effects described here include Elizabeth Aries, "Interaction patterns and themes of male, female, and mixed sex groups: Are traditional sex roles changing? *Psychological Reports* 51 (1982): 127–34; Joseph Berger, Susan J. Rosenholtz, and Morris Zelditch, Jr., "Status organizing processes," in Alex Inkeles et al., eds., *Annual Review of Sociology* (Palo Alto, Calif.: Annual Reviews, 1980), 6:479–508; Mary Parlee Brown, "Conversation politics," *Psychology Today*, May 1979, pp. 48–56; John A. Courtright, Frank E. Millar, and L. Edna Rogers Millar, "Domineeringness and dominance: Replication and expansion," *Comunication Monographs* 46 (1979): 179–92; Starkey Duncan, Jr., and Donald W. Fiske, *Face-to-Face Interaction* (Hillsdale, N.J.: Lawrence Erlbaum Associates, 1977); Barbara Eakins and Gene Eakins, "Verbal turn-taking and exchanges in faculty dialogue," in Betty Lou Dubois and Isabel Crouch, eds., *The Sociology of the Languages of American Women* (San Antonio, Tex.: Trinity University, 1976), pp. 53–62; Carole Edelsky, "Who's got the floor?" *Language in Society* 10 (1981): 383–421; Sheryle B. Eubanks, "Sex-based language

differences: A cultural reflection," in Reza Ordoubadian and Walburga
von-Raffler Engel, eds., *Views on Language* (Murfreesboro, Tenn.: Inter-
University Publishers, 1975), pp. 109–20; Pamela M. Fishman,
"Conversational insecurity," in Howard Giles, W. Peter Robinson, and
Philip M. Smith, eds., *Language: Social Psychological Perspectives* (New York:
Pergamon Press, 1980), pp. 127–32; Pamela M. Fishman, "Interaction:
The work women do," *Social Problems* 25 (1978): 397–406; Pamela M.
Fishman, "What do couples talk about when they're alone?" in Douglas
Butturff and Edmund L. Epstein, eds., *Women's Language and Style*
(Akron, Ohio: L&S Books, 1978), pp. 11–22; Nancy Henley, *Body Politics:
Power, Sex and Noverbal Communication* (Englewood Cliffs, N.J.: Prentice-
Hall, Spectrum, 1977); Susan Freeman Hoffman, "Interruptions:
Structure and tactics in dyadic conversations," paper given at the
International Communication Association convention, Acapulco, Mexico,
1980; Janet L. Johnson, "Questions and role responsibility in four
professional meetings," *Anthropological Linguistics* 22 (1980): 66–76; Carol
W. Kennedy, "Patterns of verbal interruption among women and men in
groups," paper given at Third Annual Conference on Communication,
Language, and Gender, Lawrence, Kansas, 1980; Julie R. McMillan, A.
Kay Clifton, Diane McGrath, and Wanda S. Gale, "Women's language:
Uncertainty or interpersonal sensitivity and emotionality?" *Sex Roles* 3
(1977): 545–59; Michael Natale, Elliot Entin, and Joseph Jaff, "Vocal
interruptions in dyadic communication as a function of speech and social
anxiety," *Journal of Personality and Social Psychology* 37 (1979): 865–78;
Mary Octigan and Sharon Niederman, "Male dominance in
conversations," *Frontiers* 4, no. 1 (1979): 50–54; Dale Spender, *Man Made
Language* (London: Routledge and Kegan Paul, 1980); Marjorie Swacker,
"Women's verbal behaviour at learned and professional conferences," in
Dubois and Crouch, *Sociology of the Language of American Women*, pp. 155–
60; Candace West, "Against our will: Male interruptions of females in
cross-sex conversations," in Judith Orsanu, Mariam K. Slater, and
Leonore Loeb Adler, eds., *Language, Sex and Gender* (New York: New
York Academy of Sciences, 1979), pp. 81–97; idem, "When the doctor is
a 'lady': Power, status and gender in physician-patient dialogues," in Ann
Stromberg, ed., *Women, Health and Medicine* (Palo Alto, Calif.: Mayfield,
1981); Candace West and Don Zimmerman, "Sex roles, interruptions and
silences in conversation," in Barrie Thorne and Nancy Henley, eds.,
Language and Sex: Differences and Dominance (Rowley, Mass.: Newbury
House, 1975), pp. 105–29; Frank N. Willis and Sharon J. Williams,
"Simultaneous talking in conversation and sex of speakers," *Perceptual and
Motor Skills* 43 (1976): 1067–70.
37. Celia Gilbert, *Queen of Darkness* (New York: Viking Press, 1977).
38. West, op. cit.
39. Anya Bostock, talk on the British Broadcasting Corporation Third
Programme, published in *The Listener*, August 1972.
40. Louise Bernikow, *The World Split Open: Four Centuries of Women Poets in
England and America, 1552–1950* (New York, Vintage Books, 1974).
41. Rowbotham, *Women, Resistance and Revolution.*
42. Jessie Bernard, *Academic Women* (New York: New American Library,
1964).

43. Carolyn Woods Sherif, "Bias in psychology," in Julia A. Sherman and Evelyn Torton Beck, *The Prism of Sex: Essays in the Sociology of Knowledge* (Madison: University of Wisconsin Press, 1979), pp. 93–133.
44. Doris Lessing, "The old chief Msh Langa," in *The Black Madonna* (St. Albans, England: Granada Publishing, 1966).
45. This is a particular instance where I most powerfully feel the absence of nonwhite women. For of course the texts of the white women's movement have obliterated their subjectivity and experience in ways directly parallel with those described here and here attributed to a general women's experience with the totalitarianism of male texts.

PART TWO

A Feminist Sociology

Chapter 2, "A Sociology for Women," and Chapter 3, "The Everyday World as Problematic," which make up this section, were written originally between 1977 and 1981 in a period of great excitement and challenge in the intellectual development of the women's movement. We could see possibilities of making much greater transformations of male-centered thinking than we had earlier recognized. We had only come gradually to the realization of the depth of the male biases built into the foundations of our knowledge and only gradually to a realization that the implications of beginning from the standpoint of women were much larger than we had had any notion of when we began. These two chapters take up that challenge in a sociological context.

In the early seventies I had written a paper entitled "Women's Perspective as a Radical Critique of Sociology," which I presented at a conference at the University of Oregon. Thereafter it circulated in an extraordinary manner in draft. I got letters from all over, including one, to my astonishment, from Hungary. I could not understand how a paper that had never been published could circulate so widely. It made me aware for the first time that when I wrote a paper for an academic context of presentation or publication I might actually be speaking to people. It made me aware of the possibility of using academic sites of discourse and of writing for academic occasions in ways quite different from my earlier understanding of their uses. Previously I think I had always seen producing papers as a performance for invisible judges. Writing papers for publication made me nervous. Sometimes I used to take a slug of brandy to get me going. My experience with how that paper traveled changed my view altogether. I saw that a paper could be a way of reaching other women, of talking to them. The academic linkages could be used as a medium of communication among women. I saw that I did not have to write a finally complete and perfected piece of work, but that I could write as I went along to tell other women, "this is the work I've been doing; this is where I've got to; this is how it looks right now; how does it look to you?" I understood that a discourse could be organized differently than one organized around an establishment that judged and controlled and held its practitioners to conform to its notions of how sociology should be practiced. I saw that the academic media could be used as a medium to reach other women and to hear from them. The remaining chapters in this book have been written under the tutelage of that experience.

In 1977 the Women's Research Institute of Wisconsin organized a conference called "The Prism of Sex: Towards an Equitable Pursuit of Knowledge." It was an exciting, sometimes conflicting, meeting. The intensity of those times is hard to capture in retrospect. It gave me an opportunity to pull together for presentation to other women the thinking I had been doing around a number of topics—the attempt to situate a sociology in a knowledge grounded in women's experience, the nature of the linkages of the university with other bases of power in the society, the peculiarities of the way changes occur around us (on the campus where I worked, one day there would be a grassy lawn, the next there would be hoardings and a hole in the ground), issues of Canadian cultural identity and of an independent Canadian sociology, my rediscovery of Marx, and specific critiques I had been developing of established methods of thinking and inquiry in sociology.[1] I had learned from the women's movement that I was not bound to observe the conventions laid down by men that constricted the relevances of my thinking. I understood therefore that I could move from what was going on around me to the world of theory and back. This lesson as well as these topics went into the making of "a sociology for women."

A sociology for women does not mean a sociology exclusively for women. It means a sociology that addresses society and social relations from the standpoint of women situated *outside* rather than within the relations of ruling. "A sociology for women" traces the site of women's emerging consciousness in the gender subtext of the relations of ruling, which I have outlined in the Introduction, and proposes a strategy of inquiry I have called "the everyday world as problematic," that is, an organization of inquiry that begins with where women *actually* are and addresses the problem of how our everyday worlds are put together in relations that are not wholly discoverable within the everyday world. There is work, therefore, for sociologists to do.

Locating the standpoint of women in the everyday world outside the text (in which the text is written and is read) creates a whole new set of problems to be solved, problems of the relationship between text and reader, problems of how to write texts that will not transcribe the subject's actualities into the relations of ruling, texts that will provide for their readers a way of seeing further into the relations organizing their lives. Sociology has in its history developed methods of writing its texts that would produce a representation of society and its processes as external to the reader or any other member of society. The constitution of a subject as within the society, of society and social relations as known from within, required the development of alternative methods of thinking and of writing sociological texts. The problem of locating a standpoint outside discourse also renews the problem of the relationship between sociologist and her whose experience and situation locate her own outlook. Established sociology's practices of objectification being removed, the sociologist has to rethink her relationships to those for whom she writes and reexamine the sites in which her writing is done and where it goes. Chapter 3, "The Everyday World as Problematic," explores an alternative method of thinking sociologically in the context of an examination of relationships between subjects and sociologist.

Note

1. My first formulation of this was published as "The ideological practice of sociology," *Catalyst* 8 (1974): 39–54.

2

A Sociology for Women

I The Line of Fault

This inquiry into the implications of a sociology for women begins from the discovery of a point of rupture in my/our experience as woman/women within the social forms of consciousness—the culture or ideology of our society—in relation to the world known otherwise, the world directly felt, sensed, responded to, prior to its social expression. From this starting point, the next step locates that experience in the social relations organizing and determining precisely the disjuncture, that line of fault along which the consciousness of women must emerge. Inquiry does not begin within the conceptual organization or relevances of the sociological discourse, but in actual experience as embedded in the particular historical forms of social relations that determine that experience.

As women members of an intelligentsia and therefore trained in the modes of acting, thinking, and the craft of working with words, symbols, and concepts, we have both a special responsibility and special possibility of awareness at this point of rupture. The disjuncture that provides the problematic of this inquiry is that between the forms of thought, the symbols, images, vocabularies, concepts, frames of reference, institutionalized structures of relevance, of our culture, and a world experienced at a level prior to knowledge or expression, prior to that moment at which experience can become "experience" in achieving social expression or knowledge, or can become "knowledge" by achieving that social form, in being named, being made social, becoming actionable. The work of inquiry in which I am engaged proceeds by taking this experience of mine, this experience of other women—this line of fault—and asking how it is organized, how it is determined, what the social relations are that generate it.

This actual or potential disjuncture between experience and the forms in which experience is socially expressed (becoming thereby intelligible and actionable) is the break on which much major work in the women's movement has focused. Perhaps Simone de Beauvoir's radical and scholarly analysis in *The Second Sex* failed to enliven a movement in the way Betty Friedan's *Feminine Mystique* or Kate Millett's *Sexual Politics* did, in part because these two make central the critique of ideologies at work in our everyday lives, whereas de Beauvoir does not.[1] As a participant in that period, one who shared in that change in consciousness and who had read de Beauvoir at an earlier stage, my sense is that books such as de Beauvoir's or Jessie Bernard's *Academic Women*[2] were important in establishing a sense of powers and possibilities, but that they did not do what Millett and Friedan (very different though they are) did, or what others of that period also did. Millett and Friedan unveiled the ideological nature of the "values," "norms," and "beliefs" concerning women's role and the relations between the sexes, which we had taken for granted even when we had struggled with the divergence between the normative and the actually practiced. These norms, values, and beliefs were received as a social reality, however resentfully or uneasily, or with those feelings of guilt that Pauline Bart so justly and precisely described: "not only were we depressed, but we were depressed because we were depressed. Since according to the experts we suburban housewives should have been happy, contented, fulfilled and pregnant. What was wrong with us?"[3]

Through these works and others we became aware of the feminine mystique as a mystique that served to keep us in our places by invading our own consciousness as our beliefs, our values, our sense of morality, fitness, and obligation. In Millett's *Sexual Politics*, the syntactic analysis de Beauvoir had provided of how women are constituted as other in relation to men as subject was given power and substance by Millett's analysis of the work of writers who for many of us (for my generation at least) had been held up as exemplary—not just as writers but as

What social relations Generate the line of fault.

exemplars and teachers of the legitimate forms of relations between the sexes. These forms we had learned directly or indirectly from these men, among others. Though we might have found them repellant, horrific, and humiliating, the moral practices of that ideological mode, drawing its pieces of machinery from Freud, among others, ensured that just those reactions affirmed the legitimacy and correctness of the prescription. Such responses were defined as defenses, pathologies, or resistance—causes for precisely the cure laid out plainly before us: be other than you are! Surely the dilemma I had experienced in relation to the work of D. H. Lawrence was, in various forms and in various relations, a common one. I was constrained to acknowledge his work both as genius and as moral authority. His ultimate idealization of sexual relations between women and men was one where woman's consciousness, her sensation, was so totally annulled before the man's that she should forego even orgasm and accept essentially the annihilation of her own consciousness in the sexual act. This totalitarian subordination, this annihilation of self, was something I resisted without knowing how to resist. But that rebellion at an earlier time had no ground to stand on, no rightful means of expression, and thus no authority for me. It certainly had no possibility as a topic for talk with other women, since to do so would have been to exhibit publicly the psychological flaws the ideology defines: an unwillingness to "accept our feminity," a secret desire to castrate men.

As we explored the world from this place in it, we became aware that this rupture in experience, and between experience and the social forms of its expression, was located in a relation of power between women and men, in which men dominated women. Millett, not alone and not first but in terms specifically relevant here, identified this relation of dominance as the patriarchy. The forms of thought, the means of expression, that we had available to us to formulate our experience were made or controlled by men. From that center women appeared as objects. In relation to men (of the ruling class) women's consciousness did not, and most probably generally still does not, appear as an autonomous source of knowledge, experience, relevance, and imagination. Women's experience did not appear as the source of an authoritative general expression of the world. Women did not appear to men as men do to one another, as persons who might share in the common construction of a social reality where that is essentially an ideological construction. As we have seen in chapter 1, the circle of speakers and hearers among men was a closed circle of significance into which women did not enter as such. Hence we could participate

in the intellectual life and culture thus created only by receiving its
terms and relevances as given. We could not be part of their making;
they did not speak from where we were.

As members of an intelligentsia, we had learned, furthermore, to
work inside a discourse that we did not have a part in making, that was
not "ours" as women. The discourse expresses, describes, and provides
the working concepts and vocabulary for a landscape in which women
are strangers. That strangeness is an integral part of the socially organized practices constituting it. This is the same rupture in consciousness—the line of fault from which this inquiry begins.

The ideologies of our society have provided us with forms of
thought, images, modes of expression, in which we were constrained
to treat ourselves as looked at from outside, as other. Sheila Rowbotham describes this at a point where the split has already appeared:

> *I had yet to understand the extent to which I identified with men, used their eyes.
> I was really sliced in two. Half of me was like a man surveying the passive half
> of me as a woman-thing. On Boxing Day in 1967 the Beatles' Magical Mystery
> Tour appeared on television. A group of people including the Beatles go on a
> coach trip. There is the atmosphere of excitement, of all being on the bus together
> and enjoying a treat. When they get off all kinds of things happen: tugs-of-war
> which remind you of the desperate tugging you felt you had to do when you were
> a child; a woman who eats and cries and cries until you can't imagine how a
> human being could carry so many tears around inside her. Then at one point
> all the boys in the bus are separated from the girls. You follow the boys in the
> film, wriggling around in your seat in front of the telly, in mounting excitement.
> It's like going into the Noah's Ark at Blackpool when you're six or listening to
> very loud rock music when you're thirteen. I got the same tightening down at
> the bottom of my spine. Well there I was clenching my cunt and where should
> they go but into a strip-tease. I had caught myself going to watch another
> woman as if I were a man. I was experiencing the situation of another woman
> stripping through men's eyes. I was being asked to desire myself by a film made
> by men.*
>
> *Catching myself observing myself desiring one of my selves I remained
> poised for an instant in two halves.*[5]

Women's means to reflect upon themselves is a reflection from outside themselves, the structuring of themselves not as subjects, but as
other. Furthermore, in its contemporary terms, it appears not as men's
view of women, but in impersonal and general terms. De Beauvoir describes it thus:

> *A man never begins by presenting himself as an individual of a certain sex; it
> goes without saying that he is a man. The terms masculine and feminine are
> used symmetrically only as a matter of form, as on legal paper. In actuality, the*

> *relation of the two sexes is not quite like that of two electrical poles, for man represents both the positive and the neutral, as is indicated by the common use of man to designate human beings in general; whereas woman represents only the negative, defined by limiting criteria, without reciprocity. In the midst of an abstract discussion it is vexing to hear a man say: "You think thus and so because you are a woman," but I know that my only defense is to reply: "I think thus and so because it is true," thereby removing my subjective self from the argument.*[6]

In so replying, she has already forfeited her position, because she has necessarily taken it up on his ground, an apparently neutral but covertly masculine position. Imagining this as exemplary of actual conversations, we can ask, How is it that what he says proceeds from a position on this general ground? That he speaks not merely with authority, but with authority of this kind and in this form, the authority of the impersonal, the neutral, the detached, the factual? How is it that her options are either to speak as a woman and therefore as limited, restricted, and subordinate, or else to speak on his ground, to speak as a man or rather to be neutered? Her subjectivity does not draw upon the implicit authority of the generalizing impersonal mode. His does.

The critique of the institutions that alienate women from their experience has taken many forms in the women's movement and developed very rapidly: attacks on stereotyping in advertising and the media in general; the critique of sexism in school reading materials, of the exclusion of women's interests and news relevant to women from the news media,[7] and of history for its exclusive focus on men and the historical traditions organized and maintained by men;[8] the critique of theology and religious institutions,[9] of the social and behavioral sciences,[10] of art, both in exemplary practices such as Women's House in Los Angeles and also in teaching and writing.[11] Another critical approach has focused on the professionally organized institutions of social control, the health care systems, law, and psychiatry in particular. The same line of fault is identified in their practices. The critique of medical institutions has been both of the failure to take up and treat as legitimate women's experience of their bodies[12] and of the historical transformation of the healing arts in the process of excluding women from its practice, as men came to appropriate and exert monopolistic control over the technical practices becoming dominant in contemporary Western medicine over the last two hundred years.[13] The critique of medicine and in particular of gynecology has been also a practical one. Women have developed alternatives for women, which have been radical both in providing for woman a place to begin from her knowledge of her own body and also in representing a radical departure from the professional forms of social relations in which knowledge is appropriated and controlled by "experts." The critique of psychiatry as among those institutions that serve the oppression of women has again been both of its ideologies and of its practical political dimensions in relation to the oppression of women.[14] It has also been concerned with the development of alternative approaches in therapy.[15]

In the disclosures and discoveries of the women's movement, women's experience breaks away along this line of fault. It makes thus observable an apparatus of social controls in part ideological, in the sense of being images and symbols, and in part an organization of specialized practices. This apparatus comes into view as a whole that, though loosely organized, is not made up of discrete and singular functional domains (as we have in sociology tended to conceptualize them), but rather constitutes a differentiated but coherent structure, an apparatus of "ruling," of organization and men, whose participation in it is also differentiated by social class (working-class men are not part of the structure; women are not part of the structure).

In analyzing the ideological phases of this "apparatus," I make use of Marx and Engels's concept or formulation of "ideology." In returning to their usage in *The German Ideology*,[16] I am bypassing some of the different usages that have developed since that time and are now current in the social sciences. I am not using the term to refer to political beliefs, though political beliefs would be one instance or aspect of ideology. Nor am I using the term to draw the boundaries between an impartial and disinterested social science and "ideology" as an interested and partial perspective biased by its roots in a particular group or class.[17] I am concerned, rather, with ideology as those ideas and images through which the class that rules the society by virtue of its domination of the means of production orders, organizes, and sanctions the social relations that sustain its domination. Further, in following Marx and Engels's use of ideology, I view the ideas, images, and symbols in which our experience is given social form not as that neutral floating thing called culture but as what is actually produced by specialists and by people who are part of the apparatus by which the ruling class maintains its control over the society. Thus, the concept of ideology provides us with a thread through the maze different from our more familiar notions of "culture," for it directs us to look for and at the actual practical organization of the production of images, ideas, symbols, concepts, vocabularies, as means for us to think about our world. It directs us to examine who produces what for whom, where the social forms of consciousness come from.

Marx and Engels's account of ideology allows us to make a preliminary sketch of the social relations organizing the rupture that is women's experience in this social form. Specifically, their formulation provides a method enabling us to see how ideas and social forms of consciousness may originate outside experience, coming from an external source and becoming a forced set of categories into which we must stuff the awkward and resistant actualities of our worlds. Marx and Engels held that how people think about and express themselves to one another arises out of their actual everyday working relations. Their view is not, however, as simpleminded as it has sometimes been represented. Their analysis shows how the ideas produced by a ruling class may dominate and penetrate the social consciousness of the society in general, and thus may effectively control the social process of consciousness in ways that deny expression to the actual experience people have in the working relations of their everyday world. It offers an analysis that shows how a disjuncture can arise between the world as it is known directly in experience and as it is shared with others, and the ideas and images fabricated externally to that everyday world and provided as a means to think and image it.

The social forms of thought, according to Marx and Engels, arise in people's immediate working relations, their immediate and directly experienced world as it is shared with others:

> The production of ideas, of conceptions, of consciousness, is at first directly interwoven with the material activity and the material intercourse of men, the language of real life. Conceiving, thinking, the mental intercourse of men appear at this stage as the direct efflux of their material behavior. The same applies to mental production as expressed in the language of politics, laws, morality, religion, metaphysics, etc. of a people.[18]

Before the development of a class structure, the kind of rupture I am attempting to explicate is one that could emerge only in biographical idiosyncracies and not as a "social" phenomenon. With the emergence of a class society, however, "mental production" becomes the privilege of the class that dominates the means of production and appropriates the means of mental production. The contrast the Marxist formulation allows us to conceptualize is between, on the one hand, ideas and images—the social forms of thought—directly expressive of a world known directly and shared, arising where things need to be thought, said, sung, or imaged in paint or sculpture, enacted in ritual, or formulated as rule, and, on the other hand, the social forms of thought made for us by others, which come to us from outside, and which do not arise out of experience, spoken of and shared with others, or out of the need to communicate with others in working contexts. The concept of ideology brings into focus the conscious production of the forms of thought by a ruling class or that section of a ruling class known as the intelligentsia, which serves to organize and order the expression of the local, particular, and directly known into forms concordant with its interests, aims, and perspectives. Thus, experiences, concerns, needs, aims, interests, arising among people in the everyday and working contexts of their living, are given expression in forms that articulate them to the existing practices and social relations constituting its rule.

Sociology is part of this ideological structure. Its themes and relevances are organized by and articulate the perspectives of men—not as individuals floating vaguely as sexual beings in a social void, but as persons playing determinate parts in the social relations of this form of society, occupying determinate class positions in it, and participating in networks of relations, which link their work to that of other professionals, in the health and educational institutions of the society, and to its more direct practices of ruling, whether in business, in government, or elsewhere. The perspectives and interests, the experience and anxieties that are incorporated into sociology and integrated to the sociological discourse arise out of a determinate range of social institutions forming the governing apparatus of the society—management, government, military organization, health institutions, psychiatry, education, and the social and psychological sciences, the media, and other specialized ideological institutions—the institutions that form the Marxist's understanding of the "superstructure."

In describing the ideological rupture and locating it in a ruling class, I am not using the model of manipulation of ideas from behind the scenes, the model of ideology as ideas designed to deceive and to fool the innocent, put forward consciously and with malign intent by a ruling elite. This model is quite inadequate to analyze the phenomenon we are concerned with. We are describing, rather, a set of positions in the structures that "rule" (manage, administrate, organize, and otherwise control). These constitute the bases of common perspectives. Thinking, informed by interests arising in the work of ruling and relevant to getting that work done, develops in overlapping circles of discourse. People who occupy such positions come to view the world in distinctive ways by virtue of their participation in the ruling structure. They have working relations with others similarly placed. They have similar problems, experiences, concerns, and interests. In the formally and informally organized circles of discourse the "social" or intersubjective character of their interests and experience is accomplished. A ruling class does not exist merely as an ideologically homogeneous collection of individuals standing in an identical relation to the means of production. Rather, a ruling class is the basis of an active process of organization, producing ideologies that serve to organize the class itself and its work of ruling, as well as to order and legitimize its domination. Ideologies take for granted the conditions of ruling-class experience. They give social form to its interests, relevances, and objectives. In its specific historical character ideology builds the internal social organization of the ruling class as well as its domination over others. Its overall character, however, depends upon, and takes for granted, the social relations that organize and enforce the silences of those who do not participate in the process, who are outside it. It is important to keep in mind that we are not talking about the control of ideas in an abstract sense. Rather, we are talking about control over the means of producing and disseminating ideas and images—that is, control over the educational process, over the media, and so on. The silence of those outside the apparatus is a silence in part materially organized by the preemption, indeed virtual monopoly, of communications media and the educational process as part of the ruling apparatus.

During the last fifty years the developments described above have deepened and intensified to a very great degree, with the extension of the educational process, with the development of news media, with the encompassment of so many more aspects of our lives within the framework of commodity production. We may imagine earlier the existence and persistence of folk tradition—of a working-class culture, for example—so that disjunctures such as we are describing were accessible directly to consciousness in the confrontation of local and special traditions with ideologies. In comparing women's situation with that of the working class, Rowbotham identifies just such a submerged tradition among the British working class in the "divorce between home talking and educated language." Here, experience has a language.

> There is a long inchoate period during which the struggle between the language of theory becomes a kind of agony. In the making of the working class in Britain, the conflict of silence with "their" language, the problem of paralysis and connection has been continuous. Every man who has worked up through the labour movement expressed this in some form. The embarrassment about dialect, the divorce between home talking and educated language, the otherness of "culture"—their culture—is intense and painful. The struggle is happening now every time a worker on strike has to justify his position in the alien structures of the television studio before the interrogatory camera of the dominant class, or every time a working-class child encounters a middle-class teacher. [19]

Such submerged traditions survive in many sections of our society—to some extent among black people, and in certain rural areas in Canada, notably among native peoples. But they have largely disappeared for women and most particularly for middle-class women—that is, women who have in common relatively highly developed skills in literacy and are oriented toward written media, the authority of women's magazines, professionals (psychiatrists, psychologists), and so on. For women, education has in the end meant intense exposure to the invasion of consciousness by interpretations systematically developed by such specialists as psychologists, historians, and sociologists, as well as exposure to short stories, novels, and other literature, which in other ways form our dreams, wishes, visions, and fantasies.

The penetration of the society by the ideological process includes, particularly for the relatively highly educated, an "in-depth" organization of consciousness. Freud's work represents the major technical breakthrough of extending the imperialism of "rationality" over personal experience, beyond the immediately practical organization of participation in professional, occupational, and womanly roles. In this way psychiatry provides a set of techniques for examining one's life and experience in relation to an ideology that legitimates and enhances conformities of feeling and disposition as well as of action and offers an elaborated technique for separating out what is "healthy" and putting away what is not. We have been left with very few places to hide.

In the emergence of modes of speaking our experience, of making it social and hence in this context political, there is, as Rowbotham has described, "a long inchoate period."[20] For women particularly, there has not even been a "home talking" to contrast with an educated language. In beginning to find out how and what to speak, we had to begin from nowhere, not knowing what it was we would have to say and what it was we would need to know how to speak. In almost every area of work, therefore, in opposing women's oppression we have had to resort to women's experience as yet unformulated and unformed; lacking means of expression; lacking symbolic forms, images, concepts, conceptual frameworks, methods of analysis; more straightforwardly, lacking self-information and self-knowledge. The distinctive and deep significance of consciousness-raising at an earlier period of the women's movement was precisely this process of opening up what was personal, idiosyncratic, and inchoate and discovering with others how this was shared, was objectively part of women's oppression, finding ways of speaking of it and ways of speaking it politically. It is this essential return to the experience we ourselves have directly in our everyday worlds that has been the distinctive mode of working in the women's movement—the repudiation of the professional, the expert, the already authoritative tones of the discipline; the science, the formal tradition, and the return to the seriously engaged and very difficult enterprise of discovering how to begin from ourselves.

The resort to beginning from our experience and from our own subjectivities has been a fundamental and essential resource in the work of radicalizing (remaking from the root) the various ideological structures of this social form. In art and in poetry the artist begins with the problem of having learned her craft in an alienated mode and must discover methods of working that allow her to begin from herself distinctly as a woman or, perhaps even more simply, to begin from herself who is a woman. Judy Chicago's autobiographical account of her "struggle as a woman artist" is an account of just this process by a politically conscious, feminist artist.[21] The same struggle is expressed in the work of women poets, whether consciously, as in the work of a poet such as Adrienne Rich, whose sense of the lack of language to express women's experiences is a powerful theme in her poetry, or as a submerged, but important organization of her relation to language, as Suzanne Juhasz has suggested for the work of Emily Dickinson.[22]

In their work at the point of rupture between experience and the ideological modes of interpreting and reading it, women have had to resort to their experience unmade, because there has been no alternative. We can speculate that the "subjectivity" of women, their "intuitiveness," their "insight," as qualities identified in them by men, represent incursions of an underground of unformed and unsystematically developed knowledge of experience excluded, repressed, and lacking the means to become shared. When Dorothy Richardson in the early twentieth century introduced her radical stylistic innovations, she was in search of a style that would and did express the consciousness of women, of a particular woman, as actual experiencing. Her aim to become a women's Balzac meant an exploration of the experiencing of an everyday world from within a particular individual subjectivity.[23] In Chicago's account of how the women of the Fresno Women's Program went about discovering how to express their experience as women, we find another method relying on the same basic resource:

> In one of our sessions, we discussed how we felt when we were walking down the street and we were harrassed by men. Everyone had very strong attitudes about these experiences, and we decided to try to make images of the feelings. I asked the women to deal with the sensation or experience of being psychically invaded by a man or men. There was no media restriction. They were free to paint, draw, write, make a film, or do a performance. On the day the work was presented, we were downstairs in the basement of one of the students' homes. Everyone was trembling because women were showing images of feelings and experiences that none of us had ever seen portrayed before: paintings and drawings, poems, performances, and ideas for films, all revealing the way women saw men. These perceptions were considerably different from the way men saw and depicted themselves in their art.[24]

This beginning "from the center" has been a powerful source for women poets and for women artists.[25] Juhasz has suggested that it is the emergence of this beginning that constitutes a new tradition in poetry:

The new tradition exists: wrought slowly through the century with pain and daring, it daily encounters and confronts a growing audience. No one style or form defines it, yet certain qualities do characterize the poetry of contemporary women poets; a voice that is open, intimate, particular, involved, engaged, committed. It is a poetry whose poet speaks as a woman, so that the form of her poem is an extension of herself. A poetry that is linked to experience through the active participation of the poet herself. A poetry that seeks to affect actively its audience. A poetry that is real, because the voice that speaks it is as real as the poet can be about herself. A poetry that seeks to affect actively its audience. A poetry that is real, because the voice that speaks it is as real as the poet can be about herself. A poetry that is revolutionary, because by expressing the vision of real women it challenges the patriarchal premises of society itself.[26]

Those of us who have been working in relation to disciplines such as sociology, psychology, and anthropology confront different constraints and possibilities. The problem seems to be of a different kind. In history, for example, though women historians have advanced very rapidly indeed, perhaps more so than in any other field, the problem of what it means to do a history of women, what the methodology and founding of such a history is, still remains.[27] The professional discourse has momentum of its own. The canons of science as a constitutional practice require the suppression of the personal. The structures developed become the criteria and standards of proper professional performance. Being a professional involves knowing how to do it this way, how to produce work that conforms to these standards, addressing these topics, and following these methodologies. Further, doing it this way is how we recognize ourselves as professionals. We begin from a position in the discourse as an ongoing social process of formally organized interchange. We begin from a position within a determinate conceptual framework that is identified with the discipline (though there are many), and by virtue of our training and of what it means to do the professional work in our disciplines we begin from outside ourselves to locate problematics organized by the sociological, the psychological, the historical discourse. The perspective of men institutionalized as the "field" or the "discipline" cannot, it seems, be so directly confronted with a personal source of experience, because to do so is to step outside the discipline, to cease to do sociology or history, and, with whatever virtue or value, to be found to be doing something else.

II Sociology: Women are Outside the Frame

The concepts, methods, relevances, and topics of sociology are accomplished in the social organization of the discourse. A discourse (the term is borrowed from Foucault)[28] is like a conversation in which utterances are abstracted from particular participants located in particular spatiotemporal settings. Certain journals and occasions such as classes, conventions, and the like are warranted sites for the presentation of sociological work. Work is accomplished as sociological in part by its presentation at such sites. By virtue of publication or appropriately sited public reading, a text becomes part of the literature that is sociology. This literature is exemplary in the sense that sociologists look to what has already been done and is already identifiable as a legitimate piece of sociological work to exhibit what is recognizable as sociology. The discourse is maintained by practices that determine who can participate in it as fully competent members. It develops as a process of organization and reorganization of relations among participants through the medium of their work. To be recognized as a proper participant, the member must produce work that conforms to appropriate styles and terminologies, makes the appropriate deferences, and is locatable by these and other devices in the traditions, factions, and schools whose themes it elaborates, whose interpretive procedures it intends, and by whose criteria it is to be evaluated. This system continually regulates the topics, themes, problematics, and conceptual practices of sociology and ensures that the relevances of sociological work are the relevances of the discourse.

The virtual exclusion of women from positions of influence in the discipline has meant that we have been unable until very recently to give themes and topics to the sociological discourse.[29] In proposing remedies, we have in general, as in other fields of intellectual work, drawn on women's experience as the primary source to correct the situation. Ann Oakley, for example, has made a critique of sociology as "concealing" women. She suggests that the definition of subject areas in sociology—social stratification, political institutions, religion, education, deviance, sociology of work, and so on—has been determined by a male focus of interest and that it "reduces women to a side-issue from the start." Her critique is formulated in terms of bias and distortion; the measures of these she proposes involve "the extent to which the experiences of women [are] actually represented in the study of these life-areas." She proposes that the major subject areas be evaluated with respect to "the extent to which women are studied in each subject-area, and their actual role in the sphere of social life that the subject-category represents. For example, in the case of housework the omission of this topic from both family sociology and the sociology of work clearly conveys a distorted impression of women's situation."[30] The remedy is to take women's experience into account so that the balance can be achieved and women's perspectives and experiences can be represented equally with men's.

Oakley's proposal for correction is, at that stage of her work at least, largely additive. Thelma McCormack's approach suggests a critique that aims to modify the organization of the field. She proposes that we should work by identifying the male bias in established approaches. These must be examined from the perspective of women, and the implications for the field of incorporating the perspectives and interests of women must be followed through. In her own field of specialization, political sociology, she points out that women's and men's relation to the political process is very different. Differences between women's and men's political behavior have generally been understood in terms of deviations from a male norm of political behavior. Explanations in socialization, or of "backwardness," have been used. Her own proposal is that women represent, in fact, a separate political culture, one that adds "up to a female design for political living that is dissimilar from that of the male." She insists, furthermore, that the interpretation of women's experience as a basis for modifying political sociology must not be interpreted as women's special interest in or "title" to topics traditionally and stereotypically identified with women, such as the political socialization of children.[31]

The problem is that this procedure is one that, whether additive (Oakley) or truly critical (McCormack), treats the "agenda" of the discipline as given. But this agenda, embodied in the organization of sociological "domains," is grounded in the working worlds and relations of men, whose experience and interests arise in the course of and relation to participation in the ruling apparatus of this society. The accepted fields of sociology—organizational theory, political sociology, the sociology of work, the sociology of mental illness, deviance, and the like—have been defined from the perspective of the professional, managerial, and administrative structures in terms of their concerns. The specialized functions and organizations of control over society have defined both the themes and relevances of sociology and to a considerable extent its subject matter. Indeed the universe of sociological phenomenon, the world it knows, is to a large extent constructed in the working relations of this ruling apparatus with the people whose lives it organizes and controls.

The organization of our work as sociologists begins from and re-

turns to the relevances and organization of the field as zones of interpretive and internal phenomenal coherence. We proceed from
within the received conceptual apparatus that defines the phenomenal
prospect before us—mental illness, motivation, work satisfaction, in-
strumental versus expressive, roles, and so on. The world that appears
before the sociologist in her sociological capacity is already structured
conceptually in its phenomenal aspect. We do not perhaps recognize
the degree to which our knowledge of the world is already located at a
conceptual level prior to the development of a theoretical apparatus.
In effect, it is the organization of the discourse that generates for sociology as a whole, as well as for its different subfields and schools, the
organization of the phenomenal world that it claims to study. We make
use of the world as it is as a resource from which we "return," bringing
our "findings" back to discourse as sociological findings, a contribution
to the sociological work and process. The world as we know it sociologically is largely organized by the articulation of the discourse to the
ruling apparatus of which it is part.

　　To a large extent and until recently the nature of this relation has
remained invisible precisely because sociology has operated with a conceptual apparatus that has served to detach the phenomena from the
working contexts of the social process constituting the phenomena thus
named. Mental illness, for example, as a phenomenon arises in the
relation between psychiatric agencies of various kinds and the problems brought to them to deal with. This is an organized social relation
that, like sociology, has two aspects. One is whatever is happening to
people that gets socially organized by the institutional processes themselves as an organized practice. "Mental illness" as a phenomenon
arises at the conjunction of the two. But sociology has taken the perspective of the institutional process that organizes the world as it appears for those whose professional business it is. In the context of their
work, the phenomena constituting its jurisdiction are seen as present
in or as properties of the world out there to be acted on. Sociology
shares this perspective and these presuppositions. It takes up mental
illness, for example, as a problematic phenomenon for which causes
have to be found. Earlier stages of breaking out of this way of thinking
in sociology saw psychiatric agencies as causing mental illness by assigning people to this role.[32] It has taken much further work, including
the important critique of ethnomethodology, for sociologists to begin
to relocate the phenomenal universe in the actual working practices of
the agencies and institutions that constitute it.[33]

　　Women are outside the frame. They are largely silent in the discourse that develops the conceptual apparatus, the relevances, and

themes. They are not a speaking part of the workings of the professional, administrative, and managerial apparatus into which sociology is locked. Indeed the positions typically occupied by women in the society are positions of subordination to this apparatus. As we have seen, much of the critique made by the women's movement locates women's oppression in the relation of women to its various parts—welfare, medical, and psychiatric agencies, as well as the ideological apparatus that is our chief focus here. In beginning, therefore, to speak from where we are as women, we can begin to make observable at least some of the assumptions built into the sociological discourse. Its own organized practices upon the world have treated these assumptions as features of the world itself. We have thus inserted into the world as its structure, organization, and the like the working relations and organizations of the discourse.

The agentic approach in research described by Bernard, on the basis of work by Rae Carlson,[34] as distinctively male would appear to have its base in this organization of the discourse. It is an approach that "operates by way of mastery and control."[35] Bernard has here isolated one of a family of "assumptions" that we find in various forms built into models of the social actor. Talcott Parsons, for example, represents the actor as a maker of choices among means in relation to ends; Rom Harré and Paul Secord's more recent model assumes that a "human being has the power to initiate change."[36] These assumptions are grounded in a mode of action in which the power to act and coordinate in a planned and rational manner and to exercise control over conditions and means is taken for granted.

Or take Alfred Schutz's description of the fear of death as a fundamental anxiety governing each individual's system of relevance in the working world. I have always stopped short at this assumption, since I do not personally experience that anxiety. Before I learned from the women's movement, I used to transform it into a metaphysical statement unsupported by experience, but Schutz does not mean it that way. He writes thus: "From the fundamental anxiety spring the many interrelated systems of hopes and fears, of wants and satisfactions, of chances and risks which incite man within the natural attitude to attempt the mastery of the world, to overcome obstacles, to draft projects, and to realize them."[37] This too, like the other assumptions mentioned above, is grounded in a mode of action in which the power to act and coordinate in a planned and rational manner and to exercise control as an individual over conditions and means is taken for granted.

Further, the lack of sociological interest in the social structuring of emotions to which Arlie Hochschild has drawn attention[38] also appears to be grounded in a sociological ontology that is isomorphic, with rational modes of action characteristic of this form of "ruling." The rational actor choosing and calculating is the abstracted model of organizational or bureaucratic man, whose motives, methods, and ego structure are organized by the formal rationality structuring his work role. At work his feelings have no place. Rationality is a normative practice organizing and prescribing determinate modes of action within the bureaucratic or professional form. Responses that do not conform to these modes of action, by virtue of how they are excluded from these domains, are constituted residually as a distinct mode of response and being. They are defined by contrast with what excludes them, the rational mode of action.[39] In *The Structure of Social Action*, Parsons specifically depends on the isomorphy of sociological practice and rationality. In arriving at a determination of its subject matter, sociology has simply conformed to the contours of the institutionalized boundaries it presupposes. It is no accident that women are identified with the world of feeling and emotion, not only as being more emotional than men, but also as creating and preserving for men who participate in this mode of action a place to feel.

These assumptions and the social organization in which they are grounded are drawn into question when we begin from the experience and actualities of women's situation. For then we locate our enterprises with knowers whose perspective is organized by exactly how they are located outside these structures, by how they are excluded from participation, and by their actual situation and its relation to the ruling apparatus of which sociology is a part. If we began from women's experience of the world, we would not find these assumptions built into its sociology, since they do not conform to the organization of our experience. Characteristically for women (as also for others in the society similarly excluded), the organization of daily experience, the work routines, and the structuring of our lives through time have been and to a very large extent still are determined and ordered by processes external to, and beyond, our everyday world. I think I would be by no means alone in seeing in my past not so much a career as a series of contingencies, of accidents, so that I seem to have become who I am almost by chance.

The experience of marriage, of immigration closely following marriage, of the arrival of children, of the departure of a husband rather early one morning, of the jobs that became available—all these were moments in which I had in fact little choice and certainly little foreknowledge. I had little opportunity of calculating rationally what it means to have a child, what it means to leave your own country and live among strangers, what it means to be married, and how each of these experiences would be a major transformation. When I read in autobiographies or fiction of the lives of other women, I find these same qualities and the surprises in store for the subject about whom she may become. I do not find them in the same way in the autobiographies of men.

In general, women's work routines and the organization of their daily lives do not conform to the "voluntaristic" model or to the model upon which an agentic style of sociology might be based. Women have little opportunity for the exercise of mastery and control. Their working lives are not structured in terms of a project of their own. The housewife, for example, becomes highly skilled at holding together and coordinating the threads and shreds of several lines of action, the projects of more than one individual, while herself pursuing none. The conflicts academic and professional women experience when they are also housewives are partly conflicts between opposing modes of organizing consciousness. Typically, the lives and daily routines of women are structured by an organization of action and are external to the positions that women usually occupy in hierarchical structures outside the home (indeed, it seems probable that one important aspect of organizational work roles for women is that they are designed specifically to constitute a class of persons who do not become a "part of the action"). Women are generally means to the enterprises of others, or means to the enterprise built into an organizational process. They hold only a piece of the action, sometimes a piece essential to the action, but they are not at its center. The consciousness required in this type of relation is organized quite differently from the agentic model. What is required is a subordination of attentiveness to self and a focus on others, the lack of development of an independent project organizing relevances and, in contrast, an openness and attentiveness to cues and indications of others' needs. A housewife, holding in place the simultaneous and divergent schedules and activities of a family, depends upon a diffuse and open organization of consciousness available to the various strands, which are coordinated only in her head and by her work and do not coordinate otherwise in the world. And again, we who have done or do both types of work can report on how the individually undertaken project of our work can seriously impair and disorganize our ability to sustain the modes of consciousness required for a peak performance in the role of housewife.

Over a lifetime and in the daily routines, women's lives tend to show a loose, episodic structure that reflects the ways in which their lives are organized and determined external to them and the situations they order and control. This lack of control over their lives and what happens to them can be found represented in a number of important contemporary novels about women. In *Them*, for example, Joyce Carol Oates has made a dramatic and intense amalgam of the disorder and disintegration of the lives of women and the working class.[40] When recently in Vancouver a series of plays were performed, written, and directed by women, they shared distinctly episodic structures—though otherwise their themes were quite different. The exclusively male reviewers of these plays consistently failed to make sense of how they were put together and complained of their lack of "plot." They could not find, as the women in the audience had no difficulty in finding, the expression of the structure of their own experience in the structure of the plays. Joan Didion in her extraordinary novel *Play It as It Lays* made use of the episodic structure of a film script as a stylistic device, realizing exactly the episodic discontinuities of the life of her protagonist.[41]

An important further difference between the frameworks relevant to the lives and experiences of men and those of women (as they are typically located in this society) emerged for me as a result of reading Huw Beynon's *Working for Ford*.[42] This book comes about as close as I can imagine to doing a sociology from the perspective of working-class men. True it does not become clear in that book what is implied by beginning from such a position, where a sociology that began there might go, or just what kinds of further consequences would follow (questions are and must be raised about the fundamentally academic enterprise of doing merely a sociology). But this book does describe and analyze not just workingmen's work experience but their work experience in the context of the organization, managerial practices, and economic relations of Ford. It is a limited perspective excluding much of the lives and experience of working-class women as well as of working-class men outside the factory. Working-class men are provided or may be provided with an adequate accounting of their working lives from within the organizational framework of company and union. The types of oppression experienced by working-class men in the workplace and the actual determinations of their work experience are a function of a directly present managerial structure set up in line with company policies, responsive to changes in the economic situation. The sociological researcher may not always be able to identify what the policies are, but that there are policies, management, managerial authority and power, and its use in relation to policy and planning is fundamental to the interpretive framework used in describing and analyzing what happens. The work lives and experience of those who work at Ford are determined by direct subordination to a managerial hierarchy, which shapes, among other matters, the union agenda. The standard socio-logical conceptual framework may need some stretching, but on the whole it will work because essentially the same processes are the focus. But women's existence cannot be comprehended within such frames (nor perhaps, with the following example, should we take it for granted that men's can).

Society has organized for women a different relation to the world. Attempts to apply a conceptual apparatus drawn uncritically from the standard sociological frames in these areas rest uneasily on the actual experience and situation of women as a means of analysis. Oakley, in her use of the conceptual apparatus from the sociology of work to focus on work satisfaction in the study of housework, adopts a framework that presupposes the wage relation—that is, a relation in which a worker sells his labor to an enterprise and in which his labor must therefore be managed for the benefit of the enterprise. This underly-ing structure—which is presupposed in the endless work that has been done on motivation in industrial settings—is simply not present in the relation of the housewife either to her husband or to her work.[43] Sim-ilarly, applications of time-budget methods to comparisons between the amount of work women do in the home and the amount of work men do outside and inside the home have simply adapted the distinction between work and leisure in such a way that the kinds of responsibilities women take in relation to the home and to the children do not ap-pear.[44] The work-leisure organization applies to employment. The so-ciological concepts are borrowed directly from it. If we started with housework as a basis, the categories of "work" and "leisure" would never emerge. And indeed, it is hard to image how, using housework as our basic framework, it would be possible to make "work" and "lei-sure" observable. The social organization of the roles of housewife, mother, and wife does not conform to the divisions between being at work and not being at work. Even the concept of housework as work leaves what we do as mothers without a conceptual home.

Traditionally in sociology, the problem of subordinating extra man-agerial forms to the conceptual hegemony of rational administrative forms of organization has been worked out by applying functionalist theory. Functionalism makes possible the application of a model of ra-tional action to social phenomena that could not be assimilated to that model empirically. Unfortunately, much contemporary Marxist think-ing on women and the household follows an essentially functionalist procedure by "reducing" women's characteristic work and social rela-tions in the household and family to concepts that analyze them in terms of their relation to capitalist economic processes.[45] But the work life of women escapes the scope of the bureaucratic, professional, and administrative princedoms of "the active society."[46] The phenomena of women's situation and experience fall between or outside the institutional spheres.[47] It is thus not adequate to do as Oakley suggests and divide women up as topics among the various existing subject areas in sociology, defined—as Oakley herself recognizes—by the various managerial and professional jurisdictions of the ruling apparatus. Beginning from women's experience calls into question more than the distribution of topics as between women and men. Further, the ways in which women's experience has been introduced have been largely as a resource in entering new topics or eking out old ones. But the sociological agenda and the forms of thought organized by the location of the discourse within the ruling apparatus remain unmoved. Though Bernard and others have proposed a radical critique of methods,[48] we have not known, as poets, painters, and sculptors have known, how to begin from our own experience, how to make ourselves as women the subjects of the sociological act of knowing.

III Sociology as a Constituent of a Consciousness Organized by the Abstracted, Extralocal Relations of Ruling

To help us analyze further the problem of women's relation as subjects or knowers to the sociological discourse, I shall draw on Alfred Schutz's description of the finite provinces of meaning and of the changes in the organization of consciousness associated with shifts from one province to another. The fundamental province of meaning is the paramount reality, the original and ultimate locus of consciousness, in which the subject's consciousness is organized by its own actual position in the world. In the paramount reality, the subject is located in that stratum of reality corresponding to the everyday world of working. Schutz describes this organization of consciousness thus:

> The wide-awake man within the natural attitude is primarily interested in that sector of the world of his everyday life which is within his scope and which is centered in space and time around himself. The place which my body occupies within the world, my actual Here is the starting point from which I take my bearings in space. It is, so to speak, the center 0 of my system of coordinates. Relative to my body I group the elements of my surroundings under the categories of right and left, before and behind, above and below, near and far, and so on. And in a similar way my actual Now is the origin of all the time perspec-

tives under which I organize the events within the world, such as the categories of fore and after, past and future, simultaneity and succession, etc.[49]

This organization of the world in consciousness locates the null point, the center 0, in an actual and particular locality. The subject is located by her bodily situation in the world, and her coordinates shift in relation to her as the center, changing as her position changes, changing as her "position" in time changes. It is consciousness located materially and in activities that enter the world of working.

Schutz analyzes other finite provinces of meaning. Among them (and of special relevance here) is the finite province of scientific attitude. In entering the "world" of science, consciousness is reorganized to drop away the particular and local organization from subject as the center, as well as relevances arising out of work or activity in relation to the subject's own interests or projects in the everyday world. Consciousness organized in the finite province of meaning of science sets aside the anxieties and hopes and fears arising in the paramount reality. The epoche peculiar to the scientific attitude has these characteristics:

> *In this epoche there is "bracketed" (suspended): the subjectivity of the thinker as a man among fellow-men, including his bodily existence as a psychophysical human being within the world; 2) the system of orientation by which the world of everyday life is grouped in zones within actual, restorable attainable reach, etc; 3) the fundamental anxiety and the system of pragmatic relevance originating therein.*[50]

Entry into the world of scientific theory organizes consciousness into a mode detached from the everyday world of working. In it "we" takes on a universal character, and the categories of before and after, and the like, are organized by the temporal and "spatial" organization of the discourse rather than by the subject's bodily location in the world.

What Schutz is describing, in part, is the organization of consciousness in the work of "doing" science, which necessarily involves attention to a domain constituted separately from the particular and immediate interests and concerns of the individual located in her body. It is that zone she enters in doing the kind of work we are doing now. But more than that, Schutz ascribes to this zone a definite cognitive domain organizing the subjectivity of its participant into a mode in which her particular position—the view from the center—is discarded and replaced by an impartial, detached mode. The grammatical subject identifies no particular person. Temporal and spatial coordinates that structure the referencing work of indexicals (before, after, etc.) do not intersect in a particular center.[51]

In taking up the scientific attitude as that mode in which their work is done, sociologists have sought to practice an objectivity constituted in relation to an "Archimedian" point—that is, a point external to any particular position in society. Objectivity for the social scientist has involved continual attention to the methodological and epistemological problems arising from the fact that the cognitive domain of sociology has to be organized in and—in a sense—out of the lived reality of the world the sociologist participates in in her total being. The scientific attitude sometimes enforces an exclusion of concerns and interests— an exclusion that seems artificial, strange, and wrong. The contrast between the professional starting point and an interested position identified with women can be seen in the following account by Catherine Russell of her experience at a conference among psychologists, psychiatrists, social workers, and sociologists concerning battered wives. She describes the character of the scientific attitude in this context in such a way that we can see how it locates her as subject outside herself and constitutes a social relationship of a distinct kind, not only in organizing her relation to the subject matter, battered wives, but also in organizing her relations with others so that she takes up her position in the hierarchical structure of the professions and separates herself from those whose partial and "emotional" involvement prevents "detached" and "logical" discussion of the problem. The accounts from which these quotes are drawn appear in a feminist newspaper. Catherine Russell writes:

> My attitudes on arriving at the conference were fairly consistent with those of the majority. I was there to learn by absorbing theories and facts about the specific phenomenon of violence in the family, particularly as experienced by battered wives. My purpose was to collect information that would contribute to my being a more effective worker at Transition House [a refuge in Vancouver, B.C., for women who have been violently treated at home]. Not knowing much, I accepted a position of being low on the hierarchy of people at the symposium; power and worthiness derived from being able to clearly articulate an intellectual perception of a social phenomenon and a theoretical solution to the problem.
>
> My first emotional response at the symposium was to Gene Errington's speech. She made a strong, angry statement of her reaction to the conference and to the orientation of professionals. I was very uncomfortable and felt antagonistic toward her for making a speech that stirred up the symposium and antagonized a large number of delegates. I didn't want to be identified with the feminists who were giving her a standing ovation—even though I was sitting with that group whose interests coincided with mine. I was accepting the norm that says: "Let's be calm and logical about this. There's no need to get angry." And, by so doing, I was denying the validity of Gene's anger.

The next day I started to realize how I had been affected by the norms of the majority. And in the process had been denying others the expression of their feelings and had been valuing people's contributions predominantly on the basis of intellectual consistency, articulation and coolness.

In the first workshop, one woman—in an emotional and somewhat rambling statement—expressed her feeling of being battered by the conference itself. The expression of her feelings was only briefly responded to by the workshop speaker. However, she had spoken for a lot of women at that workshop, in that there was a lot of frustration being experienced—and not spoken of—at the tone of the conference. Her speaking led other women to speak from their feelings.

And that's when I really started feeling angry. I recognized that my acceptance of the professionals' norms had been a critical factor in my discounting and criticizing Gene the previous day and others during the course of the symposium, and consequently in my feeling separated from people. Those norms value intellectual perception so highly and emotions so lowly; they are a basic cause of the violence in our culture. And that was not being dealt with.[52]

In Russell's account, distinctive properties of the scientific attitude in the social sciences come into view. By suspending the subjectivity of the thinker as a woman among sister-women,[53] she is related in a particular mode to women who have experienced violence from the men with whom they live. That relation is packaged in a social organization that aligns her with other professionals sharing the same orientation and alienates her from groups representing directly the concerns and interests of women in that situation. The relation between the knower and the object of her knowledge (constituted as such in the relation) is a socially organized practice. The cognitive domain of science is itself a social relation. Knowledge itself is a social accomplishment.[54] The conceptual practices, methodologies, instrumentalities, and so on that in the concrete instance organize the cognitive domain of the particular science in which the subject is practitioner are not merely tools to be picked up and laid down at will. They are together those practices that organize and bring into being the phenomena as such in the knower's relation to the known as object. In the example above it becomes clear that knowledge in the social sciences has this further character, namely, that both terms of the "knowledge relation" are human. The methods of inquiry and of thinking are integral not only to the relation among knowers in a discourse but constitute a determinate social relation among knowers and the human objects of their knowledge. Sociology is an organization of practices that structure our relation to others in the society of whom we speak and write, concerning whom we make assertions, into whose lives and experience we inquire, who are the objects of our study, and whose behavior we aim to explain.

That the parties to this relation are rendered specifically anonymous by procedures taken for granted in our methodologies must be viewed as a definite feature of this social relation rather than as suspending its social character. Anonymity, impersonality, detachment, impartiality, and objectivity itself are accomplished by socially organized practices that bring into being a relation of a definite form between knowers and known. Integral to the relation thus formed is its organization to suspend the particular subjectivities of knower and known in such a way that its character as a social relation disappears—very much in the way in which, according to Marx, the activities of people disappear in the social relation constituted in the commodity form, such that relations between actual people appear as relations of exchange between things, money, and commodities.

In working as sociologists within established methods of thinking and inquiry, we "enter" a social relation organizing our relations with others into determinate forms. We get into this mode very much as the driver of a car gets into the driving seat. It is true that we do the driving and can choose the direction and destination, but the way in which the car is put together, how it works, and how and where it will travel structure our relation to the world we travel in. In entering the discourse as practitioners, we enter it as subjects of the kinds of sentences it can properly generate, the assertions it can make. We have learned in our training to proceed from within the conceptual frameworks, the epistemological presuppositions, as well as to find our way around in the organization of camps, schools, and factions of the discourse. We have learned to discard our experienced worlds as a source of concerns, information, and understandings of the actualities of the social world and to confine and focus our "insights" within the conceptual frameworks and relevances given in the discipline. Should we think otherwise or experience the world in different ways, with edges or horizons passing beyond what could be conceptualized in the established forms, we have learned to practice a discipline that disattends them or to find some way of making them over so that they will fit. We have learned a way of thinking about the world, a way of knowing it, that is recognizable to its practitioners as a sociological way of thinking, and we have come to identify ourselves as professionals in these terms.

In this way the discourse organizes our social relations with those who become the objects of our study. Ordinarily, as sociologists we function in and operate this social relation. Its methods are as effective in eliminating our subject's presence as they are in suspending our recognition of our own. Occasionally, when we are doing fieldwork or interviewing, we experience this strange relation as an actual social interaction. But the conceptual procedures developed in sociology serve to suspend the presence of an actor in her actions; what people are doing, what they experience, what is happening to them become "roles," "norms," "systems," "behaviors." We have learned a method of thinking that does away with presence of the subjects in the phenomena, which only subjects can accomplish.

In attempting to develop a sociology from the standpoint of women, we find a persistent difficulty that does not yield to the critique of standard themes and topics. In any of the many ways we might do a sociology of women, women remain the objects of study. Sociologies of sex roles, of gender relations, of women, constitute women as the object of inquiry. It never quite makes sense to do a sociology of men, nor is it clear how that would differ from the sociology we do. By insisting that women be entered into sociology as its subjects, we find that we cannot escape how it transforms us into objects. As women we become objects to ourselves as subjects. We ourselves therefore can "look back"[55] as subjects constituted as objects in that relation, and in doing so, we disclose its essential contradiction. So long as "men," "he," and "his" appeared as the general and impersonal terms locating the subject of sociological assertions, the problem remained invisible. We had learned to "enter" our subjectivities into sentences beginning "he" and to disattend our sex under the convention—applying only to women since it is irrelevant for men—that the pronoun was in this context neutral. Once we had understood, however, that the male pronoun did indeed locate a male subject for whom women were constituted in the sociological relation outside the frame that organized this position, the appearance of impersonality was gone. The knower turns out after all not to be "abstract knower" perching on an Archimedian point but a member of a definite social category occupying definite positions in the society.

The problem of how women cannot escape the status of object in the sociological relation thus enlivens a general issue. The methods of thinking, empirical inquiry, and the practices accomplishing the objectivity and the recognizably sociological features of sociological work organize an object world from the perspective of a determinate position in the society. They organize a determinate relation between those who occupy the positions from which it is known and those who become the objects of its method of knowing. In questioning the sociological relation from the standpoint of women, we find we have called into question the organization of the discourse in general, its location in the world, and the social relations organizing the positions of its subjects that its objectifying practices conceal. The specific character of the sociological mode of reflecting upon society, upon social relations, upon people, in suspending the actual and particular position of the knower, must be understood as itself located. Sociology provides a mode in which people can relate to themselves and to others in a mode that locates them as subjects outside themselves, in which the coordinates are shifted to a general abstracted frame and the relation of actions, events, and the like to the local and particular is suspended or discarded. Robert Bierstedt has celebrated the educational value of sociology thus: "Sociology can liberate the mind from time and space themselves and remove it to a new and transcendental realm where it no longer depends upon these Aristotelian categories."[56]

What sociology teaches is precisely this mode of relating to the society in which it is practiced, but this mode of relating to others is not for everyone. It does not represent an impartial and general knowledge whose knower is truly Archimedian, nor does it represent knowers who might be any member of the society. We have found already that women are outside the frame and do not enter as its subjects. It is a partial view, a view that originates in a special kind of position in the society.

The basis of this position develops with the emergence of forms of corporate capitalism. Increasingly in the twentieth century we find the emergence of an abstracted conceptual mode of organization in which organizing functions become (a) differentiated as a distinct system of functions—whether as administration, management, or aspects of professional organization; (b) primarily communicative and informational (the "chief" of a corporation or a government department does not gather together the armed men of his clan and ride across the hills to attack his neighbor); (c) dependent increasingly on a secondhand knowledge organized conceptually as "facts," "information," and so on; (d) dependent increasingly on generalized systems of planning in the same mode. These practices are known as rational administrative practices and the like.[57] They constitute a generalized and generalizing practice of organization occupying an increasingly abstracted conceptual space, detached from the local and particular as the locus and center of the organizational processes.

The form of capitalism and indeed the most general form of enterprise in nineteenth-century Canada and the United States was the small-scale enterprise, whose owner also managed and controlled the enterprise. Such was the characteristic social organization of farming, as farming became more fully articulated to the market process; such was the organization of crafts, of shopkeeping, and of the various now relatively invisible roles in the market process (merchant, trader, jobber, etc.). Though the market appeared as an external force organizing relations and functioning independent of the choices and wishes of individual capitalists or workers and as the cumulated product of those choices, the immediate governance of the enterprise managed in relation to market exigencies and opportunities was local. Enterprises organized on a local basis also organized the relations of that local sector of the economy among themselves, including their relation to those who owned no property and participated in the productive process as sellers of labor. Class relations were locally based, and class organization had to build from that basis.

Toward the end of the nineteenth century, as capital accumulated, the earlier forms of individually owned enterprises organized on a local basis began to be superseded by the corporate form. An integral aspect of this was a change in the forms of property relations. Berle and Means have described it as a separation of ownership and control,[58] but it is more accurately understood as the emergence of a corporate form of property relations whereby the direct ownership of capital was vested in a corporation and the managerial process was a process of the corporation as an organizational form. The corporation is a determinate type of organizational process in which managerial practices become not only highly technical but also take on what Albert Sloan (who was one of the inventors and promulgators of this organizational form) describes as "objective organization," as contrasted with "subjective organization."[59] "Subjective" forms of organization he identified as the practices that had earlier prevailed, whereby decisions on financial issues on how the assets of an enterprise should be committed had been made on the basis of hunches by individuals or of negotiations among heads of different departments or sectors functioning somewhat like fiefdoms. The forms of organization that began to emerge depended in the first place on marked technical developments in accounting practices and on the ability to analyze the economic environment and situation, as well as on processes of demand and supply, in ways that made possible decision making from which individual hunches, intuitions, bargaining, and personal edges or power were removed. The performance of different sections or departments became measurable in relation to one another with respect to how each contributed to the overall enterprise. Management, moreover, became self-conscious of the organizational process. Social relations, organizations, and so on became conceptualized as discrete and self-conscious processes quite separable as such from the particular individuals who performed and brought them into being as concrete social activities.

During this period of development a locus of organization became predominant, requiring a viewpoint of society and social relations that was extralocal, something like a bird's-eye view, a viewpoint not situated in the local and particular places and not located in actual, particular- istic social relations. A perspective was required that organized a world at a conceptual level abstracted from the local and particular and ca- pable of locating the subjectivity of the knower in a view of society, and view of social relations, that she could not get from within her own null point, her own bodily location, where near and far, before and after, had to be organized in relation to herself as center. An institutionalized form of knowledge and practice of social control developed (in law, psychiatry, in education, in universities, in the social sciences, in soci- ology in particular) that was externalized, objectified, and not locatable in a particular place, physical or social.

The concept of ideology as it was used in the sociology I learned in graduate school was more than a purely "scientific" term. It played a critical and constitutive role among the practices that identified sources of "bias" in the idealized notion of a fully objective account of society. An objective social science depended upon the cleansing of the subject from the partial perspectives of particular groups, the rural vil- lage, the country town, the city, the political party, the particular class. In his study of *Ideology and Utopia,* Karl Mannheim saw the work of the sociologist of knowledge not merely as that of the impersonal, disinter- ested, and scientific study of the social basis of knowledge or perspec- tives of the world. His methods of analysis were developed as means to the synthesis rising above the contending views. A total perspective was to be constructed by combining and distilling the partial views, detach- ing them thereby from their local and particular basis in a particular section of social structure, in particular groups, classes, or localities.[60] The sociological or social scientific perspective must be separated from the biases of particular and subjective accounts; it must rise above the contentious views of different classes.

Work of this kind gathered sociology up into the world in which activity, practice, methods, and social relations are the practices of mind, of the "head," of speaking, of writing, rather than of the body, the hand, the material work, the working world. A sociology was cre- ated with the capacity to transform actualities into the forms in which they could be thought of in the abstracted conceptual mode of ruling. These methods of working enabled sociologists to transform phenom- ena from their original actualities in concrete material processes into observables at the conceptual level. Thus the actual practices of social relations are transformed into "social roles," individuals' activities into "norms," and people's actual words in religious or political settings into "beliefs" and "values."

These methods of conceptualizing social processes articulate the local and particular worlds in which people are concretely located into the forms of thought that organize them in relation to the abstracted conceptual mode of "ruling." Of special importance so far as sociology is concerned is the capacity of people playing their parts in the ruling apparatus to think about people, to think about social relations, to think about social action, in terms of systems and in terms of social processes external to individuals. Sociological practices of thinking do indeed locate the consciousness of the thinker in just those ways that Bierstedt describes—outside the Aristotelian categories, detached from particularities, detached from the knower's location in the world. This detachment has been part of the distinctive historical work of sociology. It provides, specifically, a mode of "entering" subjectivities into the abstracted conceptual modes of organizing this form of society. As a finite subprovince of meaning it structures a discard of the localized organization of consciousness from the "null point."[61] The knower starts already located outside herself. When we work as sociologists in this mode, we "enter" a sociology constituting our relation to the world in this way. We "enter" this relation.

IV The Standpoint of Women Is Outside the Extralocal Relations of Ruling

When we take up the standpoint of women, we take up a standpoint outside this frame (as an organization of social consciousness). To begin from such a standpoint does not imply a common viewpoint among women. What we have in common is the organization of social relations that has accomplished our exclusion. Taking up this position for the subjects of a sociology, what is the critique? A critique is more than a negative statement. It is an attempt to define an alternative.

We have asked here how it is that sociology as we practice it and recognize its practices does not allow us to begin our work from our experience as women. Women's experience has been a resource, but it has not become the basis for a position from which sociology, as the systematic study of society and social relations, proceeds.

In *The Phenomenology of Mind*, Hegel analyzes the relation of master and servant.[62] This analysis was a model for Marx's analysis of the relation between a ruling class and the working class, including the dynamic process built into the relation that transforms it. Here we have use for a limited aspect of Hegel's "parable," the relation between the master's consciousness and the labor of the servant. Hegel describes how for the master the object of his desire is available to him in a simple and obvious manner such that he can leap directly from the desire to its object, from appetite to consummation, without an intervening labor. The object appears there for him in a simple and direct way. This appearance is, however, the result or product of the servant's labor. The servant produces the object for the master. In so doing the servant conforms to the will of the master, and his work is in that sense the master's consciousness realized. The servant in relation to the master does not constitute a distinct subject, a consciousness distinctly and authentically present who looks back and reflects the master's will and has no autonomous existence. The servant's labor is present in the relation of the master to the object of his desire, the object of consciousness. The invisibility of that relation from the master's standpoint is a product of the organization of the relation between master and servant. That organization itself is not visible from the standpoint of the master. Within the consciousness of the master there is himself and the object and a servant who is merely a means. For the servant there is the master, the servant's labor producing the object, and there is the simplicity of the relation between the master and the object. The totality of the set of relations is visible.

When Hegel's parable of the master-servant relation is used to interpret Marx's view of the relationship between the consciousness of a ruling class as an ideological consciousness and a science of political economy proceeding from and grounded in the standpoint of the working class, Marx's analysis of the different bases of ideology and knowledge can be applied to the standpoint of women. Our social forms of consciousness have been created by men occupying positions in the extralocal organization of ruling. Discourses, methods of thinking, theories, sociologies take for granted the conditions of that ruling. The actual practices that make that ruling possible are not visible. Women are outside the extralocal relations of ruling, for the most part located in work processes that sustain it and are essential to its existence. There are parallels then between the claims Marx makes for a knowledge based in the class whose labor produces the conditions of existence, indeed the very existence, of a ruling class, and the claims that can be made for a knowledge of society from the standpoint of women.

Established interpretations of Marx understand him to argue that ideological forms of consciousness are determined by their social base, particularly by their base in a class, and that all social forms of consciousness are so determined. It follows, so this interpretation proceeds, that this reasoning applies also to the claims of a science from the standpoint of labor, invalidating its claims to knowledge, hence to Marx's own work.[63] If, however, we apply the Hegelian paradigm to Marx's reasoning, the argument proceeds differently. There is a difference between forms of consciousness arising in the experience of ruling and those arising in the experience of doing the work that creates the conditions of ruling. Ideological forms of consciousness are definite practices of thinking about society that reflect the experience of ruling. From the standpoint of ruling, the actual practices, the labor, and the organization of labor, which makes the existence of a ruling class and their ruling possible, are invisible. It is only possible to see how the whole thing is put together from a standpoint outside the ruling class and in that class whose part in the overall division of labor is to produce the conditions of its own ruling and the existence of a ruling class.

The basis for a political economy from the standpoint of labor, according to Marx, is precisely that it is grounded in the work and activity of actual individuals producing their existence under definite material conditions. The standpoint of labor provides, therefore, a basis for knowledge corresponding to the position of the servant in Hegel's exemplary tale. From the servant's position, the working of the whole process is available in principle since his actual practice brings into being the relation between self and object, appearing as it does from the perspective of the master. From the point of view of the ruling class, the actual practices and the material conditions that form, organize, and provide for the "appearance" of direct action are not visible. Their activities, their work, their consciousness appear simple and complete, their relations undetermined, because how they are determined is a product of the labor of the working class. The social organization of the forms of consciousness characteristic of a ruling class cannot be examined from the standpoint of the ruling class because that organization is not visible from that perspective or in that mode of action. Thus, when Marx draws attention to how Feuerbach's idealist philosophy ignores its essential dependence on the production of the philosopher's subsistence, and hence his consciousness upon the material processes of labor that produce the world he inhabits and its features (including the cherry tree before his window, whose presence is itself a historical product of trading relations), he is not engaging in cheap gibes.[64] He is drawing attention, rather, to an idealism that views the transformation of social forms as taking place in and through conceptual transformations (and therefore as simple) and to how these very idealizations are organized, provided for, and produced by the productive relations and the productive activities, the labor of a working class standing in determinate relation to a ruling class, producing not only the subsistence of a ruling class, but also the basic organization that the social forms of consciousness of the ruling class take for granted.[65] The standpoint of labor thus establishes a site for the knower from which these relations and organization can be made visible as they actually arise in the actual activities of individuals.[66]

Analogous claims can be made for a sociology from the standpoint of women. In the social division of labor the work of articulating the local and particular existence of actors to the abstracted conceptual mode of ruling is done typically by women. The abstracted conceptual mode of ruling exists in and depends upon a world known immediately and directly in the bodily mode. The suppression of that mode of being as a focus, as thematic, depends upon a social organization that produces the conditions of its suppression. To exist as subject and to act in this abstracted mode depend upon an actual work and organization of work by others who make the concrete, the particular, the bodily, thematic of their work and who also produce the invisibility of that work. It is a condition of anyone's being able to enter, become, and remain absorbed in the conceptual mode of action that she does not need to focus her attention on her labors or on her bodily existence. The organization of that work and work expectations in managerial and professional circles both constitute and depend upon the alienation of members of this class from their bodily and local existence. The structure of work in this mode and the structure of career assume the individuals can sustain a mode of consciousness in which interest in the routine aspects of bodily maintenance is never focal and can in general be suppressed. It is taken for granted in the organization of this work that such matters are provided for in a way that will not interfere with action and participation in the conceptual mode.

The sociologist enters the conceptual mode of action when she goes to work. She enters it as a member, and she enters it also as the mode in which she investigates it. She observes, analyzes, explains, and examines as if there were no problem in how that world becomes observable to her. She moves among the doings of organizations, governmental processes, bureaucracies, and so on as a person who is at home in that medium. The nature of that world itself, how it is known to her, and the conditions of its existence or her relation to it are not called into question. Her methods of observation and inquiry extend to it as procedures that are essentially of the same order as those that bring about phenomena with which she is concerned, or that she is concerned to bring under the jurisdiction of that order. Her perspectives and interests may differ, but the substance is the same. She works with facts and information that have been worked up from actualities and appear in the form of documents, which are themselves the product of organizational processes, whether her own or administered by her or of some other agency. She fits that information back into a framework of entities and organizational processes which she takes for granted as known, without asking how she knows them or what are the social processes by which the phenomena corresponding to or providing the empirical events, acts, decisions, and so forth of that world may be recognized. She passes beyond the particular and immediate setting in which she is always located in the body (the office she writes in, the libraries she consults, the streets she travels, the home she returns to) without any sense of having made a transition. She works in the same medium as she studies.

But like everyone else she also exists in the body, in the place in which it is. This, then, is also the place of her sensory organization of immediate experience; the place where her coordinates of here and now, before and after, are organized around herself as center; the place where she confronts people face to face in the physical mode in which she expresses herself to them and they to her as more and other than either can speak. Here there are textures and smells. The irrelevant birds fly away in front of the window. Here she has flu. Here she gives birth. It is a place she dies in. Into this space must come as actual material events, whether as the sounds of speech, the scratchings on the surface of paper that is constituted as document, or directly anything she knows of the world. It has to happen here somehow if she is to experience it at all.

Entering the governing mode of our kind of society lifts the actor out of the immediate local and particular place in which she is in the body. She uses what becomes present to her in this place as a means to pass beyond it to the conceptual order. This mode of action creates a bifurcation of consciousness, a bifurcation, of course, that is present for all those participating in this mode of action. It establishes two modes of knowing, experiencing, and acting—one located in the body and in the space that it occupies and moves into, the other passing beyond it. And although I have made use of the feminine pronoun in general, it is primarily men who are active in this mode.

It is a condition of a person's being able to enter and become absorbed in the conceptual mode that attention to the local and bodily remain, as Schutz says, "horizonal" rather than focal or thematic. Schutz himself, that great ethnographer of the "head" world, provides an account of just this suppression, which locates at least one form of women's work in organizing its own suppression. He writes:

> The corollary to the fact that we live simultaneously in various provinces of reality or meaning is the fact that we put into play various levels of our personality. . . . Only very superficial levels of our personality are involved in such performances as our habitual and even quasi-automatic "household chores", or eating, dressing, and (for normal adults) also in reading and performing simple arithmetical operations. To be sure, when we turn to such routine work, the activities connected with it are constituted as thematic, requiring and receiving our full attention if only momentarily.[67]

Without challenging Schutz's general picture of these various levels of personality and their organization in relation to projects in the world of working, we can also recognize what is presupposed in just that organization, namely, that the routine matters, the household chores, are not problematic, do not become a central focus of man's work, or at least "only momentarily." Once we are alerted to how women's work provides for this organization of consciousness, we can see how this structure depends in actual situations on the working relations of those providing for the logistics of the philosopher's bodily existence—those for whom household chores are not horizonal, but are thematic, and whose work makes possible for another the suppression of all but passing attention to the bodily location of consciousness.

If men are to participate fully in the abstract mode of action, they must be liberated from having to attend to their needs in the concrete and particular. Organizing the society in an abstracted conceptual order, mediated symbolically, must be articulated to the concrete and local actualities in which it is necessarily and ineluctably located. That must be a work, must be a product of labor. To a very large extent the direct work of liberating men into abstraction from the Aristotelian categories of time and space of which Bierstedt speaks[68] has been and is the work of women.

The place of women, then, in relation to this mode of action is where the work is done to facilitate men's occupation of the conceptual mode of action. Women keep house, bear and care for children, look after men when they are sick, and in general provide for the logistics of their bodily existence. But this marriage aspect of women's work is only one side of a more general relation. Women work in and around the professional and managerial scene in analogous ways.[69] They do those things that give concrete form to the conceptual activities. They do the clerical work, giving material form to the words or thoughts of the boss. They do the routine computer work, the interviewing for the survey, the nursing, the secretarial work. At almost every point women mediate for men the relation between the conceptual mode of action and the actual concrete forms on which it depends. Women's work is interposed between the abstracted modes and the local and particular actualities in which they are necessarily anchored. Also, women's work conceals from men acting in the abstract mode just this anchorage.[70]

In the health profession, for example, the routine practices that mediate the actualities of the immediately experienced world and work them up into forms corresponding to the abstracted conceptual forms under which they may be professionally (or "scientifically") known are done largely by women. The psychiatric patient is indeed present to the psychiatrist as a "whole person," but the routines that limit the psychiatrist's relation to the patient, and hence define those aspects that come strictly within his professional focus, are performed in large part by women—nurses, laboratory technicians, social workers, clerks, and so on. To a large extent women have at various points direct and immediate contact with the actual life situation of the patient, before it has been cleaned and tidied up, in all its complexity—just as anyone's life situation is always complex, rooted in others' lives, and multifaceted. Through the work of those who reconstruct the patient's life as a case history, it is obliterated as it was experienced and lived. By the time the patient gets to the psychiatrist, she is already an abstraction. She has been separated from the contexts in which what she was saying and doing were connected. Hence, the psychiatrist encounters the patient as one whose abstraction has already been socially organized. For him there is no war or tension between the direct experience he has in the settings of his work and the ideologies he uses to name, interpret, and order what he observes. He is not exposed to disjunctions between the nature of his psychiatric procedures and the actualities of his patients' lives. He is not exposed in his professional practice to the world before the practices of receptionists, nurses, secretaries, nurses' aides, social workers. Their work brings into being the forms in which what he does, thinks, and says make ordinary sense. His accomplishment of his work in the abstracted conceptual modes depends upon their work in ways that their work itself makes invisible.

Beginning from the standpoint of women locates a subject who begins in a material and local world. It shows the different cognitive domains structuring our realities, not, as Schutz describes,[71] as alternatives—a paramount reality on the one hand and the scientific domain on the other—but rather as a bifurcation of consciousness, with a world directly experienced from oneself as center (in the body) on the one hand and a world organized in the abstracted conceptual mode, external to the local and particular places of one's bodily existence. The abstracted mode of the scientific province is always located in the local and material actualities. Participation in the "head" world is accomplished in actual concrete settings making use of definite material means. Suppression of interest in that setting is organized in a division of labor that accords to others the production and maintenance of the material aspects of a total process. To those who do this work, the local and concrete conditions of the abstracted mode are thematic. The organization that divides the two becomes visible from this base. It is not visible from within the other.

We can see then how the silencing of women of which we spoke earlier suppresses not only women, but the work they represent and the dimension of existence that locates, among other things, that fear of death Schutz holds as the fundamental anxiety. The fear of death is the final announcement to the thinker that his occupancy of the conceptual mode of the bifurcated consciousness is necessarily temporary. He is precipitated into time. Women's lack of authority to speak, their exclusion from the circle of those who make the tradition, who make the discourse, means that the work that suppresses the concrete and material and, with them, the local, particular, and material locus of consciousness, is also silenced. The modes of action in the conceptual mode depend upon this silence.

The theories, concepts, and methods of our discipline claim to be capable of accounting for and analyzing the same world as that which we experience directly. But these theories, concepts, and methods have been built up out of a way of knowing the world that takes for granted the boundaries of experience in the same medium in which it is constituted. It takes for granted and subsumes without examining the conditions of its existence. Its object appears to it, as to Hegel's master, in a direct and simple relation. It is not capable of analyzing its own relation to its conditions nor of locating itself where the social relations organizing and providing for its existence can be seen. The sociologist as actual person in an actual concrete setting, the sociological knower, has been "canceled" from the act of knowing by a procedure that objectifies and separates him from his knowledge. The essential linkage that is the first clue pointing back to the conditions of his knowledge is lacking.

Locating women's experience as a place to work from in sociology does not, if we follow this line of analysis, land us in a determinante type of position or identify a category of persons from whose various and typical positions in the world we must take our starting point. Women are variously located in society. Their situations are much more various than the topics we recognize somewhat stereotypically as women's topics would suggest. Their position also differs very greatly by class. Even among housewives, who appear to share a universal fate, there are rather wider differences in the conditions, practices, and organization of housework and the social relations in which it is embedded than our studies and the ways in which they have been framed would allow. The identification of the bifurcated consciousness is a potential experience for women members of an intelligentsia or of women otherwise associated with the ruling apparatus that organizes the society. It is clearly not every woman's experience of the world. That is not the issue. At this point the concern is to develop a method of working in sociology that will make it possible to begin from where women in general are, doing the type of work with which we are a sex identified. To develop a sociology from the standpoint of subjects located materially and in a particular place does not involve simply the transfer from one conceptual frame to another, from, say, a Parsonian to a Marxist framework. It does something rather different. A Marxist framework can and has been quite readily assimilated into the modes of the sociological discourse that accord primacy to the conceptual categories and the forms of thought and that subordinate the actualities of the world to them. Nor does the answer lie, as has sometimes been suggested, in the renunciation of the rational, conceptual, scientifically rigorous method or procedure. This is to treat the two sides of the bifurcated consciousness as if they were equal and to locate what is distinctively "female" in the subjective, emotional side, so that the alienative intellectual practices of sociology are eliminated rather than transformed. It has been suggested to me that a phenomenological sociology is a feminist sociology merely because it begins with the consciousness of the knower and is hence "subjective," but the phenomenological perspective remains within the conceptual abstracted world and begins from there, taking for granted the material and social organization of the bifurcated consciousness, and does not render its organization and conditions examinable.

The two sides of the divided consciousness are not equal. As Schutz makes clear and as even minimal attention to the actualities of our own functioning in the world makes clear (you can stop this moment in your reading and attend to the material properties of your reading: chair, paper, ink marks, your own bodily presence, etc.), there is no entry to the abstracted conceptual mode of working without passing through and making use of the concretely and immediately experienced. The symbolic structures that constitute the modes in which we act are necessarily material in transcending that materiality—the sounds we hear that we take up as speech, the scratches on the paper, the material organization that provides for how our consciousness can be thematized in this mode, as well as the social division of labor that sustains us in it. These are not merely essential as prerequisites; they are integral to the organization and existence of the abstracted conceptual mode. It is indeed part of how they are integral that they do not become thematic, that they remain horizonal. The other term of the bifurcated consciousness, which is located not merely in a subjectivity but in a subjectivity located in its body and located therefore in a definite and particular spatiotemporal existence, is irremediably in what Schutz describes rather ambiguously as the world of working. Beginning, then, from there locates the knower where knowledge must begin.

If we address the problem of the conditions as well as the perceived forms and organization of immediate experience, we should include the events as they actually happen or the ordinary material world that we and others encounter as what is happening to us, to them. When we examine these events, when we examine the actual material organization of our everyday experience, we find that there are many aspects of how these things are and come about of which we have very little, as sociologists, to say. We do not even know how to begin. We have a sense that the events entering our experience originate somewhere in a human intention, but we are unable to track back to find it and to find out how it became and how it got from there to here. Take this room in which I work or that room in which you are reading and treat that as a problem. If we think about the conditions of our activity here, we could track back to how it is that there are chairs, table, walls, our clothing, our presence; how these places (yours and mine) are cleaned and maintained; and so forth. There are human activities, intentions, and relations that are not apparent as such in the actual material conditions of our work. The social organization of the setting is not wholly available to us in its appearance. What is here for us is the product of a social division of labor. If we heard in the things that we make use of—typewriter, paper, chair, table, walls—the voices of those who made them, we would hear the multitudinous voices of a whole society and beyond. Were it not for the time lapse involved, our own voices would be part of them. Locating our work as knowers in the first and fundamental term of the bifurcated consciousness also locates us in the standpoint of the working class, in the location from which Marx's political economy begins. Beginning from the standpoint of women does not follow in any direct way from beginning from the standpoint of labor, but once we have taken this other and momentous step, we can begin to take up the relation established by Marx. It becomes available to us in the mode in which it was originally conceived, namely, as having its premises not in the conceptual, abstracted mode but in actual individuals, their work, their actual productive activities, and the material conditions produced by those activities that become their conditions.[72]

V The Everyday World as Problematic

The critique of established sociological frameworks from the perspective of women's location leaves us with the problem of the structure of the sociological relation as it was described above. It does not, as such, serve to design for us a method of proceeding that offers an alternative to the concepts, relevances, and methods of a discourse that, in its very use, organizes and shapes our work into its own forms and intentions regardless of what we mean to do. We must see this problem, I believe, in how our work returns to, is aimed at, and is repossessed by knowers who are participants in the discourse or in other domains of the ruling apparatus, rather than knowers who are members of the society anywhere in it. Suppose then we began to devise a sociological enterprise not directed primarily toward the discourse and its knower, but capable of providing a sociology for women. We might attempt to develop for women analyses, descriptions, and understandings of their situation, of their everyday world, and of its determinations in the larger socioeconomic organization to which it is articulated. Then indeed we would be thinking about how to do a sociology relocating the sociological subject. Such a sociological enterprise presents an alternative conception of a science to that which depends upon a knower theoretically located in an Archimedian, that is, a purely formal space. It is a sociology whose knowers are members of the society and have positions in it outside that abstracted ruling apparatus—as an understanding of the bifurcating consciousness shows us everyone does—and who know the society from within their experience of it as an everyday world. Their experience locates for us the beginning of an inquiry. This is to constitute the everyday world as problematic, where the everyday world is taken to be various and differentiated matrices of experience—the place from within which the consciousness of the knower begins, the location of her null point.

Such a sociology would aim to make available to anyone a knowledge of the social organization and a determination of his or her directly experienced, everyday world. Its analyses would become part of our ordinary interpretations of experience and hence part of experience, just as our experience of the sun's sinking below the horizon has been transformed by our knowledge that the world turns and that our location in the world turns away from the sun—even though from where we are it seems to sink. The sociological knower, then, is not the sociologist as such. The work of the sociologist is to develop a sociology capable of explicating for members of the society the social organization of their experienced world, including in that experience the ways in which it passes beyond what is immediately and directly known, including also, therefore, the structure of a bifurcated consciousness.

Rather than explaining behavior, we begin from where people are in the world, explaining the social relations of the society of which we are part, explaining an organization that is not fully present in any one individual's everyday experience. Since the procedures, methods, and aims of present sociology give primacy to the concepts, relevances, and topics of the discourse, we cannot begin from within that frame. This would be to sustain the hegemony of the discourse over the actualities of the everyday experience of the world. It is precisely that relation that constitutes the break or fault disclosed by the women's movement.

An alternative is to turn this method on its head and to make the everyday world the locus of a sociological problematic. The everyday world is that world we experience directly. It is the world in which we are located physically and socially. Our experience arises in it as conditions, occasions, objects, possibilities, relevances, presences, and so on, organized in and by the practices and methods through which we supply and discover organization. It is necessarily local—because that is how we must be—and necessarily historical. Locating the sociological problematic in the everyday world does not mean confining the inquiry to the everyday world. Indeed, as we shall see, it is essential that the everyday world be seen as organized by social relations not observable within it. Thus, an inquiry confining itself to the everyday world of direct experience is not adequate to explicate its social organization.

One way in which the sociological discourse has maintained its hegemony over experience has been by insisting that we must begin with a conceptual apparatus or a theory drawn from the discipline, if only because to embark on inquiry without such a conceptual framework exposes us to the wild incoherennce of "history" or of the actualities of people's worlds. I am not suggesting, of course, that sociology can be done without knowing how to do it and that we can approach our work with a naïve consciousness. Indeed, I believe sociology to be rather more difficult than it has been made to seem. But the implication that the actualities of the everyday world are unformed and unorganized and that the sociologist cannot enter them without a conceptual framework to select, assemble, and order them is one that we can now understand in this special relation of a sociology constituted as part of a ruling apparatus vis-à-vis which the local and particular, the actualities of the world that is lived, are necessarily untamed, disordered, and incoherent. But we can begin from a different assumption when as premises we begin with the activities of actual individuals whose activity produces the social relations that they live.[73] Social phenomena are products of action and interpretation by actual women and men. Rational order itself, order itself, as ethnomethodologists have pointed out, is an accomplishment of members of society. The order, coherence, rationality, and sense of social situations and relations are an active work done prior to the presence and observational work of the sociologist. Further, her work itself is inseparable from such a social relation and in its preliminary phases must be constrained by the enterprise of explicating an organization of relations that is there prior to her inquiry and is to be discovered in its course.

Defining the everyday world as the locus of a sociological problematic is not the same as making it an object of study. A distinction must be made between the everyday world as problematic and as phenomenon. To aim at the everyday world as an object of study is to constitute it as a self-contained universe of inquiry. The effect of locating the knower in this way is to divorce the everyday world of experience from the larger social and economic relations that organize its distinctive character. Then when attempts are made to reunite the two, they begin, as do Lefebvre and Kosik for example,[74] with the abstracted conceptual mode and seek to grasp the everyday world as an object. From this perspective its essential organization escapes. History, for example, is viewed as erupting into the everyday world as if the two somehow existed alongside one another, largely independent except for occasional collisions. In constituting the everyday world as an object of sociological examination, we cut it off methodologically from the ways in which it is actually embedded in a socially organized context larger than may be directly known in that mode. Strategies such as Erving Goffman's or Don Zimmerman and Melvin Pollner's constitute the everyday world as a phenomenon for investigation.[75] In so doing they serve to seal it off as a discrete phenomenon within the sociological universe. Goffman's dramaturgical metaphor does two kinds of work in this respect: one in providing a way of making features and processes of the everyday world visible as appearances; and another (closely connected) in creating a set of categories (front stage and back, regions, settings, etc.) that organize a domain of inquiry to be treated as internally coherent and descriptively comprehensive. Though very different in approach, Zimmerman and Pollner's definition of the "occasioned corpus" also constitutes the everyday world as phenomenon. It is, in their approach, bounded by the constraint of observation and of knowledge arising in and as part of an "occasioned corpus." Thus, properties or organization and so on, conceived to be "in back of" the occasioned corpus, are treated as warrantably present for the observer only as they are accomplished in the present of her observation and become thereby features of the occasioned corpus. These and other strategies, focusing on the everyday world as phenomenon, constitute it as an object of the sociological inquiry and isolate it.

The concept of problematic is used to relate the sociologist and the sociological inquiry to the experience of members of a society as knowers located in actual lived situations in a new way. It is used here to constitute the everyday world as that in which questions originate. The term "problematic" is ordinarily used to talk about matters at the level of concept or theory rather than at the level of experience and action (it should not, incidentally be confused with the concept of problem.). As it is used here, we follow a procedure of going from a social actuality to develop a conceptual apparatus disclosing and explicating its properties. The problematic is property of the social organization of the everyday world. The concept of problematic explicates a property of the everyday world as a focus for sociological work. Constituting the social organization and determinations of the everyday world as a problematic is a method of guiding and focusing inquiry. The purpose and direction of inquiry is in part (and particularly at the outset of this approach to sociology) an explication or codification (to use Freire's term)[76] of a problematic that is implicit in the everyday world.

The concept of problematic is used here to direct attention to a possible set of questions that may not have been posed or a set of puzzles that do not yet exist in the form of puzzles but are "latent" in the actualities of the experienced world. The questions themselves, the inquiry, the puzzles, and perhaps the issues are the means of developing the problematic as an inquiry. What I have done in using this term, therefore, is to shift it out of its ordinary place within a scientific or philosophical discourse and treat it as a property of an actuality lived and practiced. This problematic is, I suggest, present in the everyday world as it is given to any of us to live. For the everyday world is neither transparent nor obvious. Fundamental to its organization for us in this form of society is that its inner determinations are not discoverable within it. The everyday world, the world where people are located as they live, located bodily and in that organization of their known world as one that begins from their own location in it, is generated in its varieties by an organization of social relations that originate "elsewhere." It is like a dance in which the subject participates or in which she is placed. The "shapes" taken by the dance and the part she plays in it bring into being the dance as an actual organization of social relations through time. Whether she chooses to play a part or not, or the particular movements she elects in relation to the dance, its emerging and developing forms are those that give shape to what she does. The dance, however, extends beyond the boundaries of her sight. She cannot from where she is recover its form or assess its character or movement. She picks it up as it moves its patterns into her scope of action, and she must be moved by or move with them. The conditions of our action and experience are organized by relations and processes outside them and beyond our power of control.

The everyday world is not fully understandable within its own scope. It is organized by social relations not fully apparent in it nor contained in it. This is the social organization of the sociological problematic in the actual work and practices of real individuals. Earlier forms of society do not have this double character. In simpler social forms, the character and organization of the everyday world are fully visible. The ethnographic techniques of the anthropologist have depended upon this visibility.

You may perhaps have seen an ethnographic movie called *The Hunters*, which tells the story of the stalking and killing of a giraffe by a small group of Kalahari Bushmen. Though the movie provides a strongly male-oriented picture of the people—women are represented as waiting in the werf (camp) for the men to come home with the meat, and no indication is given of the substantial contribution women make to the food of the group—it illustrates a distinctive aspect of the social relations of production in this group. When the hunters have killed, the group brings the meat back to the camp and distributes it. All members of the group are present and part of the distribution. An old man passes it to small family groupings. Each little group takes its share, divides it further, and passes on a portion to other waiting groups of kinfolk. The origin of the meat is fully known. The territory that the hunters traveled is known to other members of the group. The path of meat from animal to pot to belly is made up of known persons standing in definite and known relations to one another as persons and performing tasks familiar and observable to anyone there. The determinations of social existence are fully present to the experience of its members and are coterminous with it.

The structures and transformation of the everyday world in our own form of society are not observable in the same way. The difference is more than a difference in size. It is only vaguely indicated in the notion of "complexity." There are important differences in the fundamental form of social organization. The problematic character of the everyday world is an essential property of this social form.

To exhibit one aspect of what I mean by the everyday world as problematic, I shall use the movie adaptation of Kurt Vonnegut's *Slaughterhouse Five*.[77] Vonnegut uses this problematic to display the senselessness of modern war. In the movie there is a sequence leading up to the firebombing of Dresden. It is a straightforward sequence in contrast to the temporal discontinuities characteristic of much of the rest of the movie. There is a shot of the spires of Dresden in the morning mist and of people marketing. We see children playing, some of them wearing the grotesque masks that are used in the movie to presage death. If you have read the book or know the history, you grasp these scenes in the shadow of what is to come. By the next morning most of the people will be dead. The temporal progression toward their doomsday is marked by a countdown printed as subtitles across the bottom of each scene as the day moves toward closure.

What Vonnegut does is to allow that sequence to stand juxtaposed to the next day, doomsmorning. As a whole the sequence makes no sense in terms of the everyday world. We cannot find how it was put together in what is available to us in the ordinary business that those people carried on the day before. Nothing they did then motivated, caused, or otherwise brought about the next morning's scene of blackened and smoking ruins. Confining the sequence to the everyday world constitutes its senselessness. If Vonnegut had wanted to recover its "rationality," he would have done what so many British war movies do (you can see them on the late or late-late shows on TV)—given us the scene of the bombers taking off at dusk from somewhere in England. He would have shown the underground strategic bomber command headquarters. We would have been shown the organizational process connecting the two moments, of life and of death, in the everyday world.

This way in which events occur, their odd property of senselessness if our knowledge of them is confined to the everyday world, is not so very extraordinary. It is not out of this world. On the contrary, such events are part of a continual process transforming the environment of our lives, transforming our lives; notice next time, in this context, that hole in the ground so soon to become a high-rise apartment, a gymnasium. Events occurring in this way are happening around us all the time. If we care to, we take them for granted. They are normal features of our world. If we cease to take them for granted, if we strip away everything that we imagine we know of how they come about (and ordinarily that is very little), if we examine them as they happen within the everyday world, they become fundamentally mysterious. If we allow them to stand there as Vonnegut does, they do not make sense within the domain of the everyday world. This is what I mean by a problematic implicit in the social organization of the everyday world.

These are events creating changes in or intruding on people's lives. The changes do not arise out of a logic of organization that is part of the local setting in which they occur. People who have lived for years in communities in the interior of British Columbia, in telling their lives and experiences, show us a typical layering sequence of change—the opening of the mine, the coming of the railroad, the market gardening enterprises established by local Indians to feed the miners, the closing of the mine, the decline of market gardening, the decline of the railroad, the dependence of the native people on the Indian Affairs Department, the building of a hydro plant, a brief period of employment for the native people while it is being built, the refurbishing of the railroad, the development of a small tourist trade, the transformation of the settlement into a retirement village for hydro engineers. These changes do not arise from a logic within the local setting. They are like the flows of lava from a volcano, each transforming the landscape in radical ways, each laying over its predecessors, but unconnected with them other than by succession. The logic of transformation is elsewhere.

The sample problem is implicit in the social organization of present relations in any such actual community, as well as in the events that become its history. The present structure of local social relations is organized by social relations external to it. Noticeable in the community I am thinking of is a lack of internal coherence in relations, a lack of working relations among members of the community, within the community as such. It is stratified ethnically by the Indian reservation and the employment opportunities for native people on the one hand and by the retirement homes of professionals from the nearby hydro plant on the other. The stratification is of a special and contemporary kind, the disconnected relations of people who live alongside one another in the same locality, but whose social relations are organized by social relations external to the local area and not appearing directly in it. This is the problematic of the everyday world.

The problematic can be characterized in a preliminary way as an abstraction of organization from the everyday world and the location of organizing processes in externally structured and differentiated relations. We return, indeed, to the same processes we identified in the organizational processes differentiating the local from the abstracted conceptual modes of consciousness, though we are no longer focusing solely on the apparatus of ruling. We are addressing a more general property of the social relations of capitalism and, specifically, of corporate or monopoly capitalism, for it is in capitalism that the socially organized forms, in and through which individuals depend upon one another, become externalized as a differentiated system of relations. In drawing a contrast between feudal and capitalist forms of social relation, Marx analyzes the capitalist form as follows:

> So far from constituting the removal of a "state of dependence", these external relationships represent its disintegration into a general form, or better, they are the elaboration of the general basis of personal states of dependence. Here too individuals come into relation with one another only in a determined role. These material states of dependence, as opposed to the personal states, are also characterized by the fact that individuals are now controlled only by abstractions, whereas earlier they depended on one another. The material state of dependence is no more than autonomous social relationships opposed to apparently independent individuals. [78]

Marx locates the organization of individual relations in a system of "autonomous social relations." These are material states of dependence—those that Marx analyzes more fully in his development of the concept of commodity in *Capital*. [79] They are social relations that appear in relations of market exchange as relations between things—the products of labor socially organized as commodities. Marx's analysis, both in this passage from the *Grundrisse* and in *Capital*, locates the determination of people's lives beyond and outside the places where they confront one another directly in the same local settings. Their relations in the local setting are organized elsewhere. The conditions of their action and experience are organized by relations external to the everyday world and beyond the power of individuals to control.

In the discussion so far, I have talked as if what is being described is merely a leaching out, a "depletion" by an extractive process, which produces an essential disorganization of the relations of the everyday world. I would emphasize, however, that this must, rather, be understood as a particular form of social organization and that the local and directly known world is extensively and increasingly penetrated by these processes of material and social organization. That organization may be experienced as disorganization, incoherence, lack of sense, but it is organization in that the processes of social relations at the abstracted level can be viewed as generating the organization of the everyday world. The relations among men hanging around on Tally's corner, [80] and the relations of women to those men, can be seen as organized by the development of capitalism to the level at which work for laborers is strictly casual and at which a segregated labor force organizes an urban pool of undifferentiated workers who are on call, and by the way in which the state, through its welfare agencies, regulates the relations between women and men, and women, men, and children.

The episodic character of women's lives—the uprooting, for example, of upper- and middle-class women from localities in which their relations have been formed to follow their husbands' careers (of which Robert Seidenburg has written[81])—corresponds to an organization of corporate systems of careers and advancement at the level of managerial personnel. The wives of construction workers or of mineworkers who confront the exigencies of the primary resource market must also be prepared to pack up and move on, resettling the children and the household in the next place where there is employment.

The structures of daily life and activity organized by this form of society are peculiarly desultory and bounded temporarily to the occasion. Sex is detached from conception and birth—as in Didion's novel of disintegration and socially organized incoherence (*Play It as It Lays*), where the protagonist may not even come to rest in the continuity and purpose of her own body in pregnancy, but is forced to abort. In the same book we see how activity arises out of the instrument, the tool, the equipment, so that the thing ceases to be a means to get things done, but becomes a motive for what it has the capacity to do. So the gun becomes a motive for shooting; the automobile and freeway a motive for driving; the camera a motive for taking a picture. Ideological forms and images derived from the media generate forms of action aimed at their realization and unarticulated to a practical orgnization of working relations among people. The life world disintegrates into a collection of episodes. An organizing "logic" is located elsewhere than in an individual's own activity and experience.

The organization of social life as occasions or episodes built into some styles of contemporary sociological theory[82] and even of the self as a discontinuous presentation of appearances is not universal nor to be taken for granted. What has been left unexamined (and is indeed unexaminable within the method that focuses upon the everyday world as phenomenon) is the social organization that generates these actual properties of experience observed and named (for example) by Goffman.[83] The intermittances of relations, the structuring of regions into front and back, the lack of biographical anchorage of the self in present witnesses to the individual past—these and other features so aptly analyzed by the dramaturgical metaphor are socially organized prior to and beyond the processes that it makes observable.

Locating the subject in one's everyday world means locating oneself in one's bodily and material existence. The everyday world is not an abstracted formal "setting" transposed by the sociologist's conceptual work to an abstracted formal existence. It is an actual material setting, an actual local and particular place in the world. Its formal and generalized properties are generated as such by the social organization and the material forms produced to accomplish its formal and generalizable properties. The equivalence of actual settings that provides for their being seen readily as conceptually substitutable (the public toilets, the restaurants, the motels, etc.) is itself a product of social and material organization accomplishing the substitutability of different actual local and particular places. The social organization of the abstracted conceptual practices of ruling is provided for by a determinante material organization, a standardization of technologies of various kinds to the material and social world as a means to transform it toward forms corresponding to the categories and concepts of the organizing processes of the ruling apparatus.

VI *Conclusion*

In the course of this inquiry I have considered under different aspects the social relation now explicated as the problematic of the everyday world. At the outset, in posing the starting point of this inquiry, I identified a "line of fault" in the social consciousness separating women's experience from the social forms of thought available in which to express it and make it actionable. The disjuncture arises because women have been excluded from the making of ideological forms produced as part of the apparatus by which this form of society is ruled. Patriarchy is a metaphor of this charcteristic relation of power among women and men, in which direct and personal relations are organized and determined by an impersonal apparatus. At this stage in examining these social relations, we can define the standpoint of women only in negation to the ideological forms from which their experience as subjects has been excluded.

In exploring the distinctive ways in which sociology excludes the concerns and perspectives of women, we can observe women's standpoint as a determinate position from which society may be known. The concepts and methods of sociology as a discourse constitute women as object rather than subject. Subject is then seen not as situated on an Archimedian point outside the world, but as a position within the ruling apparatus. The social relations explicated as the problematic here came into view in a new form. Sociology was seen as part of a differentiated practice of organizing a society constituted in an abstracted conceptual mode detached from the actual local and particular places in which individuals necessarily exist (and in which social relations themselves are necessarily grounded). Sociology as an ideological mode provides means of thinking social relations and social action into this abstracted conceptual mode. Locating ourselves as subjects in this relation places our knowledge of society and social relations outside experience and cuts us off from the actual grounding of our world.

The ideological relation formed by sociology also locates ourselves as subjects outside our experience and outside the local and particular places in which our knowing necessarily originates. The practices mediating and accomplishing the differentiation of the abstracted conceptual mode as a mode of action from the local and particular places of our bodily existence are not visible from within it. But since women's work has been characteristically that which directly mediates at the personal and individual level, the relation between women's two standpoints brings this relation into view.

My final step, then, has been to propose a method of relocating the sociological subject as actual individuals located in an everyday world. The conception of an everyday world as a sociological problematic presents a basis for a sociology that, like Marx and Engel's conception of the materialist method, begins not within the discourse but in the actual daily social relations between individuals. The problematic explicates, as the basis of inquiry, an actual socially organized relation between the everyday world of experience and the social relations of capitalism. The conceptualization of the problematic is intended to "hold" a relation between the sociological subject and a (possible) sociology (a systematic knowledge of the social relations of her society) in which the latter may become a means to disclose to the former the social relations determining her everyday world. The standpoint of women becomes now defined fully in such a way that we see it has been a "transformer" rather than a final position. It has served to direct the inquiry and at each point has made us restless with solutions that fail to meet the criteria it imposes. In arriving at the formulation of the everyday world as problematic, we find a sociological subject who may be anyone, but who is always located just as she or he is actually located in a particular material setting.

The constitution of the problematic of the everyday world establishes something like a Copernican shift in sociology. The significance of Copernican innovations was less that the sun rather than the earth was declared to be the center of the solar system than that the position of the observer was no longer fixed and could no longer be disattended in interpreting observations. She had no longer a fixed, central position but had to be seen as located in a position itself in motion in relation to what she observed. Hence, the observed movements of the planets could no longer be seen simply as their movements, but had to be understood as movements seen from a moving position. The effect of locating the knower in the everyday world of experience pulls what we know as the "microsociological" level of the everyday world and the "macrosociological" level, which we make observable as "power elites," "formal organization," "stratification," and the "state," into a determinate relation. From a standpoint within the ruling apparatus, the actual organization of these relations remains unexaminable and disorganized to thought by the conceptual apparatus that constitutes its observability. The pieces of a world—"power elites," "formal organization," "stratification," "social class," the "state"—are thus littered all over a sociological landscape. Locating the knower in the everyday world and constituting our inquiry in terms of the problematic arising from how it is actually organized in a social process enable us to see the "micro" and the "macro" sociological levels in a determinate relation— though it is one that scarcely makes sense any more in these terms. The determination of our worlds by relations and processes that do not appear fully in them are matters for investigation and inquiry, not for speculation.

Making the everyday world our problematic instructs us to look for the "inner" organization generating its ordinary features, its orders and disorders, its contingencies and conditions, and to look for that inner organization in the externalized and abstracted relations of economic processes and of the ruling apparatus in general. Our inquiry then can begin from the position of women, of women in whatever relation determines their experience as it is. It can begin from the position of any member of the society, explicating the problematic of her or his experience as a sociological problematic. The implications of a sociology for women in contemporary corporate capitalistic society pose again, though with a different grounding, the problematic originally formulated by Marx and Engels: "Individuals always started, and always start, from themselves. Their relations are the relations of their real life. How does it happen that their relations assume an independent existence over against them? And that the forces of their own life overpower them?"[84]

Notes

1. Simone de Beauvoir, *The Second Sex* (New York: Bantam Books, 1961); Betty Friedan, *The Feminine Mystique* (New York: W. W. Norton, 1963); Kate Millett, *Sexual Politics* (New York: Avon Books, 1971).
2. Jessie Bernard, *Academic Women* (New York: New American Library, 1964).
3. Pauline Bart, "Sexism in social science: From the iron cage to the gilded cage—The perils of Pauline," *Journal of Marriage and Family* 33 (November 1971): 742.
4. Millett, *Sexual Politics.*
5. Sheila Rowbotham, *Women's Consciousness, Man's World* (Harmondsworth, England: Penguin Books, 1973), p. 41.
6. De Beauvoir, *Second Sex,* p. xv.
7. Media Women's Association, with Ethel Strainchamps, ed., *Rooms with No View: A Woman's Guide to the Man's World of Media* (New York: Harper and Row, 1974).
8. See, among others, Gerda Lerner, "New approaches to the study of women in American history" and "Placing women in history," in Bernice A. Carroll, ed., *Liberating Women's History* (Urbana: University of Illinois Press, 1976); Dorothy E. Smith, "Some implications for a sociology for women," in Nona Glazer and Helen Y. Waehrer, eds., *Woman in a Man-made World* (Chicago: Rand McNally, 1976), pp. 15–39.
9. Mary Daly, *Beyond God the Father: Towards a Philosophy of Women's Liberation* (Boston: Beacon Press, 1973); Rosemary R. Ruether, *Religion and Sexism: Images of Women in the Jewish and Christian Traditions* (New York: Harper & Row, 1974).
10. See, among others, Jessie Bernard, "My four revolutions: An autobiographical history of the ASA," in Joan Huber, ed., *Changing Women in a Changing Society* (Chicago: University of Chicago Press, 1973); Naomi Weisstein, "Pyschology constructs the female, or the fantasy life of the male psychologist," in Michele Hoffnung Garskof, ed., *The Roles Women Play* (Belmont, Calif.: Brooks/Cole Publishing, 1971); Sandra L. Bem and Daryl J. Bem, "Training the woman to know her place: The power of a nonconscious ideology," in Garskof, *Roles Women Play;* Dorothy E. Smith, "The ideological practice of sociology," *Catalyst* 8 (1974): 39–54.; Meredith Kimball, "Women, sex role stereotypes, and mental health: Catch 22," in Dorothy E. Smith and Sara David, eds., *Women Look at Psychiatry* (Vancouver, Canada: Press Gang, 1975); Ann Oakley, *The Sociology of Housework* (London: Martin Robertson Ltd., 1975).
11. Judy Chicago, *Through the Flower* (New York: Doubleday, 1975); Lucy R. Lippard, *From the Center: Feminist Essays on Women's Art* (New York: E. P. Dutton, 1973).

12. Among others, the Boston Women's Health Collective, *Our Bodies, Our Selves* (New York: Simon and Schuster, 1973).
13. Barbara Ehrenreich and Deidre English, "Complaints and disorders: The sexual politics of sickness," Glass Mountain Pamphlet No. 2 (New York: Feminist Press, 1973); Ann Oakley, "Wise woman and medicine man: Changes in the management of childbirth," in Juliet Mitchell and Ann Oakley, eds., *The Rights and Wrongs of Women* (Harmondsworth, England: Penguin Books, 1976); Jean Donnison, *Midwives and Medical Men: A History of Inter-Professional Rivalries and Women's Rights* (London: Heinemann, 1977).
14. Phyllis Chesler, *Women and Madness* (New York: Doubleday, 1972); Bart, "Sexism in social science"; Dorothy E. Smith, "Women and psychiatry," in Smith and David, *Women Look at Psychiatry.*
15. Sara J. David, "Becoming a non-sexist therapist," in Smith and David, *Women Look at Psychiatry.*
16. Karl Marx and Frederick Engels, *The German Ideology, Part I* (New York: International Publishers, 1970).
17. See Karl Mannheim, *Ideology and Utopia* (New York: Doubleday/Anchor, 1965).
18. Marx and Engels, *German Ideology, Part I*, p. 47.
19. Rowbotham, *Women's Consciousness*, p. 33.
20. Ibid.
21. Chicago, *Through the Flower.*
22. Adrienne Rich, *Poems: Selected and New, 1950–1974* (New York: W. W. Norton, 1975); Suzanne Juhasz, *Naked and Fiery Forms: Modern American Poetry by Women, A New Tradition* (New York: Harper Colophon, 1976).
23. Dorothy Richardson, *Pilgrimage* (London: Virago, 1979).
24. Chicago, *Through the Flower*, pp. 78–79.
25. From the title of Lucy Lippard's book exploring the emergence of women as the creative subject in art, *From the Center: Feminist Essays on Women's Art* (New York: E. P. Dutton, 1973).
26. Juhasz, *Naked and Fiery Forms*, p. 205.
27. Lerner, "New approaches to the study of women"; idem, "Placing women in history."
28. Michel Foucault, *The Archaeology of Knowledge* (London: Tavistock Publications, 1974).
29. Bernard, "My four revolutions."
30. Oakley, *Sociology of Housework* (London: Martin Robertson, 1974), p. 4.
31. Thelma McCormack, "Towards a non-sexist perspective on social and political change," in Marcia Millman and Rosabeth Moss Kanter, eds., *Another Voice: Feminist Perspectives on Social Life and Social Sciences* (Garden City, N.Y.: Anchor Books, 1975).
32. Thomas J. Scheff, *Being Mentally Ill: A Sociological Theory* (Chicago: Aldine Press, 1962); R. D. Laing, *The Divided Self: A Study of Sanity and Madness* (Chicago: Quadrangle Books, 1960).
33. Aaron V. Cicourel, *The Social Organization of Juvenile Justice* (New York: John Wiley, 1968); Dorothy E. Smith, "The statistics on mental illness: What they will and will not tell us and why," in Smith and David, *Women Look at Psychiatry.*
34. Rae Carlson, "Understanding women: Implications for personality theory and research," *Journal of Social Issues* 28, no. 2 (1972): 17–32.

35. Bernard, "My four revolutions," p. 23.
36. Talcott Parsons, *The Structure of Social Action*, vol. 1 (New York: Free Press, 1968); Rom Harré and Paul F. Second, *The Explanation of Social Behavior* (Oxford: Basil Blackwell, 1972).
37. Alfred Schutz, "On multiple realities," in *Collected Papers* (The Hague: Martinus Nijhoff, 1962), 1:228.
38. Arlie Russell Hochschild, "The sociology of feeling and emotion: Selected possibilities," in Millman and Kanter, *Another Voice*.
39. Max Weber, *Economy and Society*, ed. Guenther Roth and Claus Wittich (New York: Bedminster Press, 1968), I:6.
40. Joyce Carol Oates, *Them* (New York: Fawcett Publications, 1970).
41. Joan Didion, *Play It as It Lays* (New York: Bantam Books, 1971).
42. Huw Beynon, *Working for Ford* (Harmondsworth, England: Penguin Books, 1973).
43. Oakley, *Sociology of Housework*, p. 4.
44. Martin Meissner, Elizabeth Humphreys, Scott M. Meis, and William J. Scheu, "No exit for wives: Sexual division of labor and the cumulation of household demands," *Canadian Review of Sociology and Anthropology* 12 (1975): 424–39.
45. Wally Seccombe, "The housewife and her labour under capitalism," *New Left Review*, no. 83 (January–February 1974): 3–24; Jean Gardiner, "The role of domestic labour," *New Left Review*, no. 89 (January–February 1975): 47–58; Marlene Dixon, "Women's liberation: Opening chapter two," *Canadian Dimension* 10 (June 1975): 56–58; Margaret Coulson, Branka Magas, and Hilary Wainwright, "The housewife and her labour under capitalism: A critique," *New Left Review*, no. 89 (January–February 75): 59–71.
46. Amitai Etzioni, *The Active Society: A Theory of Societal and Political Process* (New York: Free Press, 1968).
47. McCormack, "Towards a non-sexist perspective."
48. Bernard, "My four revolutions."
49. Alfred Schutz, "On multiple realities," 1:222–23.
50. Ibid., 1:249.
51. Dorothy E. Smith, "The intersubjective structuring of time," *Analytic Sociology* 1, no. 2 (1977).
52. Catherine Russell, letter in *Kinesis* (Vancouver, B.C.) 5 (February 1977).
53. Schutz, "On multiple realities."
54. Roy Turner, "Introduction," in R. Turner, ed., *Ethnomethodology* (Harmondsworth, England: Penguin Books, 1974).
55. De Beauvoir, *Second Sex*, pp. xvii–xiv.
56. Robert Bierstedt, "Sociology and general education," in Charles H. Page, ed., *Sociology and Contemporary Education* (New York: Random House, 1966).
57. See Max Weber's discussion of the rational type of legitimate authority in *Economy and Society*, I:215–26.
58. Adolphe Berle and Gardiner C. Means, *The Modern Corporation and Private Property* (New York: Harcourt, Brace and World, 1968).
59. Albert Sloan, *My Years with General Motors* (New York: Doubleday, 1964); Alfred D. Chandler, Jr., *Strategy and Structure: Chapters in the History of American Industrial Enterprise* (New York: Doubleday, 1966).

60. Mannheim, *Ideology and Utopia.*
61. Schutz, "On multiple realities."
62. Georg Wilhelm Friedrich Hegel, *The Phenomenology of Mind,* trans. A. V. Miller (Oxford: Oxford University Press, 1977).
63. An outstanding current example of this misinterpretation of Marx can be found in Martin Seliger, *The Marxist Conception of Ideology* (Cambridge: Cambridge University Press, 1977).
64. Karl Marx and Frederick Engels, *The German Ideology, Part I* (New York: International Publishers, 1976), p. 62.
65. Marx and Engels, *German Ideology.*
66. In *The German Ideology,* Marx and Engels formulate the premises of a "positive science" as "the real individuals, their activity, and the material conditions of their life" (p. 42).
67. Alfred Schutz, *Reflections on the Problem of Relevance,* ed. Richard Zaner (New Haven: Yale University Press, 1970), p. 11.
68. Bierstedt, "Sociology and general education." See sec. 3 of this chapter, "Sociology as a Constituent of a Consciousness Organized by the Abstracted, Extralocal Relations of Ruling."
69. Rosabeth Moss Kanter, *Men and Women of the Corporation* (New York: Basic Books, 1977).
70. It is this continual and invisible work in all its aspects to which some "wages for housework" theorists have generalized the concept of "housework." See, for example, Suzie Fleming, "All women are housewives," in *The Activists: A Student Journal of Politics and Opinion* 15, nos. 1–2 (1975): 27–33.
71. Schutz, "On multiple realities."
72. Marx and Engels, *German Ideology.*
73. Ibid.
74. Henri Lefebvre, *Everyday Life in the Modern World* (London: Allen Lane, 1971); Karel Kosik, *Dialectics of the Concrete: A Study of Problems of Man and World,* Boston Studies in the Philosophy of Science, vol. 52 (Dordrecht, Holland: D. Reidel Publishing, 1976).
75. Erving Goffman, *The Presentation of Self in Everyday Life* (New York: Doubleday/Anchor, 1959); Don H. Zimmerman and Melvin Pollner, "The everyday world as phenomenon," in Jack Douglas, ed., *Understanding Everyday Life: Towards the Reconstruction of Sociological Knowledge* (London: Routledge and Kegan Paul, 1971).
76. Paulo Freire, *Cultural Action for Freedom* (Harmondsworth, England: Penguin Books, 1972).
77. Kurt Vonnegut, *Slaughterhouse Five, or The Children's Crusade: A Duty-Dance with Death* (New York: Delacourte Press, 1969).
78. Karl Marx, *Grundrisse: Foundations of the Critique of Political Economy* (New York: Random House, 1976), p. 73.
79. Karl Marx, *Capital: A Theory of Political Economy* (New York: Vintage Books, 1977), 1:163–77.
80. Elliot Liebow, *Tally's Corner: A Study of Negro Streetcorner Men* (Boston: Little, Brown, 1976).
81. Robert Seidenberg, *Corporate Wives, Corporate Casualties* (Garden City, N.Y.: Doubleday/Anchor Books, 1975).
82. Harre and Second, *Explanation of Social Behavior.*

83. Goffman, *Presentation of Self.*
84. Karl Marx and Frederick Engels, *Feuerbach: Opposition of the Materialist and Idealist Outlooks* (London: Lawrence and Wishart, 1973), p. 30. This is an edition of the first part of *The German Ideology,* reedited to correct mistranslations and arrangements of the text that do not conform to the original. The International Publishers' version of *The German Ideology,* Part I, which I have made use of elsewhere in this book, does not include this passage. It does, however, appear in a somewhat different translation in the complete version of *The German Ideology* published by Progress Publishers, Moscow. The latter version does not make a different sense but it is far less clear and incisive. It is on page 102 and reads like this: "Individuals always proceeded, and always proceed, from themselves. Their relations are the relations of their real life-process. How does it happen that their relations assume an independent existence over against them? and that the forces of their own life become superior to them?"

3

The Everyday World as Problematic:
A Feminist Methodology

I The Standpoint of Women in the Everyday World

In previous chapters I began to define the distinctive standpoint of
women and to explore the problematic yielded by that standpoint.
Here I am concerned with the methods of thinking that will realize the
project of a sociology for women. The chapter is built on a series of
encounters between sociologist or subject, or between Two and One.
One is always the subject whose subjectivity as organizer of her knowledge is imperiled by the texts Two might or does write in political or
intellectual contexts. Alternative methods of thinking and methods of
writing sociological texts are explored in the context of dilemmas and
problems posed in these encounters.

The fulcrum of a sociology for women is the standpoint of the subject. A sociology for women preserves the presence of subjects as knowers and as actors. It does not transform subjects into the objects of study
or make use of conceptual devices for eliminating the active presence
of subjects. Its methods of thinking and its analytic procedures must
preserve the presence of the active and experiencing subject. A sociology is a systematically developed knowledge of society and social relations. The knower who is construed in the sociological texts of a so-

ciology for women is she whose grasp of the world *from where she stands* is enlarged thereby. For actual subjects situated in the actualities of their everyday worlds, a sociology for women offers an understanding of how those worlds are organized and determined by social relations immanent in and extending beyond them.

Methods of thinking could, I suppose, be described as "theories," but to do so is to suggest that I am concerned with formulations that will explain phenomena, when what I am primarily concerned with is how to conceptualize or how to constitute the textuality of social phenomena. I am concerned with how to *write* the social, to make it visible in sociological texts, in ways that will explicate a problematic, the actuality of which is immanent in the everyday world. In part what is meant by methods of thinking will emerge in the course of the chapter. This is an exploration rather than an account of a destination. We are in search of conceptual practices with which to explicate the actual social relations disclosed in investigation and analysis. We are looking, in other words, for methods and principles for generating sociological texts, for selecting syntax and indexical forms preserving the presence of subjects in our accounts, in short for methods of *writing* sociology. Such methods must recognize that the subject of our sociological texts exists outside them, that, as Marx says, "The real subject [matter] retains its autonomous existence outside the head just as before."[1] Or perhaps we go further than Marx in insisting that both subject matter and the "head" that theorizes it as well as its theorizing are enfolded in the existence of our subject matter. A sociology for women must be conscious of its necessary indexicality and hence that its meaning remains to be completed by a reader who is situated just as she is—a particular woman reading somewhere at a particular time amid the particularities of her everyday world—and that it is the capacity of our sociological texts, as she enlivens them, to reflect upon, to expand, and to enlarge her grasp of the world she reads in, and that is the world that completes the meaning of the text as she reads.

So this chapter is concerned with how to write a sociology that will do this. It does not go so far as the practicalities of how to do it. That will be a later topic. Here the focus is on those aspects of standard methods of thinking sociologically that deny us the presence of subjects and on formulating alternatives and suggesting how we might proceed in exploring the everyday world from the standpoint of women.

To avoid potential misunderstanding, I should state first what I do not mean by the standpoint of women. A sociology for women should not be mistaken for an ideological position that represents women's oppression as having a determinate character and takes up the analysis of social forms with a view to discovering in them the lineaments of what the ideologist already supposes that she knows. The standpoint of women therefore as I am deploying it here cannot be equated with perspective or worldview. It does not universalize a particular experience. It is rather a method that, at the outset of inquiry, creates the space for an absent subject, and an absent experience that is to be filled with the presence and spoken experience of actual women speaking of and in the actualities of their everyday worlds.

In chapter I, I explored issues for women arising from a culture and politics developed almost exclusively by men and written from the standpoint of men and not of women. This statement was as true of intellectual and scientific discourses as of TV commercials. To begin with, therefore, we had to discover *how* to take the standpoint of women. We did not know—there were no precedents—how to view the world from where we were, We discovered that what we had known as *our* history was not in fact ours at all but theirs. We discovered the same of our sociology. We had not realized what and who was not there in the texts in which we had learned to understand ourselves. Becoming a feminist in these contexts means taking this disjuncture up deliberately as an enterprise. The very forms of our oppression require a deliberate remaking of our relations with others and of these the relations of our knowledge must be key, for the dimensions of our oppression are only fully revealed in discoveries that go beyond what direct experience will teach us. But such a remaking cannot be prejudged, for in the very nature of the case we cannot know in advance what we will discover, what we will have to learn, and how it will be conceptualized. Remaking, in the context of intellectual enterprise, is itself a course of inquiry.

The exclusion of women is not the only one. The ruling apparatus is an organization of class and as such implicates dominant classes. The working class is excluded from the ruling apparatus. It also excludes the many voices of women and men of color, of native peoples, and of homosexual women and men. From different standpoints different aspects of the ruling apparatus and of class come into view. But, as I have argued in chapter 2, the standpoint of women is distinctive and has distinctive implications for the practice of sociology as a systematically developed consciousness of society.

I proposed women's standpoint as one situated outside textually mediated discourses in the actualities of our everyday lives. This is a standpoint designed in part by our exclusion from the making of cultural and intellectual discourse and the strategies of resorting to our experience as the ground of a new knowledge, a new culture. But it is also designed by an organization of work that has typically been ours, for women's work, as wives, secretaries, and in other ancillary roles, has been that which anchors the impersonal and objectified forms of action and relations to particular individuals, particular local places, particular relationships. Whatever other part women play in the social division of labor, they have been assigned and confined predominantly to work roles mediating the relation of the impersonal and objectified forms of action to the concrete local and particular worlds in which all of us necessarily exist.

The standpoint of women therefore directs us to an "embodied" subject located in a particular actual local historical setting. Her world presents itself to her in its full particularity—the books on her shelves, the Cowichan sweaters she has bought for her sons' birthdays, the Rainforest chair she bought three years ago in a sale, the portable computer she is using to write on, the eighteenth-century chair, made of long-since-exhausted Caribbean mahogany, one of a set of four given her by her mother years ago—each is particularized by insertion into her biography and projects as well as by its immediacy in the now in which she writes. The abstracted constructions of discourse or bureaucracy are accomplishments in and of her everyday world. Her reading and writing are done in actual locations at actual times and under definite material conditions. Though discourse, bureaucracy, and the exchange of money for commodities create forms of social relations that transcend the local and particular, they are constituted, created, and practiced always *within* the local and particular. It is the special magic of the ubiquity of text and its capacity to manifest itself as the same in diverse multiple settings that provide for the local practices of transcendence.

A standpoint in the everyday world is the fundamental grounding of modes of knowing developed in a ruling apparatus. The ruling apparatus is that familiar complex of management, government administration, professions, and intelligentsia, as well as the textually mediated discourses that coordinate and interpenetrate it. Its special capacity is the organization of particular actual places, persons, and events into generalized and abstracted modes vested in categorial systems, rules, laws, and conceptual practices. The former thereby become subject to an abstracted and universalized system of ruling mediated by texts. A mode of ruling has been created that transcends local particularities but at the same time exists only in them. The ruling apparatus of this loosely coordinated collection of varied sites of power has been largely if not exclusively the sphere of men. From within its textual modes the embodied subject and the everyday world as its site are present only as object and never as subject's standpoint. But from the standpoint of women whose work has served to complete the invisibility of the actual as the locus of the subject, from the standpoint of she who stands at the beginning of her work, the grounding of an abstracted conceptual organization of ruling comes into view as a product in and of the everyday world.

Sociology is part of the ruling apparatus. Its relevances and subtending organization are given by the relation of the ruling apparatus to the social world it governs. The institutional forms of ruling constitute its major topics—the sociology of organizations, of education, of health, of work, of mental illness, of deviance, of law, of knowledge, and the like. The organization of sociological thinking and knowledge is articulated to this institutional structure. It pioneers methods of thinking and the systematics of articulating particular actualities to a generalized conceptual order that serves it. To a significant extent, sociology has been busy clarifying, organizing, mapping, and extending the relations of the institutional forms of ruling to the actualities of their domains.

Women's lives have been outside or subordinate to the ruling apparatus. Its conceptual practices do not work for us in the development of a sociological consciousness of our own. The grid of political sociology, the sociology of the family, of organizations, of mental illness, of education, and so forth, does not map the unknown that extends before us as what is to be discovered and explored; it does not fit when we ask how we should organize a sociology beginning from the standpoint of women. We start, as we must, with women's experience (for what other resource do we have?); the available concepts and frameworks do not work because they have already posited a subject situated outside a local and actual experience, a particularized knowledge of the world. Women are readily made the objects of sociological study precisely because they have not been its subjects. Beneath the apparent gender neutrality of the impersonal or absent subject of an objective sociology is the reality of the masculine author of the texts of its tradition and his membership in the circle of men participating in the division of the labor of ruling. The problem confronted here is how to do a sociology that is for women and that takes women as its subjects and its knowers when the methods of thinking, which we have learned as sociologists as the methods of producing recognizably sociological texts, reconstruct us as objects.

If we begin where people are actually located in that independently existing world outside texts, we begin in the particularities of an actual everyday world. As a first step in entering that standpoint into a textually mediated discourse, we constitute the everyday world as our problematic. We do so by interesting ourselves in its opacity for we cannot understand how it is organized or comes about by remaining within it. The concept of problematic transfers this opacity to the level of discourse. It directs attention to a possible set of questions that have yet to be posed or of puzzles that are not yet formulated as such but are "latent" in the actualities of our experienced worlds.[2] The problematic of the everyday world is an explicit discursive formulation of an actual property of the organization of the everyday world. I am talking about a reality as it arises for those who live it—the reality, for example, that effects arise that do not originate in it. Yet I *am talking* (or rather writing) about it. I am entering it into discourse. The term "problematic" enters an actual aspect of the organization of the everyday world (as it is ongoingly produced by actual individuals) into a systematic inquiry. It responds to our practical ignorance of the determinations of our local worlds so long as we look for them within their limits. In this sense the puzzle or puzzles are really there. Hence an inquiry defined by such a problematic addresses a problem of how we are related to the worlds we live in. We may not experience our ignorance as such, but we are nonetheless ignorant.

The problematic, located by our ignorance of how our everyday worlds are shaped and determined by relation and forces external to them, must not be taken to imply that we are dopes or dupes. Within our everyday worlds, we are expert practitioners of their quiddity, of the way they are just the way they are. Our everyday worlds are in part our own accomplishments, and our special and expert knowledge is continually demonstrated in their ordinary familiarity and unsurprising ongoing presence. But how they are knitted into the extended social relations of a contemporary capitalist economy and society is not discoverable with them. The relations among multiple everyday worlds and the accomplishment of those relations within them create a dynamic organization that, in the context of contemporary capitalism, continually feeds change through to our local experience. In the research context this means that so far as their everyday worlds are concerned, we rely entirely on what women tell us, what people tell us, about what they do and what happens. But we cannot rely upon them for an understanding of the relations that shape and determine the everyday. Here then is our business as social scientists for the investigation of these relations and the exploration of the ways they are present in the everyday are and must be a specialized enterprise, a work, the work of a social scientist.

The contemporary feminist critique has emphasized problems in the relationship between researcher and "subject"[3] and has proposed and practiced methods of interview that do not objectify the research "other." Important as such methods are, they are not in themselves sufficient to ground a feminist sociology. Changes in the relationship of researcher and "subjects" do not resolve the kinds of problems we have been discussing. They are not solutions so long as the sociological methods of thinking and analysis objectify what our "subjects" have told us about their lives. We are restricted to the descriptive, to allowing the voices of women's experience to be heard, unless we can go beyond what our respondents themselves have to tell us. Important as it has been and is to hear the authentic speaking of women, it is not sufficient to ground and guide a sociological inquiry. The development of a feminist method in sociology has to go beyond our interviewing practices and our research relationships to explore methods of thinking that will organize our inquiry and write our sociological texts so as to preserve the presence of actual subjects while exploring and explicating the relations in which our everyday worlds are embedded.

II Problems in the Relationship of Observer and Observed

Beginning from the standpoint of women implies beginning at a point prior to the moment that organizes the detached scientific consciousness. It means therefore beginning in the world that both sociologist and those she observes and questions inhabit on the same basis. Taking the standpoint of women means recognizing that as inquirers we are thereby brought into determinate relations with those whose experience we intend to express. The concepts and frameworks, our methods of inquiry, of writing texts, and so forth are integral aspects of that relation. Furthermore what has been argued of the everyday world of women in general applies equally to that everyday moment in which we encounter those we will write about in some form or other. The relations with others organized by our inquiry are also shaped by social relations subtending it and entering into the inquiry in unseen ways.

The purpose of raising this issue is not to shift from inquiry into the problematic of other women's worlds to inquiry into the problematic of the relationship between sociological inquirer and her respondents. It is rather to display the relational organization within which the sociological work goes on. The objectifying practices of established sociology make such subtending organization inaccessible to exploration. But here we are in search of a method of inquiry giving ourselves as inquirers and our subjects a presence in our methods of writing sociological texts.

To give substance to the issue, here is an example I used in an earlier paper.[4] I did not analyze it at that time as I shall now. It is, at least in certain highly relevant respects, paradigmatic of the set of relations routinely involved in sociological inquiry.

> *Riding a train not long ago in Ontario I saw a family of Indians: woman, man, and three children standing together on a spur above a river watching the train go by. There was (for me) that moment—the train, those five people seen on the other side of the glass. I saw first that I could tell this incident as it was, but that telling as a description built in my position and my interpretations. I have called them a family; I have said they were watching the train. My understanding has already subsumed theirs. Everything may have been quite other for them. My description is privileged to stand as what actually happened, because theirs is not heard in the contexts in which I may speak.[5]*

The sociologist here enters into a relation with those observed in which they become her puppets who speak, see, and think the words, sights, and thoughts she attributes to them. The passing of the train provides a metaphor for a kind of distance between observer and observed in which the observed are silenced. Here, of course, the break is deeper than ordinary because the observer could not have been even an individuated presence for those she watched. The train passes, and all that could have been available to the watcher are those white faces at the windows. The communicative break is extreme but the silence of those observed in the little story is routine. Those she sees are a resource for a telling entered already into the social relations of the discourse at the very moment of observation (she keeps a notebook and has written this observation and some of these reflections down). Her ordinary descriptive procedures incorporate interpretations unchecked by the experience of those she describes. She has called them a "family," but were they a "family"? Were they actually watching the train? But the issue is not only that of accuracy. It is also that she has laid down the agenda of description and its terms. It is she who has seen them as a family and has seen the family watching and has inserted that organization into the world as its feature. So even questions of accuracy and fact revolve within the frame she has already established. In the discussion that follows we will move back and forth between this immediate level of contact and experience, the level of direct encounters with others, and exploration of the relations subtending the immediate level. The immediate level of relationships is embedded in determinate relations that provide its underlying structure.

In the paradigmatic instance above, the moving train structures the encounter (if indeed it can be described as such) between sociologist and those standing by the railroad and structures also the specific differences in how each can have appeared to the other. The moving train is the matrix of anything that was observed to be told. It sets up a distinctive intersection of differing temporal structures arising from the passage of the train carrying the sociologist toward and away from those standing and perhaps waiting for the train to pass by. Sitting in the train, the sociologist is merely looking out. She is not otherwise actively engaged. The movement of the train and her mere looking create for her the structure of a "moment," an "incident." Her seeing of those people has a beginning and an end structured by the train's passage. They come into view, they are abreast, they are disappearing from view (she peers backward at the corner of the window to catch a last sight of them before the bush intervenes). Of course, we do not know how it was structured for those she observed, though we know it could not have been structured in anything like the same way if only because it is for them the train that passes and the event is its passage.

Beyond the local organization provided by the train and its passing is a further political and social organization of the historical relation of native peoples to the railroad, their displacement from former modes of living, their confinement to reservations in areas where there is little or no possibility of developing a livelihood other than dependence in some degree on the state. In its contemporary forms, this state is integrated with the relations I have described earlier as a ruling apparatus. The sociological discourse is also located there. It is indeed the administrative practice of the state that, from the multiplicity of tribal groups once peopling North America, has generated this category "Indian" (as I used it in the earlier paper) and its updated contemporary, "native peoples," of which I avail myself so naturally and unthinkingly in my description.

I am white, English-speaking, a paid member of the Canadian intelligentsia. I have my place in this same organization of relations that generates the experience of the world of those I observed. Such considerations as these suggest yet other possibilities in the relationship. Could there have been hostility among those on the spur above the railroad, looking toward the train against the white faces looking out? I remember then another incident from many years ago. The first time I traveled across Canada by train, when the train was passing through part of northern Ontario (country not too different from this) a native women killed herself by throwing herself on the tracks in front of the train. At first all we knew as passengers was that there was delay. Then the news was passed by word of mouth down the train. Then a young native woman came down the tracks and, sitting beside us on the ground, cried and screamed at us in a language we did not understand. We had no idea what she was saying to us or why she was screaming at us—after all we were not driving the train; we were not in control; we did not have anything to do with what had happened. We can only see what this might have been about if we shift from the immediate level of the relationship to the underlying historically determined structure of relations.

The one-sided relationship of observing and telling that is embedded in these extended relations organizes the sociologist's account. For the sociologist in the train, what can be told as an event is already structured by its passage. It is constituted as an "event" in her account. For those who stood on the knoll, what was an "event" for her could not appear in the same way to them. There was a different temporal structure, different intentions and purposes (they had their destination; they were, we can imagine, going somewhere).

Even when the observer has no presence in the text so that what she has observed appears as an unmediated object, the "structure" of the original relation of observation is still implicit in the account. Here is a nonsociological instance demonstrating such an effect. *Round about a Pound a Week* by Mrs. Pember Reeves reports a pre–First World War investigation of the effects of increased nourishment before and after childbirth on working-class mothers and their children. Participants were selected on the basis of an income neither significantly above nor below a sum just enabling them to subsist. Supplementary nourishment was provided for three weeks before birth and until the child was a year old. The family was visited every week. Mrs. Reeves's book describes the living situation of these families, their housing, their weekly budget, their diet, and in general their management of their daily lives. I want to show the presence of social relations *in* the text. Here is the opening passage to the book.

> *Take the tram from Victoria to Vauxhall Station. Get out under the railway arch which faces Vauxhall Bridge, and there you will find Kennington Lane. The railway arch roofs in a din which reduces the roar of trains continually passing overhead to a vibrating, muffled rumble. From either end of the arch comes a close procession of trams, motor-buses, brewers' drays, coal-lorries, carts filled with unspeakable material for glue factory and tannery, motor-cars, coster-barrows, and people. It is a topping place for tramcars and motor-buses; therefore little knots of agitated persons continually collect on both pathways and dive between the vehicles and descending passengers in order to board the particular bus or tram they desire. At rhythmic intervals all traffic through the arch is suspended to allow a flood of trams, buses, drays and vans to surge and rattle and bang across the opening of the archway which faces the river.*[6]

Let me draw your attention first to the description of the scene as one of noise, bustle, and confusion. The focus is on movement and the flow of a miscellaneous collection of vehicles. It is an effect of the writer's art to bring that scene to the view of our imaginations with its activity, its noise (even its smells), and its multifarious sources of movement coordinated into a "flow" of traffic. This scenic structure arises in the relation of an outsider to the scene. It is presented to outsiders as an outsider's view. The author/observer gives us directions for how to find it. They are rhetorical. We are not expected to follow them. Like the observer, we come to this place from a distance. Our journey starts from one of the major railway terminals in London. We might have come from anywhere. Directed to this place by the observer/author, her seeing of it organizes the scene for us. She does not belong to it as one who is herself engaged in it. She is not one of those habitually among "the knots of agitated persons" collecting on the pathways to catch the motor bus or tram. She does not drive a bus or tram; she does not drive the brewer's dray or the coal lorry; she does not push (or pull) the coster-barrow. She is an outsider; she is *an observer.* Her relationship to the scene is given by her business there, which is to observe; that is part of the research enterprise. Observation has a distinctive temporal structure. The confusion and chaos of the scene are framed by an observational stasis. The account would be very differently organized if it were presented from the standpoint of someone involved as an actor in the setting. His or her purpose and direction would organize the constituents Mrs. Reeves describes quite differently—what the traffic was like to the driver of the dray, for example, would not be chaos but a familiar setting and condition of his work. For him that moment conjured by the observer would not exist as such. He passes through the same setting as that of the observer with a temporal perspective organized by his work. But the moment of observation congeals the bustle and action into "events" in themselves. The actual substrate of what has been produced textually as a "scene" containing "events" has been "sectioned off" by the author/observer. The continuities of action, purpose, and direction that provide the materials of the author/observer's scene are not preserved. The "sectioning off" is an effect of framing the moment of observation, the moment of "looking at." It is the outsider's point of entry into a living process; she not only looks at the scene, but constitutes it as a scene in that looking. Her looking is organized by her intention to speak of it to those who are not there. Implicit in this passage, then, is an organization of the social relations of which the passage does not speak. The relations that underlie it organize the account over and above the observer's privileged interpretations of what was there and what happened. That very privileging is itself an "expression" of those relations.

From the perspective of the passenger in the train, an event is constituted as those five people come into view and disappear from sight. Her account is informed by a structure latent in the relationship. Similarly Mrs. Reeves's introduction to Kennington Lane is organized by her external relationship to the processes she describes. The sociologist's normal working relationship to the world is of the same order. She is thinking in discourse terms; she makes her observation not as something merely noticed, or as a remark to a fellow passenger, but as one that gets written, which intends the discourse of sociology. The relevances of the discourse isolate *this* as an instance, as something to be told. The account she writes—this account you have had before you—is specifically structured by these as well as by the silences of those who are also present. The "structure" of the observational moment is implicit in the account.

Thus, beyond the encounter on the common ground of an everyday world there is another level of organization. In the everyday work of sociological inquiry, the sociologist or her hireling interviews a "subject." "Subject" or respondent answers the sociologist's questions. She does just that. She does not tell the sociologist what questions to ask. She is not a participant in the textually mediated discourse to which the sociologist will return from the field with her trophies. As we shall see below, Mrs. Reeves works in the same way, taking for granted the privileges of speaking for those who are not members of the discourses embedded in the relations of ruling in which she has a voice. The sociologist exercises the same privilege. The relations of ruling are immanent in the sociologist's observations, the way in which her interview is conceived, what she will do with the "material" she collects when she takes it back home and works it up, but these remain unexplicated. The fact that I am in the train and the Indians are standing on the spur above the river, and that my observations are entered into a discourse articulated to the relations of ruling which oppress them, is continually at work in the (immediate if transitory) relationship and in the account of it that I write.

We will take up this drama at the paradigmatic level by naming our two characters, subject and sociologist, One and Two. In the everyday work of observation, Two observes One driving a dray, waiting for a motorbus, cutting wood, or standing on a knoll by the railroad. Or perhaps Two interviews One, who answers Two's questions. If so, One does just that. She does not tell Two what questions to ask her, and she is not a participant in the discourse to which Two will return from the field with her trophies. Like it or not, Two speaks from and assumes the privileges of her participation in a discourse embedded in relations of ruling. The latter are immanent in Two's observations, in the way in which her interview is conceived, in her use of the "material" she collects when she takes it back home and works it up, and as we have seen, in the texts that are her product and the methods of writing them.

III Sociological Methods of Writing Texts

Established sociology is preoccupied with suppressing the presence of the sociological subject.[7] This points to an underlying contradiction. While objectivity, in the sense of the detached scientific knower, has come to be seen as an essential property of its scientific texts, actuality has continued to resist this discursive production. However flexible her joints and acrobatic her postures, the sociological knower is always and cannot escape being part of the world that goes on outside her head, as well as inside it, and is her object of inquiry. Her head and her inquiry are as much part of it as the object of her investigation. Scientific detachment itself is a product of distinctive and specialized social organization, consisting, on the one hand, of methods of writing and reading the texts of scientific discourse and, on the other, as Schutz has shown us,[8] of the subject's own practices of suppressing and discarding her biographical and local setting and the pragmatic concerns of her world of working to enter the cognitive domain of science as reader of scientific texts. To forget her bodily being is also to forget her own historicity.

The sociologist's methods of writing texts produce a world for her readers such that they too stand outside it. Those of us who have had the experience of being members of a category that is the object of sociological inquiry can recognize the strangeness of finding ourselves as subjects transformed in a course of reading into objects and of the unspoken sociological stipulation instructing us to disregard what we know of ourselves as embodied subjects. The unspoken relationship between sociologist and those she observes is hidden in the conceptual practices that externalize their activities and practices as properties of structures or systems, and reinterprets the daily actualities of their lives into the alienated constructs of sociological discourse, subordinating their experienced worlds to the categories of ruling.

Methods of writing sociological texts construct out of the one-sided privilege of the sociologist a text that claims to stand outside the "subjectivity" of both sociologist and "subject." Sociological claims for the objectivity of its accounts have been based on methods that will generate a sociological account overriding and independent of divergent and localized perspectives. Sociology claims to provide a "third" version among the contending or potentially contending accounts of other parties.[9] The sociological "third" version is more than an additional perspective added to the previous collection. Rather it is a version that is (a) specifically independent of the partial and subjective perspectives of particular individuals or groups involved in the action to be described and analyzed; and (b) a metaversion constructed so that it will subsume and account for the other versions and hence can be substituted for them as the authoritative account. In the making of such accounts, sociology has developed vocabulary, concepts, and syntactic modes that enable Two's one-sided version to be represented as objective, as standing outside the world it surveys.

It would seem that sociologies that isolate meaning as the defining property of the social,[10] and propose as their necessary ground the interpretation of the meaning of social actors, would preserve the presence and force of subjects in the sociological texts. The sociologist's knowledge or apprehension of what is going on or what someone is doing is an interpretive act if only in the very fundamental sense that to describe what someone does in action language incorporates intention. People who act have something "in mind." She is scratching her nose, for example; she is unpacking her groceries; she is making her bed; she is cutting wood for the winter; she is letting Rosa the cat in. But interpretive sociologies go beyond this point to an ontology of the social that projects the sociologist's necessary grasp, the interpretive act, onto the world as its mode of being, its ontology. Such an ontology grounds methods of writing "third versions," which supersede those of the actual individuals in which they originate. Typically body and mind are taken apart and "mind"—or its refractions—"meaning," "motive," "interpretation,"—are given the principal parts as agents or operators. The shared meanings or expectations, consensus, the "known-in-common," the "intersubjective," "culture," are modes in which the actualities of the social are given subjectless presence in the sociological text. The sociology of Alfred Schutz, for example, builds sociological constructs on the constructs of actors and locates the essentially social in the sharing of knowledge, in the idealizations and achievement of intersubjectivity.[11]

Such practices and devices build in the one-sided relationship between Two and One in which Two speaks for One's capacities as subject. They presuppose a discourse in which only Two is privileged to speak.

This building in is made visible in passages from the foundations of interpretive sociology in the work of Max Weber. In setting out the grounds for sociology as "a science concerning itself with the interpretive understanding of social action and thereby with a causal explanation of its course and consequences,"[12] Weber distinguishes between different types of understanding. The first is the direct observational understanding of the subjective meaning of a given act as such, including verbal utterances.[13] Among the examples he gives is that of "the action of a wood-cutter" in cutting wood. This is an instance of an immediate understanding of someone's actions. A second and more complex type of understanding is "explanatory understanding." Here Weber introduces the concept of motive. Motive is "the meaning an actor attaches to" actions that themselves are grasped by direct observational understanding.

Motive is "what makes him do this at precisely this moment and in these circumstances."[14] The concept of motivation provides explanatory understanding of actions that are understood by direct observation:

> Rational understanding of motivation . . . consists in placing the act in an intelligible and more inclusive context of meaning. Thus we understand the chopping of wood or aiming of a gun in terms of motive in addition to direct observation if we know that the woodchopper is working for a wage or is chopping a supply of fire-wood for his own use or possibly he is doing it for recreation. But he might also be working off a fit of rage, in the irrational case.[15]

The posture of the sociologist has been built into the presuppositions of inquiry and then into the concepts developed to generate sociological texts. The sociologist can see that the woodchopper is chopping wood. It seems as though her problem is to figure out why he is doing it. The concept of motive traps this moment and transposes it into our conceptual equipment. The behavior to be explained is unproblematic; it is immediately available to observation. Motive is a second-order concept that will explain it. The woodchopper may be chopping wood to sell; he may be working for a wage or for his own uses; or he may be in a rage. These are motivational explanations. This methodological practice is structured analogous to Reeves's method of writing her description of Kennington Lane. The moment of chopping wood, of "direct observational understanding," is "sectioned out." In this way the temporal structure of the observational moment is imposed upon a lived and moving actuality. The observer looks, notices, and leaves. She returns to her study (or perhaps more likely to the kitchen table), and there she writes down what she has observed directly. She isolates that moment, the seeing of the woodchopper at work. The sectioning off is part of her sociological work. She has posed as a problem what she does not know—those aspects of the lived actuality that have escaped her observation.

It is here that the problem of explanatory understanding arises. It does not arise at all for the woodchopper who continued to cut wood, has stacked it in this cart, and is already making his round of nearby homes to whose owners he has promised a bundle of wood. It is not unproblematic for the woodchopper simply because the woodchopper knows why he is doing it. It is unproblematic because chopping wood is part of an ongoing course of action in which he is engaged. His work is coordinated with that of others in a temporally ordered sequence of actions; the depth of the relations in which this particular sequence is embedded is present in his ax, cart, clothes, horse, and so forth which are themselves the product of other and preceding similar complexly concerted sequences of work. Yet the sociological method of producing an account deprives us precisely of that grasp of the other's active participation in the extended relations of the market that would enable us to pass beyond opacity rather than transferring it to the level of sociological discourse.

The continuity of his actions and the ordered sequences of actions linking his work to that of others do not isolate anything corresponding to the sociologist's moment of observation. That "moment" exists only as a product of the sociologist's work and of her relationship, as sociologist, to the woodchopper. The concept of direct observational understanding, the second level of explanatory understanding, as well as the methodological value of the concept of motive, build a one-sided relationship between One (the woodchopper) and Two (the sociologist) into a sociological method for *writing texts*. The conceptual practices that organize her sociological text produce an account of the social process as if she stood outside it.

The observer's problem of "explaining" what the drive of the brewer's dray or the woodchopper is doing results from the sectioning out of a moment of observation as a practice situated in a determinate social relation. Such a moment arises only as Two is positioned so that he or she can speak of One's life in texts in which One does not appear as subject (indeed in which the presence of subjects is altogether suppressed). Indeed it can appear only in a relation in which One is already other to Two. The observer's moment of separation is incorporated into sociological methods of thinking as conceptual practices are elaborated in the construction of the phenomenal world of sociological discourse. Concepts such as 'motive' provide structuring devices reproducing the original relation in the sociological text.

Yet seeking an alternative incorporating the standpoint of subjects as they are actually located, we seem to have stuck ourselves in the traditional sociological dilemma of "multiple perspectives." If we renounce a sociological rereading of what the people we talk to tell us and at the same time want to say something more or other than they can see and say, we seem to resign ourselves to a dual vision in which either account is equally valid and neither has the power to supersede the other. Perhaps more problematic is the issue of how we are to decide among differing products of inquiry, among differing sociological versions? If we forgo the move of objectivity, are there procedures enabling us to determine which among differing versions of the world we can rely on as an account of how it is? What is the status of our version if we forgo our claim to write the "third" and overriding version?

Can we, as Sandra Harding suggests,[16] come to rest in an acceptance of intrinsic many-sidedness of our worlds and therefore of the many stories that may be told of it, of which ours is only one? Postmodernists have celebrated and theorized the overthrow of the transcendental subject, replacing it with a recognition of multiple alternative narratives, none of which can claim a privileged status over others. Harding has described this move as follows:

> Once the Archimedean, transhistorical agent of knowledge is deconstructed into constantly shifting, wavering, recombining, historical groups, then a world that can be understood and navigated with the assistance of Archimedes' map of perfect perspective also disappears. As Flax put the issue, "Perhaps 'reality' can have 'a' structure only from the falsely universalizing perspective of the master. That is, only to the extent that one person or group can dominate the whole, can 'reality' appear to be governed by one set of rules or be constituted by one privileged set of social relation-ships?"[17]

Harding concludes that "by giving up the ghost of telling "one true story," we embrace instead the permanent partiality of feminist inquiry."[18] The "one true story" is nothing more than a partial perspective claiming generality on the basis of social privilege and power.

But suppose we posed the problem at a more mundane level where we are not grappling with notions of truth, but more simply and rudely with how to write a sociology that will somehow lay out for women, for people, how our everyday worlds are organized and how they are shaped and determined by relations that extend beyond them. Inquiry itself does not make sense unless we suppose that there is something to be found and that that something can be spoken of to another, as we might say "Well, this is the way it is. This is how it works." It would not be enough to be able to say "This is how it looks to me" when that is not just a way station toward something more final, but is all we are going to be able to say. If we want to be able to offer something like a map or diagram of the swarming relations in which our lives are enmeshed so that we can find our ways better among them, then we want to be able to claim that we are describing is actual in the same way as our everyday worlds are actual. We want to be able to say with confidence that we can speak of it truthfully and faithfully.

The problems of multiple perspectives for sociology and the decision rules provided by sociological methods of constituting objectivity arise in the context of a sociology that has built into its methods the assumption that we cannot encounter the world without a concept, that knowing it relies on the ordering procedures already established in the theoretical armamentarium of the discourse. If we move then to a sociology whose business is making out a world that is put together in determinate ways prior to our thinking it and that makes as its enterprise the discovery of just how it is done, then the issues are no longer at the level of "truth" but rather, in assessing the products of inquiry, "Has she got it right? Is this how it really works? Is it accurate? Faithful to the character of the organization and relations investigated?" Such questions can be asked only if there exists the practical possibility of another account that *can* invalidate hers. If it is a power play, as Harding suggests,[19] to claim the veracity of one version, is it not also essential to the most modest possibilities of knowing how things work that a social scientific account can be called into question? And therefore that another version can be on some grounds preferred?

So the epistemology must also be an ontology, a method of thinking (a theory if you like) about how the social can be said to exist so that we can describe it in ways that can be checked back to how it actually is. Therefore, I shall argue that by the very character of the social itself that lies in the ongoing active recreation of a world in common, this possibility exists.

IV   A Method of Thinking for a Sociology for Women

Though the standpoint of women commits us to a subject discovering the social process from *inside,* hence subjectively, we have also insisted upon subject's embodiment and her existence therefore in a world of time and activity and of materiality. In search of a method of thinking that denies neither the subjective mode in which the social exists nor its "objectivity" (in the minimal sense that we can "test" different accounts against the actuality of which both speak and therefore that somehow or other "it" has an existence independent of the interpretation of the accounts), we turn to the materialist method as Marx and Engels formulated it in *The German Ideology*. For theirs is an ontology that first shifts us out of the discourse among texts as a place to start. The premises they declare are not in imagination. They insist we start in the same world as the one we live in, among real individuals, their activities, and the material conditions of their activities. What is there to be investigated are the ongoing actual activities of real people. Nothing more or less. We are talking about a world that *actually happens* and can be observed, spoken of, and returned to to check up on the accuracy of an account or whether a given version of it is faithful to how it actually works (in principle at least; the practice may at times prove more complicated).

But what has happened to the subject? Has she been swallowed up, as some readings of Marx have argued, in a reduction of consciousness to an epiphenomenon of material being? *The German Ideology* provides a decisively simple response. Far from viewing consciousness as a mere function of material process, Marx and Engels in *The German Ideology* insist that we cannot detach individual and consciousness.[20] The distinctive stance of Marx's materialism (we cannot be quite so confident of Engels's if we follow his later work) is the assertion that consciousness is inseparable from the individual. In contrasting their method to the idealism of the German ideologists, who treat consciousness as if it were an active agent in history, they assert *the inseparability of consciousness and individual:* "In the first method [idealism] the starting point is consciousness taken as the living individual; in the second method, which conforms to real life, it is the real living individuals themselves, and *consciousness is considered solely as their consciousness.*"[21] This conception is of the social as existing in and only in actual people's actual activities and practices, where the terms "individual," "activity," and "practice" are taken to include the "subjective side" or consciousness.

Of course it is not just activities and practices as such that give us the social as an object of inquiry but the concerting or coordination of activities or, as Marx and Engels put it, the forms of cooperation.[22] If we take the ongoing concerting of activities in all the complex ways in which that concerting is accomplished and in all the complex forms of what Harold Garfinkel refers to as the quiddity of local historical process,[23] we are no longer stuck with shared meanings or intersubjectivity as the guarantor and ground of the social. Rather the coordering or concerting of actual activities by actual individuals is continually being worked out in the course of working together, competing with one another, conversing, and all the other ways in which people coact. People work together in concrete actual situations; the coordination or concerting of their activities is both in movement in time and in and through talk and other "expressive" modes such as music. The existence of a common environment of objects comes into being at whatever level of complexity, in and of an ongoing local historical organization of practices. See George Herbert Mead, for example, who writes: "The social environment . . . is an organization of objective relations which arise in relation to a group engaged in such activities in processes of social experience and behavior. Certain characteristics of the external world are possessed by, only with reference to, or in relation to an interacting social group of individual organisms."[24]

We can see the fully socially organized existence of a table in how a small child does not know, for example, how to constitute a table as the space that at its simplest separates what may be done with head and hands from the (dirty) floor of feet. The very ordinary presence of the objects of our daily lives, chairs, tables, are not what they are simply because of their physical properties, but are socially organized in our everyday practices and organize their concerting. The terms for socially constituted objects are anchored in and anchor a social organization of actual practices in and through which table becomes table. Indeed the meaning of their terms, rather than arising in a referential process, consists in that anchorage of a socially organized form. Our everyday world of practical activities continually confirms for us and others a shared world of objects and people.[25] In a study of the discovery of a pulsar, Garfinkel, Lynch, and Livingstone show the ongoing concerted practices in which the pulsar comes into social existence as an object. At the beginning of the taped record of the talk among astronomers at work, that pulsar did not exist; in the course of that talk, observations are made indicating "pulsar"; further observations affirm "pulsar"; it then exists. A feature of its social organization is that it was already there to be discovered prior to its discovery; this is the sense and social organization of a "discovery." Its existence is a socially organized product of the specialized work of astronomers in an actual local historical context and as an actual local historical process.

This coming into being of a particular object provides a paradigm of how objects exist for us, for their existence is continually renewed for us in daily practices, our own and those of others. The objectivity of simple objects is an ongoing social accomplishment. The women who gets up from her chair and walks over to the cigarette machine in a cafeteria, puts her money in the slot, and gets her packet of cigarettes affirms for me and anyone else there present in multiple ways a world we hold in common. Further, as she acts, she discovers those objects as reliably and appropriately what they are—the chair, the money in her handbag which fits the slot in the machine and produces the cigarettes, the floor she walks on, and so on. If, leaving the cafeteria, our paths crossed, we would adjust our movements to one another. The concerting, the coordination of the world, both produces and is present in the material environment she so naturally takes for granted—the chair, the money, the cigarette machine, the package of cigarettes, each produced to intend its complementary act and social in this double mode.

Such methods of thinking enable us to see realities as social and as arising in an ongoing organization of practices that continually and routinely reaffirm a world in common at the most basic grounding of our life in the concrete daily realities as well as in more complex social forms. Our world is continually being brought into being as it is and as it is becoming, in the daily practices of actual individuals.

Such an ontology analyzes social processes as the ongoing concerting of actual practices of actual individuals. We see, then, people very much as they are, the competent practitioners of their everyday worlds, active in definite material and social contexts, desiring, thinking, feeling, and actively engaged with others in producing the actualities of the world they have in common with one another. A social reality, in this line of thinking, is a local historical process created by those involved for themselves and each other. It is essentially a process in time. Sociological analysis explicates what members accomplish, their actual practices and methods of producing the order they find and are active in bringing into being.

These practices, these objects, our world, are continually created again and again and are already social. Because they arise in actual activities, they are always coming into being as a local historical process, falling away behind us as we move forward into the future. They are being brought into being. But this does not mean that they exist in different ways for different people. It does not mean that our realities are not substantial nor that how they are differs from person to person depending on meaning or perspective. The social construction of reality is precisely that of creating a world we have in common. It is the work of continually accomplishing a world that does exist as a reality that is the same for me as it is for you. Where you see chair, I see chair. Or if I do not recognize that strange humpy lumpy object as a chair, you tell me "that's a chair" and I know then how it works as object coming to hand or rather to seat. And, rather gingerly, I sit down to wait while you put the kettle on. Its capacity as chair arises as you announce its social organization, and we both then know how to enter it into the concerting of our joint work of having a cup of coffee and a conversation together. In exploring the social then we are exploring what is being accomplished as what we have in common *ongoingly* and as what we know and rely on as the same for us as it is for others. This effect is not produced by the mysterious "idealizations of intersubjectivity" which Schutz's cognitively based conception of social reality requires.[27] It is brought into being for us ongoingly in the concerting of actual activities in which language plays the essential role of storing and re-membering social organization.

Here, there is no implication that a social reality is fixed or final, nor that it is always a simple matter to verify "premises" in a purely empirical way.[28] What we are trying to make visible in this way is an ongoing production. The social process is always in the making; it is also always coming into being as a condition of our own activity, confirmed in the very process of coordinating our own moves with those of others, corrected as it is found to fail as a condition of theirs. A socially organized reality is known as such not as "objective,"[29] but as an ongoing practical matter of accomplishing presence by and among subjects.

Marx and Engels say of their method that it "conforms to real life," which *is* the actual activities of actual individuals under definite material conditions. Ethnomethodology specifies its ontology very similarly. "In doing sociology [says Garfinkel] . . . every reference to the "real world," even where the reference is to physical or biological events, is a reference to the organized activities of everyday life."[30]

The organized activities of everyday life have been the focus of ethnomethodological inquiry. The method of analyzing naturally occurring conversations, for example, *explicates* the orderliness that members themselves produce for each other:

> If the materials (records of natural conversation) were orderly, they were so because they had been methodically produced by members of the society for one another, and it was a feature of the conversations we treated as data that they were produced so as to allow the display by the co-participants to each other of their orderliness, and to allow the participants to display to each other their analysis, appreciation and use of that orderliness.[31]

The practice of inquiry proposed will *explicate* rather than *explain* the actual ongoing concerting of human activity.

In any given context of action, the social arises in how individuals enter actual courses of action coordinating with others, with objects, with an environment that is already socially organized and that is becoming organized as it is again (in its quiddity) as they act. Questions of what become less significant than questions of how—how it gets done, how it works. So while we draw back from the somewhat smug oversimplification of Marx and Engels's conclusion to their announcement of the premises of the new materialist method, "These premises can be verified in a purely empirical way," we can hold with them that the social itself (as we have been specifying it) creates the conditions of its own observability. We do not therefore rely on a technical methodology for producing objectivity but on an inquiry (necessarily technical) oriented by prospective questions from others: "Is it really so?" "Does it really happen like that?" Such questions rely on the possibility that others could return to the object of our inquiry and on the basis of their own work respond, "No, she is wrong, it does not work like that but like this," and so forth. In contrast to the established methodologies constructing a third version out of contending versions and thus constituting the objectivity of the world as a product of inquiry, we propose a method of inquiry that relies on the existence of a world in common ongoingly created and recreated in human sensuous activities. It is a method of inquiry that proposes to explicate the same world as that of people's action and experience. Indeed the work of inquiry itself goes forward in and is part of the same world as it explicates.

V Sociological Inhibitions to Exploring the Everyday World as Problematic

Opening an inquiry from the standpoint of women means accepting our ineluctable embeddedness in the same world as is the object of our inquiry. It means recognizing that our work enters us into relationships with others that are structured by relations not fully present in them and that our textual pretensions to objectivity are betrayed by the secret presence of those relations in the text itself and the conceptual and other devices that we make use of in producing it. To work then from the standpoint of women as a method of thinking and of writing the subject into texts, we must cede from the outset our discursive privilege to substitute our understandings for those whose stories instruct us in their experience of lived actualities. Yet clearly if we move to an investigation of the relations that are not plain either to our interlocutor or ourselves, she cannot be our resource for everything we want to know. We want to know more so that she can also.

Beyond the encounter on the common ground of an everyday world, we have shown dimly the workings of another level of organization. Individuals' accounts of their experience may disclose a level of organization beyond that experience. Here are instances of other encounters displaying a rift not fully analyzable within the local historical settings of meeting. Our first two are accounts by workers of their experience as participants in radical left-wing organizations in the United States and our third an instance of issues arising in the women's movement between middle- and working-class feminists.

> *I remember once they were having this discussion on feudalism. Of course, three-fourths of the discussion I didn't understand. So finally, I asked a question. One of the women in the group told me my question was "too simple"—that the issue was "actually much more complicated" than that. There were two worlds meeting there and they couldn't be reconciled. I couldn't imagine those people doing the same work as we did or relating like we did. I'd go to work the next day after one of those meetings and it was a totally different reality.*[30]

Another worker told of a similar experience:

> *I remember how shocked one of these people was when they heard me griping about all the shitty jobs I'd had. One of them asked me, "haven't you ever had a job you felt good about?" I said, "No." It was beyond him, outside his reality. Factory workers are exotic creatures to these people.*[31]

There are similar examples from the women's movement. Berson describes how she learned to confront the realities of her own class experience as she lived and worked politically with working-class women.

> *I learned that class is not only how much you have relative to everybody else, but what kind of economic security you have. My family never had to worry about whether we would eat, or whether my father would have work. We worried about how often we could eat at restaurants, and the kind of work my father would have to do. For lower class women those worries are so far removed from their lives that they seem ludicrous. Eating and working are questions of survival, not taste.*[34]

The two may meet and work together, but their meeting and working together are determined (in the sense of "shaped") by underlying social relations that enter a deep rift into their relationship.

The level at which One or Two encounter one another is grasped as being embedded in relations of class, which shapes that encounter and how it is experienced. Figure 3.1 shows how the different levels are conceived. The one-sided relationship of observing and telling which is embedded in the extended relations of class also organizes Two's sociological account.

The practical problem that arises as we attempt to explore the class

Figure 3.1

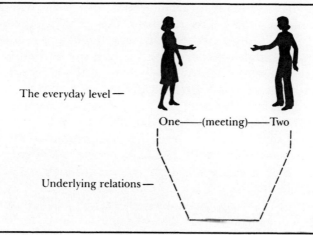

The everyday level —

One——(meeting)——Two

Underlying relations —

relations in which the encounter between One and Two is embedded is that the methods of thinking and conceptual practices that we ordinarily use to talk "class" sociologically, and often politically too, make such underlying determinations invisible. We have already seen how these tranpose what arises necessarily in a determinate relationship with its determinate underlying properties into a single, unidimensional account. The standpoint of one position only, that of Two, the sociologist, becomes the source of an account that is represented as written from a position transcending that of particular subjects.

Sociological methods of thinking of "levels" of "structure" beyond and determining the local historical matrices of our experience will capture such underlying relations only at the cost of dispensing with the presence of subjects. It seems that here we have no alternative other than to move to conceptual practices suppressing the presence of subjects. Methods of macrosociological thinking are specialized to produce an account of a social process as if it were external to the individuals who necessarily bring it into being. They create a wholly external relation between those whose lives are the source of whatever textual "structure" is erected to represent them. They also create a wholly external relationship between inquirer and object of her inquiry so that the latter appears to exist altogether independent of the practices and project through which she knows it. They constitute a standpoint within the texts of discourse, severing them from their ground in an original world of active subjects.

Thus in practicing the methods of thinking of sociological discourse, the sociological inquirer participates in the world of discursive objects they have brought into being and that are sustained as the known-in-common world of its members. The complex organization of activities of actual individuals and their actual relations is entered into the discourse through concepts such as class, modernization, formal organization. A realm of theoretically constituted objects is created, freeing the discursive realm from its ground in the lives and work of actual individuals and liberating sociological inquiry to graze on a field of conceptual entities that now can be combined in ways unconstrained by the original actual relations organizing and organized by actual individuals. Agency can be transferred from people to a discursive object originating in and reflecting the social relations of their actual lives and work—"the effects of modernization on the family" or "class as a determinant of political consciousness." In research, classes of variables are constructed and generalized across populations to disclose particular refractions of discursive entities. The products may be entered into the purely formal space constituted by statistical manipulations of data.

The samples through which the world has been given textual presence here have all been ones in which "class" has been or could be used to interpret relations between One and Two. Using sociological methods of thinking, how does "class" operate on an array of subjects? Here is a little population of eight people. They are represented by asterisks in figure 3.2.

Figure 3.2

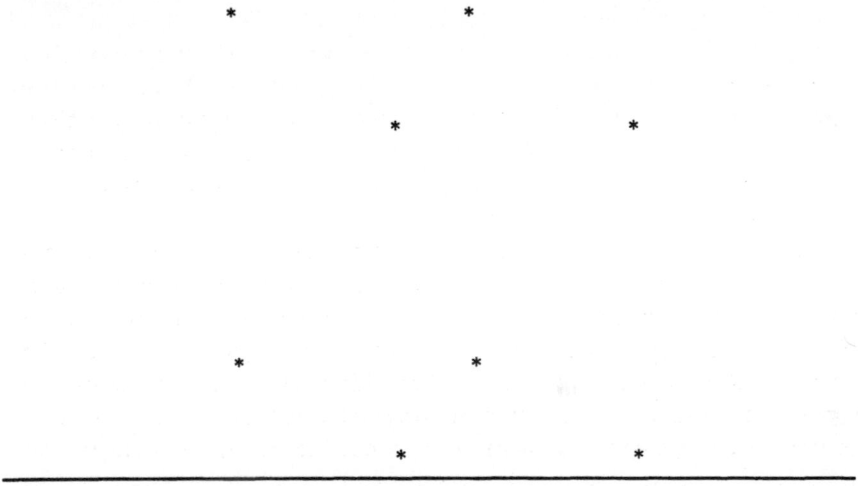

To emphasize that everything depends upon the method of thinking and not upon the term itself, I shall use the neo-Marxist concepts of bourgeoisie, new and old petty bourgeoisie, and proletariat. Imagine then that we have interviewed our eight subjects; some of them might have been those already represented in the text. We now have the problem of assigning them to the different categories of class—what sort of work do they do? If they are women, what are their husbands' jobs. And so forth. And although I am not going to confine our little model to the cases of One and Two's encounters that we have before us, we can begin by thinking through how we might analyze some of them in terms of class. Immediately of course we have the problem of how to locate the native people who are not proletariat. They do not work for a wage and are therefore not proletariat. But what then shall we call them? We could argue that they are situated in a different mode of production and hence need a different classification altogether. It is a bit peculiar to do this, since clearly their current economic relations are within a capitalist mode of production. So maybe we had better just leave them out. Then we do not know exactly who the people were the two politically involved workers were talking about; most likely, however, they were university students or, judging by their style of work, at least members of an intelligentsia. So they might be members or proto-members of a new petty bourgeoisie. And Mrs. Pember Reeves and Weber? Well perhaps not exactly old petty bourgeoisie nor exactly new, but precursors in their own time of the new petty bourgeois intelligentsia. Perhaps we should leave them out too. Or maybe if we could learn something about their sources of income, we might feel quite comfortable then in assigning Mrs. Pember Reeves to the bourgeoisie regardless of her Fabian socialist linkage.

And so we would go, imposing the categories on the people by using the criteria that clean them up to make a better fit between the world and the discursive entity expressed in the categories. We shall suppose for the sake of figurative drama as well as simplicity that each individual represented by a star in figure 3.3 can be plotted unambiguously into the four categories of class.

We could then grasp the relations among them *now expressed as properties of a formal system*. While the formalization does not tell us much about the characteristic of the encounters between One and Two which we have been keeping in mind, we can see that as the categories are tied into the theories, so we could perhaps raise suspicion about the possible contradictory character of the allegiance of the members of the new petty bourgeoisie, who were encountered by workers in the context of political organization, to the cause of working-class

Figure 3.3

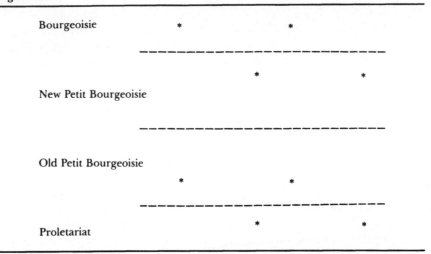

struggle.[35] The categories of class thus used do not analyze the specific character of the relations in which their encounter is embedded, but they do tie that moment back into a theoretical analysis that "predicts" to properties of a theoretically postulated process of class struggle in which such moments as those we have identified are embedded. So the encounters of our stories are given a new interpretation; we see them in a new light, as we cast the protagonists in the theoretical script by classifying them under the categories of a system. But it is not the story as they told it. Nor does it enable us to go beneath the surface of the passing reflection to display underlying relations at work within it, for these relations are collapsed into a "flat" two-dimensional surface by our methods of producing the sociological account. The problem of the one-sidedness of our accounts is the same as those that prevent us from exploring the extended relations in which people's differing lives and experiences are embedded.

VI *Exploring the Social Relations Determining the Everyday*

It is essential to extend the methods of thinking proposed in sections 3 and 4 to the explication of the social relations present in and shaping the local historical process and constituting the problematic of the everyday world. We do so by recognizing that the activities of actual

individuals are not only concerted in the immediacy of the everyday.
They are implicated also in the organization of extended social relations or in sequences of socially coordinated action in which many individuals unknown to one another may be active. These appear distinctively as a level of organization superimposed on the concretely and
immediately known: "A cotton spinning Jenny is a machine for spinning cotton. It becomes *capital* only in certain relations. Torn from
these relationships it is no more capital than gold itself is money or
sugar is the price of sugar." [36] Similarly table, chair, coffee, cigarette may
be constituted as commodities in the social relations of the market in
which goods are produced to be exchanged for money. In Marx's analysis, the character of the commodity as a social relation is distinct from
the character of a particular object. As the latter it has a use-value, but
as constituted in the social relations of the market the object "is
changed into something transcendent." [37]

In *The German Ideology* Marx and Engels pose this question: if social
relations exist only in the activities of actual individuals and invididuals
always start from themselves, how could those relations take on the
character of forces standing over against them and overpowering their
lives? [38] Marx's analysis of the commodity in *Capital* establishes the
bridge over which activities pass in entering into a realm in which relations function as impersonal "forces." The social relations constituting commodities are distinctive. They are relations in which individuals
are necessarily present and active but in which they do not appear as
such. They are the relations of an economy in which money is exchanged for commodities and commodities for money. The invisibility
of subjects in the commodity as a social relation is not a conceptual
effect, but a feature of the particular way in which exchange relations
are organized in a capitalist mode of production. The "objectivity" of
the relations is an effect of the activities of individuals concerted in
determinate forms of social relations. Such a concept of social relations
enables us to see how "explanations" in terms of intentions or motives
are quite insufficient as accounts of social phenomena, for the activities
of individuals are articulated to and organized by the social relations
that express no intention but, arising out of the multiple intentions of
many, coordinate and determine (in the sense of shaping or giving determinate form to) people's intentions.

Social relations in this sense do not exist in an abstract formal space
organized purely conceptually, but as determinate actual processes.
Just as table takes on its specific character as people coordinate their
activities in relation to it, so commodity only comes into being as such
as an object is entered into the coordinated sequences of action consti-

tuting relations of exchange. Thus a commodity begins in one place as an object actually produced for sale and in the process of being exchanged for money; it is fully realized as such only at its final destination where it passes out of the commodity mode and its uses as an object come into play.[39] It takes only a little imagination to see that all such relations are present in and produced in the organization of activities at the everyday level as well as entering the everyday into relations that pass beyond the control of individual subjects. The child who goes to the corner grocery store to spend her quarter on candy or pop enters into just such a complex of relations. Her simple act and the ordinary intelligibility of the sentence describing it depend upon and are structured by that complex.

This method of thinking shows us a way of examining the actual and immediate organization of the experienced world to disclose its articulation to extended social relations. We begin with a knower, a subject, whose everyday world is determined, shaped, organized by social processes beyond her experience and arising out of the interrelations of many such experienced worlds. They are relations that coordinate and codetermine the worlds, activities, and experiences of people entered into them at different points. Their experience and knowledge of their worlds arise in their active relation to them and are necessarily various; that variety of experience and knowledge is itself organized by the complex of extended relations. The latter necessarily generate different positions and different worlds of experience. Some of these are the ineradicable differences of opposition that enter into and arise out of class struggle. The problematic of the everyday world organizes inquiry into the social relations in back of the everyday worlds in which people's experience is embedded. It opens up the possibility of exploring these relations as they really are, of discovering how they work and how they enter into the organization of the local historical settings of our work and experience and of our encounters with others. The relationships between our Ones and Twos that we tried to fit to the frame of class conceived as a set of formal categories are no longer confined to the imaginary construction of positions in a wholly conceptually structured space. Rather, we can explore the extended social relations that, even in the moment of immediate encounter between One and Two, enter into and structure it, shaping their different bases of experience within it. Working with the everyday world as problematic avoids collapsing differences in perspectives into one another by the methodologies for constructing a metaversion; rather, the object of our inquiry is the social relations establishing the matrices of such differences. And these social relations are real.

Working with the concept of social relation does not deprive subjects of activity. Class is not understood as a secret power behind our backs, determining how we think, how we understand the world, and how we act. Rather class is seen as a complex of social relations coordinating the activities of our everyday worlds with those of others with whom we are not directly connected. Such relations exist only as active practices. While we work and struggle, our everyday acts and intentions are locked into the underlying dynamic of the relations and forces of production and governed by the powers they give rise to.

Figure 3.4 shows the points linked into an intelligible structure as a cube. All at once we can grasp how they are related. The links between points represent the underlying relations determining the positions and how they stand in relation to one another. Figure 3.4 dramatizes how the mutual determination of relationships between positions can be grasped once the underlying relations are brought into view. Each point represents a matrix of the everyday world into which the individual's activities are entered and in which her experience is shaped. Those matrices of the everyday world are substructed by relations we read as relations of class. From any one of these matrices, inquiry leads back into the same set of relations. We can start anywhere and, though seen from a different perspective and experienced differently, the same complex of relations comes into view. We can see One and Two (the sociologist) within the figure, each located at different relational coordinates.

Figure 3.4

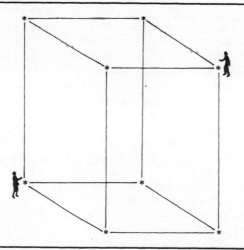

Let us explore, in a very preliminary way, such a set of extended relations as they have been crystallized in Mrs. Pember Reeves's book on the household economies of working-class mothers in London in the early twentieth century.[40] We reach back through an account that has transformed an original multivocality into one voice to a complex of relations in which different matrices of consciousness and experience are generated.

In Mrs. Reeves's study, she tells, among others, of the working day of a working-class woman she calls Mrs. T. Here then is Two, telling of One's life in a text intended for others certainly more like herself than like One. In the textual context, One is the stranger, the other whose life must be told because to the implicit "we" of the readerly conspiracy it is not familiar (their own daily routines are not a topic). Mrs. Reeves is at work organizing our relationship to Mrs. T., drawing us imperceptibly into the presuppositions of the relations that are both strangely visible but also silenced in the text. Here then we will not take the text as it appears in "document time,"[41] detached from the social relations in which it was made *and of which it formed an operative part.* It is treated rather as it gives textual presence to the actualities of the lives of working-class women in a definite and historically specific context of reading.

Much of Mrs. Pember Reeves's account of Mrs. T.'s working day is based on Mrs. T.'s own account, though we are not given the latter verbatim. Though Mrs. T. does not speak to us directly, she is present in the text as that subject whose experience is its necessary condition.

> *We now come to the day of a mother of six children with two rooms to keep. Mrs. T. . . . is the wife of a builder's handyman on 25s a week. The two rooms are upstairs in a small house, and, as there is no water above ground floor, Mrs. T. has a good deal of carrying of heavy pails of water both upstairs and down. She is gentle and big and slow, never lifts her voice or gets angry, but seems always tired and dragged. She is very clean and orderly. Her husband is away all day; but he dislikes the noise of a family meal and insists on having both breakfast and tea cooked specially for himself, and eats alone.*

> *6:00   Nurses baby.*
> *6:30   Gets up, calls five children, puts kettle on, washes "necks" and "backs" of all the children, dresses the little ones, does hair of three girls.*
> *7:30   Gets husband's breakfast, cooks bloater, and makes tea.*
> *8:00   Gives him breakfast alone, nurses baby while he has it, and cuts slices of bread and dripping for children.*
> *8:30   He goes; gives children breakfast, sends them off to school at 8:50, and has her own.*
> *9:00   Clears away and washes up breakfast things.*

9:30   *Carries down slops, and carries up water from the yard; makes beds.*
10:00   *Washes and dresses baby, nurses him, and puts him to bed.*
11:00   *Sweeps out bedroom, scrubs stairs and passage.*
12:00   *Goes out and buys food for the day. Children at home.*
12:25   *Cooks dinner; lays it.*
1:00   *Gives children dinner and nurses baby.*
1:45   *Washes hands and faces, and sees children off to school.*
2:00   *Washes up dinner things, scrubs out kitchen, cleans grate, empties dirty water, and fetches more clean from yard.*
3:00   *Nurses baby.*
3:30   *Cleans herself and begins to mend clothes.*
4:15   *Children all back.*
4:30   *Gives them tea.*
5:00   *Clears away and washes up, nurses the baby, and mends clothes till 6:30.*
6:30   *Cooks husband's tea.*
7:00   *Gives husband tea alone.*
7:30   *Puts younger children to bed.*
8:00   *Tidies up, washes husband's tea things, sweeps kitchen, mends clothes, nurses baby, puts elder children to bed.*
8:45   *Gets husband's supper; mends clothes.*
10:00   *Nurses baby, and makes him comfortable for the night.*
10:30   *Goes to bed.*[42]

The text is the product of a project undertaken by Reeves as a member of the Fabian Women's Group. It reports on a study of whether improving the nutrition of working-class women in late pregnancy and while nursing their babies improved their and the child's overall health. Its very existence is grounded in class relations, and class relations are at work in how the text is constructed as an account of the lives of working-class women *for* an "educated" middle class. The project itself, the need for a *study* rather than hearing from the women themselves; the taken-for-granted entitlement of the visitor to inquire into the family lives and domestic work and routines of working-class women; the unmentioned quid pro quo that adds to Mrs. T.'s daily work the additional task of keeping a record of her daily routines and weekly budget; the work of editing her account into readable English (for the women Mrs. Reeves wrote about practiced, according to her, at best a phonetic spelling), and its entry into the textual discourse of early twentieth-century English socialists: all these are practices articulated to the class relations of the England of that period. This was a time in which women of the dominant classes were active in the management of the working-class family. They were involved in what we have in the past described rather contemptuously as "charities"; they supported women's organization in trade unions; they were concerned with work-ing-class housing, with working-class health and nutrition, with the training of working-class women for motherhood, and so forth. This text is situated in this context of an active organization of class in which women of the dominant classes played a leading role. The interests of the Fabian Women's Group in the nutrition and health of working-class mothers and their newborn children are located in a class-based con-cern about the health, nutrition, living conditions, and education of the working class, which first arose, in Britain, in the context of recruiting for imperialist wars that exhibited the physical inadequacies of work-ing-class men as military "material."[43] This then is the site of the text and of the relevances that organize it.

Returning to the text, we can see aspects of the structuring of Mrs. T.'s work and experience and how these are organized in relations be-yond her narrow domestic world. Her daily routine is powerfully struc-tured by the employment and school schedules of her husband and children. Let us focus on the children and their relationship to school. First, school attendance is required, and the timing of the children's coming and going and its meshing with her husband's employment schedule are primary organizers of meal times and bedtimes and hence of how her domestic work has to be allocated to spaces in between the disjunctures created by the timing of their meals and the like. Her work cannot be organized in accordance with its own logic. But more is in-volved than cooking and scheduling meals to fit these external sched-ules. Mrs. T. includes in her daily routine washing the children's necks and backs, those parts of their bodies that the children themselves either cannot easily reach or see and might miss or skip. She washes them before school in the morning, and she also washes their hands and faces before they return to school after lunch. We notice that Mrs. T. must fetch water from the yard and carry it upstairs, and then she must carry the slops downstairs to dispose of. At school these children will be inspected by the teacher for their cleanliness. They are going to have the backs of their necks and their hands scrutinized. The chil-dren's cleanliness and Mrs. T.'s care to ensure they go to school clean are enforced by the school, whatever personal pride Mrs. T. may take in her children's appearance. The school's concern, enforced by the teacher, with the cleanliness of working-class children has arisen as part of the same concern as that which motivates Mrs. Reeves's study. The dominant classes have taken steps to manage the health of the working class and the working-class family, and the school is one agent through which these new managerial concerns are implemented. When we make the link between the work organization of Mrs. T.'s day and the school, the way in which the state through the school enters into that organization can be discerned in the background.

We can see thus how Mrs. T. in a curious way comes to act as an agent of this external authority vis-à-vis her children, at least in this matter. She is constrained to enforce in the home the order imposed by the school. But the relation does not appear in this way. We begin to see that the working relationships among women and men and parents and children sharing a household cannot be understood as if families formed autonomous systems. While Reeves's orientation and description isolate Mrs. T.'s work process, giving it a self-contained character, ours anchors it in the same complex of social relations in which the study arises and which the text "expresses."

The use of a historical example bars us forever from moving beyond the text or outside it, to talk to Mrs. T. directly. But the explication of experience as such is not the objective of this sociology for women. The use of a historical example places it in any case out of reach. Yet we see that there is a way of addressing the other side of the dissevered relationship between the women sociologist or Fabian socialist who tells the tale and those others mute but for her text who are somehow given presence in it. To take up the exploration and analysis of the social relations in which One's life is embedded is to take up the organization of her experience not as an external system but as a world, the social character of which arises in the constant ongoing intercoordination of actual activities. The reality of the relations that organize the encounter between One and Two and the ways in which Two may represent One in the texts of her discourse are an ongoing accomplishment. All the features of the world that Reeves puts before us exist (are constituted?) in social relations in which these named objects are accomplished in their quiddity.

The work of women such as Mrs. T. enters social relations such as these and is part of their formation. These relations also organize and determine their work. We understand then the reciprocal or dialectical character of social relations, for they arise in the coordering of people's work while their specific properties also organize the work process at the local historical level. Mrs. T.'s household and family are organized in determinate ways in the context of school and wage labor. They do not stand suspended as an instance of an abstract family located in an abstracted conceptual space. Rather they are clearly a work organization sustained on a daily basis by its members and continually organized and reorganized by how its members' work practices take up such material exigencies as a capitalist market in real estate and rental properties; as the enforcement of school and the authority of school authorities to examine children's cleanliness; by the specific character of the local organization of retail stores, transportation, and the like; by opportunity for additional nutritional support conditional upon allowing Mrs. Reeves and others like her to come into the home, to look about, and to approve or disapprove the housewife's dispositions. Here is the matrix of experience and an everyday world, the problematic of which we have sought to open up (in a very preliminary way). The conjunction in this book of Mrs. T.'s absent but determining experience and Mrs. Reeves's own speaking is not irrelevant. It is precisely here that we can explore the relations in which both are implicated and active and in which the account itself, *Round about a Pound a Week*, is embedded. It is precisely in these relations that we discover class and its actual character as a routine, daily accomplishment.

VII *The Sociologist inside the Whale*

Mrs. Reeves's study enables us to hold at a historical distance the relations we are concerned with exploring. Reaching through her work, we discover the presence of others who do not speak directly to us; through her work we have discovered the relations at work in it through which those others have been silenced. We see her text as a moment in the organization of those relations. In returning from the past to reflect upon our present, we discover our own sociological texts as moments in the organization of relations within which our work is embedded. Redesigning the relationship between sociologist and those she learns from in her investigations is not enough. Any such reconstruction still bears the determinations of the extended relations within which the encounters between sociologist and the subject are embedded. The methodology of its writing structures how it enters into the organization of the social relations that it bears.

Texts are organizers of social relations. Methods of writing them produce their capacity to organize. Sociological methods of writing texts produce accounts relating ourselves as readers to those of whom they speak in a relation of ruling. Of course we do not magically transform those relations by writing our texts in different ways. We have to recognize the real limitations of what our work can do. But a discipline such as sociology has developed powerful methods for producing texts that will operate in the extended relations of ruling. What we have focused upon here is how to produce alternatives that will go beyond the reporting of experience to the development of a knowledge of the social relations within which we work and struggle as subjects. We are seeking methods of inquiry *and* of writing sociology that organize the relation between the text and those of whom the text speaks as "cosubjects" in a world we make—and destroy—together.

The alternative I have been developing here begins with people as subjects active in the same world as we are situated in as bodies. Subject is located at the beginning of her acts—work and other practical activities; through these she joins with others, known and unknown, in bringing into being a world that they have, but do not necessarily know, in common. The objects of our worlds, whether concrete (cigarettes, tables, horses, or microchips) or relational (commodities, gifts, capital), are accomplishments of ongoing courses of action in which many are implicated. These are actual activities; their concerting or coordering is an ongoing process.

The multiple perspectives of subjects, the multiple possible versions of the world arising in subjects' experience, create a problem for sociology only when our project is to establish a sociological version superseding theirs. It is a difficulty that arises largely from grounding sociology in "meaning," "interpretation, "common understandings" and the like rather than in an ongoing coordering of actual activities accomplished in definite local historical settings. But when the latter is our ontology (the mode in which the social can be conceived as existing), then our business is to explore the ongoing socially ordered matrices differentiating experience and the extended social relations immanent in the everyday. These are actual in the simple sense that they arise in the coordering of actual activities, and they go beyond or underneath the stories people know how to tell about their lives through which what we call their experience or perspectives become part of the same world as that we are investigating. We recognize actual social relations arising in the concerting of human sensuous activity, hence objectively. Though such relations may not be already known-in-common, they may indeed be known. They may be explored, discovered, analyzed, and described.

The relation of subject to the extended relations organizing her local and immediate experience is that limned in the formulation of Marx's problematic quoted at the end of chapter 2: "Individuals always started, and always start, from themselves. Their relations are the relations of their real life. How does it happen that their relations assume an independent existence over against them? And that the forces of their own life overpower them?"[44] As Marx developed his investigation it came to focus exclusively upon the impersonal relations in which subjects disappear as such. While he was careful to mark the shift from

the concrete and "subjective" to the constitution of the objective relations of the economy, those who have followed him have not. As his
theories have been developed, subjects have been seen as totally sub-
dued to the driving historical dynamic of capitalist forces and relations.
In the thinking of some notable contemporaries they have been wholly
displaced, surviving on the ontological margins, inhabiting the fox-
holes of functional positions, subjected to the massive on-rolling of
structures lurching toward obscure destinies. Whether these are
proper extensions of Marx's thinking or not is not an issue here. They
are certainly totally at odds with this, perhaps any, feminist method of
inquiry, for we insist on preserving the subject as active and competent
and as the knower of inquiry, the knower to whom our texts should
speak. We insist on recognizing our active presence as doer as well as
knower and our active part in the making of relations that pass beyond
the scope of our direct knowledge and power to change. I am not concerned to be faithful to Marx or to a Marxist tradition, but only to seize
upon what it offers us as a means of exploring the dynamic of relations
in which our lives are caught up and which are continually at work in
transforming the bases and contexts of our existence and our struggles.
It is only a Marxist ontology that is capable of projecting an ontology
grounded in the activities of actual subjects beyond the immediately
observable and known. We need such an ontological consistency if we
are going to be able to move from the local matrices of experience,
directly known, to extended relations beyond our direct knowledge. At
the same time the standpoint of women anchors Marxist methods of
thinking and inquiry. It insists that its grasp of the world be constrained
not by a discourse organized for the theoretical subject tucking his own
life out of sight, but for subjects situated outside discourse in the actualities of their everyday worlds. Among them, of course, is the sociological inquirer herself, a member of the same world she explores, active in the same relations as those for whom she writes.

Like Jonah, she is inside the whale. Only of course she is one
among the multiplicity of subjects whose coordered activity constitutes
whale. Like the astronomer, she is of and inside the cosmos she seeks
to understand. Her opportunities, her curiosities, as well as her limitations derive from just this necessary standpoint. To discover and explicate its actual character and relations depend upon recognizing that
she is indeed located, that her seeing is mediated (by texts for example),
that her work is located in definite social relations, that she is always
and ineluctably an insider. Her own seeing arises in a context structured by the same system of social relations structuring the everyday
worlds of those whose experience provides the problematic of her in-

quiry. Her only route to a faithful telling that does not privilege the perspectives arising in the sites of her sociological project and her participation in a sociological discourse is to commit herself to an inquiry that is ontologically faithful, faithful to the presence and activity of subjects and faithful to the actualities of the world that arises for her, for them, for all of us, in the ongoing coordering of our actual practices, both those within and those beyond our reach.

Notes

1. Karl Marx, *Grundrisse: Foundations of the Critique of Political Economy* (New York: Random House, 1976).
2. See chap. 2 above.
3. A number of feminist sociologists have raised these problems, notably Ann Oakley, in "Interviewing women: A contradiction in terms," in Helen Roberts, ed., *Doing Feminist Research* (London: Routledge and Kegan Paul, 1981).
4. See Dorothy E. Smith, "Women's perspective as a radical critique of sociology," *Sociological Inquiry* 44, no. 1 (1974): 7–13.
5. Ibid., p. 12.
6. Mrs. Pember Reeves, *Round about a pound a Week* (London: G. Bell and Sons, 1913), p. 1.
7. See Dorothy E. Smith, "The ideological practice of sociology," *Catalyst* 8 (1974): 39–54, for an analysis of the sociological methods that suppress the presence of actual subjects.
8. Alfred Schutz, "On multiple realities," in *Collected Papers,* vol. 1 (The Hague: Martinus Nijhoff, 1962).
9. This vivid notion of sociology as writing a third version superseding that of two contending parties originates in Alan Ryan, *The Philosophy of the Social Sciences* (Oxford: Oxford University Press, 1970).
10. Max Weber, *Economy and Society,* ed. Guenther Roth and Claus Wittich (New York: Bedminster Press, 1968), I:4.
11. Alfred Schutz, "Concept and theory formation in the social sciences," in *Collected Papers,* 1:48–66.
12. Max Weber, *Economy and Society,* I:4.
13. Ibid., I:8.
14. Ibid., I:4.
15. Ibid., I:8.
16. Sandra Harding, *The Science Question in Feminism* (Ithaca: Cornell University Press, 1986).
17. Ibid., p. 193; the reference is to Jane Flax, "Gender as a social problem: In and for feminist theory," *American Studies/Amerika Studien,* journal of the German Association for American Studies, 1986.
18. Harding, *Science Question in Feminism,* p. 194.
19. Ibid., p. 193.
20. It is unfortunate that the exposition of this method in *The German Ideology*

has so often been read out of context and using the interpretive frame of the idealist-materialist dichotomy of classic philosophical thought. If Marx criticized the idealism of German philosophy, it is thought that his alternative must be its inverse. If the German philosophers he contended with treated mind and consciousness as if they shaped social existence and the historical process, it is assumed that his own method of thinking must be one that subordinates consciousness to a thoroughgoing materialist version of society and history in which consciousness is a mere epiphenomenon.

But Marx's materialism does not cleave to the old dichotomy. In the *Theses on Feuerbach* he dumps Feuerbach's materialism because "it is conceived only in the form of the *object* or of contemplation" and has no notion of "human sensuous activity, practice." The active aspect, he writes, has been taken over by idealism. But idealism also has forgotten about "real, sensuous activity." The active side thus remains abstract. His materialism unites and sublates the materialism of Feuerbach and idealism. The sensuous and the active are combined in the conception of "real, sensuous activity," "practice," or, in the formulation of *The German Ideology*, "real individuals, their activity and the material conditions of their life" which ground "positive science" (Karl Marx and Friedrich Engels, *The German Ideology* [New York: International Publishers, 1970], pp. 36–37). And, I suggest, it also grounds a feminist sociology. Clearly, body is there when we speak of "sensuous activity." The activity or practices are "sensuous," done with or in the body.

21. Karl Marx and Frederick Engels, *Feuerbach: Opposition of the Materialist and Idealist Outlooks* (London: Lawrence and Wishart, 1973), p. 25 (my emphasis).
22. Marx and Engels, *The German Ideology*, p. 50.
23. This term is introduced in Harold Garfinkel, Michael Lynch, and Edward Livingstone, "The work of a discovering science construed with materials from the optically discoverd pulsar," *Philosophy of the Social Sciences* 11, (1981): 131–58.
24. George Herbert Mead, *On Social Psychology: Selected Papers*, ed. Anselm Strauss (Chicago: University of Chicago Press, 1964).
25. Nancy Jackson has developed an ethnographic strategy based on such an ontology; Nancy S. Jackson, *Describing News: Towards an Alternative Account*, M.A. thesis, Department of Anthropology and Sociology, University of British Columbia, July 1977.
26. Garfinkel, Lynch, and Livingstone, "The work of a discovering science construed with materials from the optically discovered pulsar."
27. Schutz, "Commonsense and scientific interpretation of human action," in *Collected Papers* (The Hague: Martinus Nijhoff, 1962), I:3–47.
28. As Marx and Engels implied in their energetic and self-confident youth (ibid., p. 42).
29. As some of Garfinkel's earlier work would suggest. For example, his formulation of ethnomethodology in "What is ethnomethodology?" in Roy Turner, ed., *Ethnomethodology* (Harmondsworth, England: Penguin Books, 1974).
30. Harold Garfinkel, *Studies in Ethnomethodology* (Englewood Cliffs, N. J.: Prentice-Hall, 1967), p. vii.

31. Emmanual Schegloff and Harvey Sacks, "Opening-up closings," in Roy Turner, ed., *Ethnomethodology* (Harmondsworth, England: Penguin, 1974), pp. 197–215.
32. Sandy Carter, "Class conflict: The human dimension," in Pat Walker, ed., *Between Labor and Capital: The Professional-Managerial Class* (Montreal: Black Rose Books, 1978), pp. 97–119.
33. Ibid.
34. Ginny Berson, "Slumming it in the middle class," in Charlotte Bunch and Nancy Myron, eds., *Class and Feminism: A Collection of Essays from THE FURIES* (Baltimore: Diana Press, 1974), pp. 60–61.
35. See as a basis for such an interpretation Eric Olin Wright's analysis of the new petty bourgeoisie as occupying a contradictory class status. Eric Olin Wright, *Class, Crisis and the State* (London: Verso, 1974), pp. 74–83.
36. Karl Marx, *Wage-labour and Capital* (Moscow: Progress Publishers, 1970), p. 28.
37. Marx, *Capital: A Critique of Political Economy* (New York: Vintage Books, 1977), pp. 163–77.
38. Marx and Engels, *German Ideology.*
39. See Marx, *Capital.*
40. Reeves, *Round about a Pound a Week.*
41. Cf. Dorothy E. Smith, "The social construction of documentary reality," *Social Inquiry* 44, no. 4 (1974): 257–68.
42. Reeves, *Round about a Pound a Week*, pp. 167–68.
43. See Anna Davin, "Imperialism and motherhood," *History Workshop: A Journal of Socialist Historians*, no. 5 (Spring 1978): 9–65.
44. Marx and Engels, *Feuerbach*, p. 90.

PART THREE

Research Strategies
for a Sociology
for Women

Having developed a theoretical formulation of the standpoint of women and of a feminist sociology, I wanted to work out research strategies giving practical substance to such an inquiry. My sociological lifetime had seen many, many instances of bold and cogent criticisms of sociology, bold and cogent proposals for alternative approaches, which failed to be carried forward into research practices. Doing a sociology for women made little sense if it used research strategies that were busy transforming us back into objects. Finding or developing alternatives was the essential next step in the project.

The first chapter in this section, chapter 4, "Institutional Ethnography: A Feminist Research Strategy," is the more general;[1] it works with the problem of going from the particular setting and experience to the generalized and generalizing relations of the apparatus of ruling and of the economy. The idea of an institutional ethnography emphasizes that the inquiry is one of discovering "how things work," "how they are actually put together." The notion of an ethnography lays stress on the project of being faithful to the actualities of social organization and relations. In contrast to research practices beginning with the concepts or theories of sociological discourse, the methods of this feminist sociology begin in an actual situation and explore the actual relations that organize it.

Chapter 4 sketches how such an ethnography might be designed. It begins from my own experience as a "single parent." The analysis of the relations in which that experience was embedded was intended as a preliminary coordination of a collection of researches being undertaken by other women as well as myself, approaching the institutional organization of mothers' work, teaching and schooling from different actual sites in the overall complex. My notion was that this "institutional" complex might be explored from a number of different sites in women's experience, each one bringing into view an aspect unavailable to the other and together making it possible to piece together a picture of its organization and the relations it organizes.

In 1984 Alison Griffith and I developed a research project to investigate the work that mothers do in relation to their children's school and the aspects of school organization that shape and organize the work.[2] We meant it to take up the everyday world as problematic, and we had to work out what that would mean as a research practice. The second chapter in this section, chapter 5, "Researching the Everyday World as Problematic," is based on a working paper I wrote to figure out how to proceed from interviews in which women described their work, to treating that as a problematic and hence as a source of questions that we would address to schoolteachers and school administrators. It translates the problematic of the everyday into a research practice.

These proposed research strategies are not intended to establish an orthodoxy. What is written means more (and sometimes other) than its author could intend; its interpretation is not exclusively here. The strategies described in the following chapters have, however, been developed out of the direction given by previous work and they carry forward the enterprise in ways fully consistent with what has gone before. It is in any case vital to a rethought sociology to develop research strategies that will transform rethinking into a research practice. I have learned in the course of thinking about and writing the papers forming the chapters of this book that to take the standpoint of women is more than critique, conceptual organization, or a construction of subjectivity in the text; it must also be realized in practices of investigation and inquiry.

Notes

1. An abridged version of "Institutional Ethnography" was published in *Resources for Feminist Research* 15, no. 1 (March 1986): 6–13.
2. This research was supported by Social Science and Humanities Research Council Grant no. 410–84–0450.

4

Institutional Ethnography:
A Feminist Research Strategy

I The Reconstruction of Sociological Inquiry

In previous chapters I have laid out the problematic and methods of
thinking for this sociology for women. These, however, are formulated
at the most general level. They need specifying as a research practice.
This chapter proposes a research strategy for doing a sociology for
women.

As we have seen, developing a sociology from the standpoint of
women implies different approaches to familiar sociological objects.
Rather than taking up issues and problems as they have been defined
and established in the discipline, the aim is to explicate the actual social
processes and practices organizing people's everyday experience from
a standpoint in the everyday world. As I have emphasized, this means
a sociology that does not transform people into objects, but preserves
their presence as subjects. It means taking seriously the notion of a
sociology concerned with how the phenomena known to sociology express the actual activities of actual individuals. It means exploring how
these phenomena are organized as social relations, indeed as a complex
of social relations beyond the scope of any one individual's experience.
It means finding a method that does not begin with the categories of

the discourse, approaching the actualities of the social world with a view to discovering in it the lineaments of the theoretical object. Rather it proposes an inquiry intended to disclose how activities are organized and how they are articulated to the social relations of the larger social and economic process. A sociology for women must be able to disclose for women how our own situations are organized and determined by social processes that extend outside the scope of the everyday world and are not discoverable within it.

It has been argued extensively that,[1] until recently, established sociology had a concealed gender subtext, that it was thought, investigated, and written largely from the perspective of men. The critique has addressed many aspects of sociology, with the dominant focus being upon what has been excluded by the absence of women from the making of the topics and relevances of the discourse. However, a second major theme in the critique has questioned established sociological methods. It has been concerned with the implications for research method of making women's situation and experience the basis for social inquiry.[2] My own critical work in this area has addressed the epistemological and methodological issues arising from the standpoint of an experience situated, as women's has generally been, outside the institutional order that governs contemporary advanced capitalist societies.[3]

Sociology has emerged and taken on its characteristic relevances and conceptual organization in the context of an apparatus, consisting of the varieties of administration, management, and professional organization, interwoven by the multiple forms of textually mediated discourse. The traditional methods of sociology objectify the social process, eliminating from its representation the presence of subjects as active in bringing a concerted social world into being. The relations of people's real lives have been conceived as formal conceptual relations between factors or variables, expressing properties of social objects. These objects themselves have been elaborated as the constructs of sociological discourse embedded in its texts. Much of the phenomenal universe of sociology has its ground in these institutional processes, which together organize, coordinate, regulate, guide, and control contemporary societies. They perform a work of ruling. Phenomena providing much of the familiar stuff of sociology, such as mental illness, violence, juvenile delinquency, intelligence, unemployment, poverty, motivation, and the like, come into being as integral constituents and products of the bureaucratic, legal, and professional operations of this apparatus. They exist as properties of the relations in and through which the society is ruled. Their objectified forms are not expressions of the actualities of a naturally existing world but are the artful constructions of text-based methodologies and the practices of formal organization. They constitute a world known in common through the medium of texts and vested in organizational systems of record keeping. These organizational and discursive forms of knowledge are specifically independent of particular individuals. Sociology has built upon, elaborated, and extended a world coming into being and known in this way.

In chapters 1 and 2, women's exclusion from this ruling apparatus and its processes of textual discourse and organization were described and analyzed. At best we have played a subordinate role, being accorded the manual and nonspecific tasks that are essential to its functioning. As secretaries, we have done the secretarial work translating thought and design into the material forms in which the latter are efficacious as communication; as wives we have provided the bodily and emotional supports for men who have been actors and movers in the ruling apparatus; our work as mothers has complemented the educational work of the school and educational system. In these and other ways we have supplied the local supports to the work of men in the institutional process.

A sociology beginning from the standpoint of women thus takes up the relation to this ruling apparatus of those whose work has been both necessary to and unrecognized by it. The problem of reconstructing sociology is more than that of introducing new topics or of addressing experience of sociological subjects with renewed respect. We are confronted with the problem of how to create a knowledge that is "for us," that will explicate the social determinations of our own lives and experience as women. The forms of social knowledge that have made the work processes underpinning them invisible must be remade. To enlarge our understanding as women of how things come about for us as they do, we need a method beginning from where women are as subjects. As subjects, as knowers, women are located in their actual everyday worlds rather than in an imaginary space constituted by the objectified forms of sociological knowledge built upon the relations of the ruling apparatus and into its practices.

This is not to recommend a sociology concerned exclusively with the world of women's experience or with the subjectivity of the sociologist herself. Rather our search must be for a sociology that does not transpose knowing into the objective forms in which the situated subject and her actual experience and location are discarded. It must provide for subjects the means of grasping the social relations organizing the worlds of their experience. The problematic structuring inquiry from the standpoint of women I have described in chapter 2 as the problematic of the everyday world. It is posed by actual properties of the social organization of the everyday world in contemporary society, namely, that its social organization is only partially discoverable within its scope and the scope of the individual's daily activities. Its local organization is determined by the social relations of an immensely complex division of labor knitting local lives and local settings to national and international social, economic, and political processes. Here, then, is where the sociologist enters.

Her specialized work, I propose, is that of inquiry organized by this problematic—how does it happen to us as it does? How is this world in which we act and suffer put together? The immediately experienced and the activities in which the immediately experienced arises as such are organized and given shape by social relations that can be disclosed fully only by specialized investigation.

But though this inquiry calls for specialized skills, it must be considered as a work of cooperation between sociologists and those who want to understand the social matrices of their experience. For each of us is an expert practitioner of our everyday world, knowledgeable in the most intimate ways of how it is put together and of its routine daily accomplishment. It is the individual's working knowledge of her everyday world that provides the beginning of the inquiry. The end product is not, of course, intended to be private. The sociologist is not an astrologer giving private consultations. Rather the approach attempted here offers something comparable to consciousness-raising. Perhaps indeed it is a form of it, aiming to find the objective correlates of what had seemed a private experience of oppression. Like consciousness-raising it is also to be shared. The strategy of institutional analysis explicates generalized bases of the experience of oppression. Hence, it offers a mode in which women can find the lineaments of the oppression they share with others and of different oppressions rooted in the same matrix of relations.

II Institutional Relations as Generalizers of Actual Local Experience

Let me give an everyday example of what I mean by the "problematic of the everyday world." When I take my dog for a walk in the morning, I observe a number of what we might call "conventions." I myself walk on the sidewalk; I do not walk on the neighbors' lawns. My dog, however, freely runs over the lawns. My dog also, if I am not careful, may shit on a neighbor's lawn, and there are certainly some neighbors who do not like this. I am, of course, aware of this problem, and I try to arrange for my dog to do his business in places that are appropriate. I am particularly careful to see that he avoids the well-kept lawns because those are the ones I know I am most likely to be in trouble over should I/he slip up—which does happen occasionally. The neighborhood I live in is a mixture of single-family residences and rental units, and the differences between the well- and ill-kept lawns are related to this. On the whole, those living in rental units do not care so much about the appearance of their front lawn, whereas those who own their own residences are more likely to give care and attention to the grass and sometimes to the flower beds in front of the house.

So as I walk down the street keeping an eye on my dog I am observing some of the niceties of different forms of property ownership. I try to regulate my dog's behavior with particular scrupulousness in relation to the property rights of the owners of single-family dwellings and am a little more casual where I know the house consists of rented apartments or bachelor units, or, as in one case, a fraternity house.[4]

Customarily in sociology we talk about this behavior in terms of norms. Then we see my selection of a path of behavior for my dog as guided by certain norms held in common by myself and my neighbors. But something important escapes this. The notion of "norm" provides for the surface properties of my behavior, what I can be seen to be doing—in general preventing my dog from shitting on others' lawns and being particularly careful where negative sanctions are more likely to be incurred. A description of the kind I have given is in this way transposed into a normative statement.

As a norm it is represented as governing the observed behavior. What is missing, however, is an account of the constitutive work that is going on. This account arises from a process of practical reasoning. How I walk my dog attends to and constitutes in an active way different forms of property as a locally realized organization. The normative analysis misses how this local course of action is articulated to social relations. Social relations here mean concerted sequences or courses of social action implicating more than one individual whose participants are not necessarily present or known to one another. There are social relations that are not encompassed by the setting in which my dog is walked, but they nonetheless enter in and organize it. The existence of single-family dwellings, of rental units, and the like has reference to and depends upon the organization of the state at various levels, its local by-laws, zoning laws, and so forth determining the "real estate" character of the neighborhood; it has reference to and depends upon the organization of a real estate market in houses and apartments, and the work of the legal profession and others; it has reference to and organizes the ways in which individual ownership is expressed in local practices that maintain the value of the property both in itself and as part of a respectable neighborhood. Thus this ordinary daily scene, doubtless enacted by many in various forms and settings, has an implicit organization tying each particular local setting to a larger generalized complex of social relations.

The organization of the immediate and local by social relations extending beyond it is also present in the language used in my description. Its categories express social as well as semantic organization. In chapter 3 I made use of Mrs. Pember Reeves's introduction to her investigation of the household economies of working-class women in London in the early years of the twentieth century. In that passage she refers to a brewer's dray. This seems straightforward, if obscure, to generations younger than mine. It refers to a type of wagon drawn by two, or perhaps more, draft horses and used to carry large loads of draught ale from the brewery to the public houses. Its characteristic form was dictated by the method of stacking barrels on the wagon. The definition of a brewer's dray appears to need little further elaboration beyond perhaps a visual image enabling us to use the term referentially. But more is involved.

A brewer's dray comes into being as a material entity that enters into definite social relations. A brewer's dray arises as such in a complex organization of the brewing industry, its transportation and distribution processes, and so forth. These presuppose a capitalist organization of economic and productive relations including, therefore, wage labor, including the wage and labor of the man who drives the dray and therefore, we may suppose, the fact that it is the vehicle and not the driver that is visible to Reeves (and that it is the dray of the brewer and not of its driver). The dray is not reducible to the object that we can in imagination bring before us when we name it. The terms tie the material entity into social relations that constitute it as what it is in terms of uses, functions, entitlements, ownership.

The language of the everyday world as it is incorporated into the description of that world is rooted in social relations beyond it and expresses relations not peculiar to the particular setting it describes. In my account of walking the dog, there are categories anchored in and depending for their meaning on a larger complex of social relations.

The meaning of such terms as "single-family residence" and "rental units," for example, resides in social relations organizing local settings but not fully present in them. The particularizing description gives access to that which is not particular since it is embedded in categories whose meaning reaches into the complex of social relations our inquiry would explicate. Ordinary descriptions, ordinary talk, trail along with them as a property of the meaning of their terms, the extended social relations they name as phenomena.

Thus taking the everyday world as problematic does not confine us to particular descriptions of local settings without possibility of generalization. This has been seen to be the problem with sociological ethnographies, which, however fascinating as accounts of people's lived worlds, cannot stand as general or typical statements about society and social relations. They have been seen in themselves as only a way station to the development of systematic research procedures that would establish the level of generality or typicality of what has been observed of such-and-such categories of persons. Or they may be read as instances of a general sociological principle. This procedure has been turned on its head in an ingenious fashion in "grounded theory," which proposes a method of distilling generalizing concepts from the social organization of the local setting observed whereupon the latter becomes an instance of the general principles distilled from it.[5] The popularity of this device testifies to the extent to which the problem of generalizability is felt by sociologists. The single case has no significance unless it can in some way or another be extrapolated to some general statement either about society or some subgroup represented methodologically as a population of individuals, or connecting the local and particular with a generalizing concept of sociological discourse.

Beginning with the everyday world as problematic bypasses this issue. The relation of the local and particular to generalized social relations is not a conceptual or methodological issue, it is a property of social organization. The particular "case" is not particular in the aspects that are of concern to the inquirer. Indeed, it is not a "case" for it presents itself to us rather as a point of entry, the locus of an experiencing subject or subjects, into a larger social and economic process. The problematic of the everyday world arises precisely at the juncture of particular experience, with generalizing and abstracted forms of social relations organizing a division of labor in society at large.

One process is that by which the actual work that people do in its particular forms—using a lathe, building wooden forms for pouring concrete, welding on an assembly line, washing dishes in a restaurant, typing on a VDT—is entered into relations in which the particular character of the work drops out of sight. Producing things and services for exchange on a market in which an uncountable multiplicity of others is involved enters people into relations that abstract from these local actualities. In these relations, the value of a product or service, or of labor power itself, is, as it were, purified of its particular uses to become merely its value in exchange against other products. Similarly, concrete forms of labor are resolved into abstract labor, or the average labor time socially necessary to produce a given good. The notion of a commodity locates the social organization of this dual relation, uniting in it the concrete uses of an object produced for sale on the one hand and on the other its entry into the extended relations of the market in which exchange value arises. Money is the form in which exchange value is expressed; money is therefore the generalizer par excellence of capitalist society, enabling, as Marx shows us,[6] quite disparate objects and services to be evaluated against and exchanged for one another. Thus the social relations of capitalism have the special character of translating the particular and concrete into abstracted and generalized forms.

The properties of these relations organize our everyday world pervasively. We have had no problems in seeing the accounts of work and social organization in a factory or other work settings as organized by them. But the effects are more general. They include the ways in which the customer plays a role in the work organization of the supermarket.[7] Or when my friend and I sit down over lunch to discuss epistemological issues in the social sciences, we take for granted the social organization of the restaurant producing our meal. We are local participants in it. Our exclusive access to a table and shelter during the period of the eating of the meal, the appropriate behavior vis-à-vis other diners, the elements of a meal, and so forth—these are the locally organized constituents of the extended commodity relations of capitalism. The generalized character of such local social organization is determined by the generalized social relations (of the market) to which it is articulated.

Complementing economic relations in transforming the local, the concrete, and the particular into general and abstract forms is the ruling apparatus itself in its multifarious aspects. These have in common the articulation of the actual to abstract conceptual forms, resolving the idiosyncratic, the concrete, and the particular into the categories whereby they are rendered actionable within bureaucratic, professional, or managerial modes. The distinctive property of the ruling apparatus is its capacity to organize the locally and inexhaustibly various character of the actual into standard forms of organizational action. In an analysis of the social construction of mental illness I described this process in the psychiatric context as follows:

> Professional and bureaucratic procedures and terminologies are part of an abstracted system. Abstracted systems are set up to be independent of the particular, the individual, the idiosyncratic and the local. . . . In actual operation . . . the abstracted forms must be fitted to the actual local situations in which they must function and which they control. In practice, the abstracted system has to be tied to the local and particular. Psychiatric agencies develop ways of working which fit situations and people which are not standardized, don't present standardized problems and are not already shaped up into the forms under which they can be recognized in the terms which make them actionable. What actually happens, what people actually do and experience, the real situations they function in, how they get to agencies—none of these things is neatly shaped up. There is a process of practical interchange between an inexhaustibly messy and different and indefinite real world and the bureaucratic and professional system which controls and acts upon it. The professional is trained to produce out of this the order which he believes he discovers in it.[8]

In other institutional contexts, the local and particular forms are not "messy" but are worked up to intend the categories and concepts through which they are entered into organizational courses of action.[9]

Investigating the everyday world as problematic involves an inquiry into relations that are themselves generalized through exploration of the character of those relations from the standpoint of everyday experience. It is important to stress that the enterprise never becomes one of the production of an account of relations as a system in and of themselves. The standpoint of actual individuals located in the everyday world is always the point d'appui. To illustrate, let me adumbrate an example to be developed at length later in the chapter. The example originates in my own experience as a mother and as a single parent in relation to my children's schooling. The investigation and thinking of Alison Griffith, Ann Manicom, and Joey Noble[10] among others enable me to embed that experience in the extended social relations that organized it. The experience was my own, but using it not as object but as point d'appui, and exploring the relations in which it is situated, shows how it is organized by generalizing relations. The very concept of single parent, as Griffith shows, is an "operator" in just such relations; to locate my experience as that of a single parent enters it into the generalized and generalizing relations of an institutional process. The concept of single parent is a constituent of a complex of relations articulating families to the specialized functions of the ruling apparatus. In examining these relations from the standpoint of that experience, the aim is not, as it might be in standard sociological practice, to identify the typical features and variations among the class of single parents in relation to the schooling process, or to represent the institutional order as a system in itself, but to explicate—though in this context only in a preliminary way—institutional relations determining everyday worlds and hence how the local organization of the latter may be explored to uncover their ordinary invisible determinations in relations that generalize and are generalized. This is the method of institutional ethnography.

I am using the terms "institutional" and "institution" to identify a complex of relations forming part of the ruling apparatus, organized around a distinctive function—education, health care, law, and the like. In contrast to such concepts as bureaucracy, "institution" does not identify a determinate form of social organization, but rather the intersection and coordination of more than one relational mode of the ruling apparatus. Characteristically, state agencies are tied in with professional forms of organization, and both are interpenetrated by relations of discourse of more than one order. We might imagine institutions as nodes or knots in the relations of the ruling apparatus to class, coordinating multiple strands of action into a functional complex. Integral to the coordinating process are ideologies systematically developed to provide categories and concepts expressing the relation of local courses of action to the institutional function (a point to be elaborated later), providing a currency or currencies enabling interchange between different specialized parts of the complex and a common conceptual organization coordinating its diverse sites. The notion of ethnography is introduced to commit us to an exploration, description, and analysis of such a complex of relations, not conceived in the abstract but from the entry point of some particular person or persons whose everyday world of working is organized thereby.

Ethnography does not here mean, as it sometimes does in sociology, restriction to methods of observation and interviewing. It is rather a commitment to an investigation and explication of how "it" actually is, of how "it" actually works, of actual practices and relations. Questions of validity involve reference back to those processes themselves as issues of "does it indeed work in that way?" "is it indeed so?" Institutional ethnography explores the social relations individuals bring into being in and through their actual practices. Its methods, whether of observation, interviewing, recollection of work experience, use of archives, textual analysis, or other, are constrained by the practicalities of investigation of social relations as actual practices. Note however that the institutional ethnography as a way of investigating the problematic of the everyday world does not involve substituting the analysis, the perspectives and views of subjects, for the investigation by the sociologist. Though women are indeed the expert practitioners of their everyday worlds, the notion of the everyday world as problematic assumes that disclosure of the extralocal determinations of our experience does not lie within the scope of everyday practices. We can see only so much without specialized investigation, and the latter should be the sociologist's special business.

III Ideology, Institutions, and the Concept of Work as Ethnographic Ground

The coordination of institutional processes is mediated ideologically. The categories and concepts of ideology express the relation of members' actual practices—their work—to the institutional function. Ethnomethodology has developed the notion of accountability to identify members' methods of accomplishing the orderliness and sense of local processes. Members themselves and for themselves constitute the observability and reportability of what has happened or is going on, in how they take it up as a matter for anyone to find and recognize.[11] Members make use of categories and concepts to analyze settings for features thus made observable. The apparently referential operation of locally applied categories and concepts is constitutive of the reference itself.[12] When applied to the institutional context, the notion of accountability locates practices tying local settings to the nonlocal organization of the ruling apparatus. Indeed, the institutional process itself can be seen as a dialectic between what members do intending the categories and concepts of institutional ideology and the analytic and descriptive practices of those categories and concepts deployed in accomplishing the observability of what is done, has happened, is going on, and so forth. Thus local practices in their historical particularity and irreversibility are made accountable in terms of categories and concepts expressing the function of the institution. Members' interpretive practices analyzing the work processes that bring the institutional process into being in actuality constitute those work processes as institutional courses of action.[13]

Institutional ideologies are acquired by members as methods of analyzing experiences located in the work process of the institution. Professional training in particular teaches people how to recycle the actualities of their experience into the forms in which it is recognizable within institutional discourse. For example, when teachers are in training they learn a vocabulary and analytic procedures that accomplish the classroom in the institutional mode. They learn to analyze and name the behavior of students as "appropriate" or "inappropriate" and to analyze and name their own (and others') responses. In responding to "inappropriate" behavior, they have been taught to avoid "undermining the student's ego" and hence to avoid such practices as "sarcasm." They should, rather, be "supportive." This ideological package provides a procedure for subsuming what goes on in the classroom under professional educational discourse, making classroom processes observable-reportable within an institutional order.[14] In this way the work and practical reasoning of individuals and the locally accomplished order that is their product become an expression of the non-local relations of the professional and bureaucratic discourse of the ruling apparatus.

The accountability procedures of institutions make some things visible, while others as much a part of the overall work organization that performs the institution do not come into view at all or as other than themselves. Local practices glossed by the categories of the discourse are provided with boundaries of observability beneath which a subterranean life continues. What is observable does not appear as the work of individuals, and not all the work and practices of individuals become observable. When my son was in elementary school, his homework one day was to write up an experiment he had done in science class that day. He asked me how to do it and I replied (not very helpfully), "Well, just write down everything you did." He told me not to be so stupid. "Of course," he said, "they don't mean you write about *everything*, like about filling the jar with water from the tap and taking it to the bench." Clearly there were things done around the doing of an experiment that were essential to, but not entered into or made accountable within, the "experimental procedure." Its boundaries were organized conceptually to select from a locally indivisible work process, some aspects to be taken as part of the experiment and others to be discounted. All were done. All were necessary. But only some were to be made observable-reportable within the textual mode of the teaching of science. In like ways, institutional ideologies analyze local settings, drawing boundaries and the like. They provide analytic procedures for those settings that attend selectively to work processes, thus making only selective aspects of them accountable within the institutional order.

An examination of some institutional ideologies suggests indeed that the work processes of actual individuals are specifically obscured.

The categories and concepts of ideologies substitute for actual relations, actual practices, work processes and organization, and the practical knowledge and reasoning of actual individuals, the expressions of
a textually mediated discourse.[15] Typically work processes are recon-
structed as social or psychological processes, depriving them of their
necessary anchorage in an economy of material conditions, time, and
effort. Thus social workers, as an outcome of the conceptual work of
sociology and psychology, have come to address families in terms of
interpersonal relations and roles, a language that has rendered the institutional presence of the home as a work setting for women and as an
economy invisible.[16] Or when Ray Rist describes how kindergarten
teachers place children in reading groups that "reflect" the social-class
composition of the class, he does so in a way that translates problems
of work organization of the classroom into the functional terms of an
institutional ideology:

> There occurs within the classroom a social process whereby, out of a large group
> of children and an adult unknown to one another prior to the beginning of the
> school year, there emerge patterns of behaviour, expectations of performance,
> and a mutually accepted stratification system delineating those doing well from
> those doing poorly. Of particular concern will be the relation of the teacher's
> expectations of potential academic performance to the social status of the stu-
> dent. Emphasis will be placed on the initial presuppositions of the teacher re-
> garding the intellectual ability of certain groups of children and their conse-
> quences for the children's socialization into the school system.[17]

Here the concepts and categories of social science are deployed to
tie the classroom process into the institutional function conceived in
terms of liberal discourse on equality. The problems of how a classroom
is to be organized to get teaching done that will articulate adequately
and competently to other parts of the division of labor within the
school are transposed into a language in which a relation to "values" is
substituted for problems of work organization. The ideological language conceals, for example, the work organization that produces in
one class in one year the expected levels and proportions of reading
skills with given resources of space and materials, given numbers of
children, as well as the setting of that classroom in the school and the
school in a particular area with particular socio-economic characteristics.

Similarly, the conceptual practices of the sociological literature on
family, social class, and school achievement analyze what mothers do in
relation to school so that it does not appear as work. Indeed, in this
literature mothers appear in a peculiar way as necessary links in a

causal process, but without agency. Their thinking, the effort and time they have put in, and the varying material conditions under which their work is done do not appear. Their presence as actual subjects is suspended. The actualities of their work in local settings, and of the social relations in which it is embedded and through which it forms part of a division of labor, are emptied out. The findings of social class differences, for example, in language capacity are not related to different class conceptions of and training in the transmission of language skills by mothers to children.[18]

Here is one example of conceptual strategies that obliterate women as active agents. A writer discussing demographic calculations showing how the effects of social-class variations on the achievement of children in secondary and higher education may translate into differential "life chances" says, however, that these "tell us little of the subcultural processes (social class attitudes), or of the more intricate psychosocial processes of the individual family which together provide the motivation to excel and the implementary values which turn school achievement into career success."[19] Somewhere buried in "subcultural process," "social-class attitudes," and the "intricate psychosocial processes of the individual family" is a work organization of families creating the material and moral conditions, the routine order, and the relations with school that concretely accomplish what here is made accountable as school achievement and career success. And in this work organization the role of women is central both in the work that is done and in the management of its routine daily order, whether we focus on the provision of conditions under which homework goes forward, the management of relations with school, the work of entertaining, and the like through which the middle-class families socialize children into styles of middle-class sociability, or some other process. Whatever the relation between school achievement, career success, and the "intricate psychosocial processes" of the family, the conscious, planful, thoughtful work of women as mothers has been part of its actuality. But it is not made accountable.

The language of social science is the language of the institutional process. Its conceptual practices are of the same order and indeed have contributed to it. We cannot therefore vest in it and depend upon its analyses and naming to organize our inquiry. If we committed ourselves to its conceptual practices we would be committed to the boundaries it draws, to its selective attention to work processes and organization, to its methods of analyzing social processes to produce their sociological accountability. We would be committed to seeing it institutionally. And even in inventing a new vocabulary, a new set of concepts in which a different and politically acceptable set of boundaries and analysis is precipitated, we would still find ourselves the prisoners of its method, unable to break out of the institutional presuppositions and making our analysis in terms of the functions of the institution.

The alternative to beginning in discourse is to begin in the work and practical reasoning of actual individuals as the matrix of experience in the everyday world. An actual work organization accomplishes the relations between mothers, children, and schooling—a work organization that is situated in determinate material contexts and therefore in an economy of conditions, effort, and time. Inquiry therefore must begin with this work organization. But we have learned already that its observability must not be defined and analyzed for us by the categories and concepts of institutional ideology. Indeed, when we take up inquiry from the standpoint of women, we are specially conscious of work essential to the accomplishment of accountable order, that is not itself made observable-reportable as work. We are familiar now with the way in which the concept of work had not been extended in the past to women's work in the home, as housewife. Our notion of work had to be expanded to include housework, and in doing so we discovered some of its presuppositions—the implicit contrast, for example, between work and leisure, which is based upon work as paid employment and does not apply to housework. Expanding the concept of work for our purposes requires its remaking in more ample and generous form. Some wages-for-housework theorists have developed an expanded concept of housework, which I shall use as a model.[20] They have used it to include all the work done by women (and sometimes by men too) to sustain and service their and men's functioning in the wage relation and hence indirectly to sustain and service the enterprises employing their labor. This generous concept of housework includes not only domestic labor proper but such activities as driving to one's place of employment, eating lunch in the cafeteria or making and eating sandwiches, purchasing and maintaining clothes worn on the job, and so forth. All these aspects of everyday life are essential to the economy though they would not ordinarily be described as work, let alone as housework. For wages-for-housework theorists, housework becomes an economic category identifying those work processes that are in fact part of the economy but are not represented as work, being described as consumption or not at all. In an analogous procedure, the concept of work is extended here to what people do that requires some effort, that they mean to do, and that involves some acquired competence. The notion of work directs us to its anchorage in material conditions and means and that it is done in "real time"—all of which are consequential for how the individual can proceed. Addressing the institutional process as a work organization in this sense means taking as our field of investigation the totality of work processes that actually accomplish it: hence it means going beyond the functional boundaries as these are defined by its ideological practices to explore those aspects of the work organization that are essential to its operation. For these are an integral part of its operation, whether they are recognized or not and whether or not they might be considered positive (or functional) in relation to its objectives. By locating institutional ethnography in the work people do we are not concerned so much to mark a distinction between what is work and what is not work, but rather to deploy a concept that will return us to the actualities of what people do on a day-to-day basis under definite conditions and in definite situations. We return thus to those processes that both produce and are ordered by the social relations of the institutional process, and to actualities that are observable, that people can describe, and that in their concerting accomplish its orderly processes as ordered.

Such a notion of work breaks through to the penumbra not comprehended by institutional accounting practices. We can see then that *our* account of the learning of a scientific experiment will include these other practices upon which the experiment depends but which are not made observble-reportable as the experiment, as well as the conceptual procedure that is part of how that work process is organized and made accountable. We can recognize, for example, that there is an organization of work articulating the work of mothering in the home to the work of the teacher in the classroom. We can examine the classroom as an actual work organization in which problems of the allocation of time and other resources in the performance of tasks for which the teacher is held responsible must be solved. We can recognize that the work organization of the classroom depends upon the work organization of mothering. In so doing we anchor our analysis in a mode that fully recognizes individuals as the competent practitioners of their everyday worlds and takes in its organization and determinations as they arise in the active ways in which people participate in how their everyday worlds come about.

In sum then institutional ethnography involves three main procedures. First, there is the analysis of the ideological procedures used to render its work organization accountable. These ideological procedures are constituents of the social relations articulating the work process to the institutional function. Second, I have proposed a "generous" notion of work enabling us to engage with the ways in which people are actually involved in the production of their everyday world, examined with respect to how that world is organized by and sustains the institutional process. It is these that ideology analyzes, interprets, and hence renders accountable within the institutional context. Finally the concept of social relation analyzes the concerting of these work processes as social courses of action. Work is articulated to such concerted sequences of action, performed by more than one and perhaps sometimes by a multiplicity of individuals not necessarily known to one another. The knitting of work processes in social relations is by no means always a conscious effect. What becomes conscious and planful is structured by the ideological processes that are constituents of social relations.

The notion of social relation cannot be collapsed into people's goals, objectives, or intentions. It is a notion transcending that of work or work organization. In chapter 3 I described a child going to the store to buy some candy. As she makes her decision and puts her quarter down, she enters into a complex of relations of exchange that are not part of her intention. Yet in however small a way, her act enters into the daily accomplishment of that complex of social relations. These reach back from her moment, through storekeeper or clerk, to marketing and production processes, which both relate and organize the conditions of her intention, its means, and characteristic order, and which themselves only exist and are sustained in the multiplicity of acts of which hers is one. That is what is meant here by the notion of social relation. It provides a procedure for analyzing local work practices— the locus of the experience of the subject—as articulated to and determined by the generalized and generalizing relations of economy and ruling apparatus.

IV Ideology and Work in the Experience of a Single Parent: Sketching an Institutional Ethnography

To illustrate the institutional ethnography as a method of inquiry that makes the everyday world its problematic, I shall draw on my own experience as the point d'appui of an inquiry that will be sketched in to show what it might look like. As I said earlier, I was for several years a "single parent." That concept provides for me a method of analyzing my biographical experience. That experience itself was situated in actual settings in which its minidramas went on—the home we lived in with its untidiness, the fruit trees, blackberries in the hedge between garden and lane, the view of the mountains from the kitchen window, the kitchen floor that would never come clean, the roads to and from the various schools my children attended. The children themselves as they were then are more difficult to re-envisage, overlaid as their images have been by their more recent being. I remember them playing soccer in the front yard and complicated games of fantasy in the back. In these fragmentary memories, there is no experience of *being* a single parent, though the work processes through which I engaged with those settings and relationships surely had that distinctive character because I was alone in charge of my children in a world of two-parent families. The notion "single parent" did not serve to analyze that work organization and its disjunctures. It does, as Griffith shows,[21] something rather different. It organizes and organized for me my relation to a school in the context of problems one of my children had in learning to read. Other women in similar situations know what this problem is. One woman I know who is a teacher and a "single parent" has concealed this information from her child's school. A child's problem in school, when it is made accountable in terms of the concept of the single parenthood of her or his mother, marshals procedures entering child, parent, teacher, and school administration into courses of action specialized to this category of "problem." This concept then becomes a basis on which the work of mothering is organized and interpreted in relation to the schooling process. It does so not merely in providing for school staff a method of analyzing, assembling, and describing how a child is a problem and how that problem ties in to his or her home background. Provided the mother is competent in its conceptual methods, it gives her a procedure for analyzing her own work practices as a mother in terms of how their defects produce the child's problem in the school setting.

The force of this effect is enhanced by how the interpretive practices rendering mothering accountable in this context do not identify it as work. Notions of good mothering practices take no account of the actual material and social conditions of mothering work. The Ontario Ministry of Education publishes for parents a little pamphlet containing suggestions about how parents (but in fact mothers) can improve their/her child's reading and writing. The specific exclusion of the suggested practices from the category of work is marked in recommendations for what mothers can do to promote reading skills that can be done "as you go about your daily work." Work and encouraging reading skills are mutually exclusive. The suggestions include such items as these:

> *Have a place where your children can paint and crayon or cut-and-paste without having to worry about making a mess. It will take them a while to develop*

the co-ordination required to make small letters. Give them large sheets of paper to work with at first so that they'll have space for large printing.

Examine photographs and works of art with your children. Discuss what they see. Extend the parts of their vocabulary that deal with shape, colour, and form.

Use home-made puppets. Have your children dramatize stories they have read. They can write scripts and put on their own shows, but they need an audience— you!

These are typical of the inventory of suggestions. All presuppose expenditures of time and effort. Most also presuppose other material conditions—the availability of paints, crayons, scissors, paper, photographs, and works of art. Some, such as the last example quoted above, presuppose preparatory work on the part of the parent—in making puppets or, which may be quite as time consuming, organizing the making of puppets as play with children. Nearly all involve time in securing materials, time sitting down with children to discuss, read, and act as audience, time in preparing play settings and materials, time in cleaning up afterward. They also presuppose in many instances the availability of space. For example, having a place where children can paint and crayon without having to worry about making a mess presupposes a size of house; so does putting on puppet shows. Many of the recommendations also presuppose that the parents possess special skills, such as knowing how to discuss photographs and works of art or how to play word games such as Scrabble or Spill-and-Spell.

Along with work involved in "developing the child,"[22] there is work involved in scheduling the comings and goings of different family members in relation to their external commitments. The providing of household services facilitating the child's working schedule, supervising homework, providing cultural activities such as visits to museums, movies, and the like, taking care of emotional stresses arising in the schooling process, covering for a child so that minor delinquencies such as being late or missing school do not appear as defects on her or his record, helping with the school library, baking a cake for the bake sale, driving the car when the team plays another school, and so forth—all these along with the routine and basic housework (feeding, clothing, health care, etc.) contribute to the child's capacity to function normally at school.

The work of mothering done by women in the home is consequential for the school as well as the child. It is consequential for the school *through* the child. The work of the teacher in the classroom, particularly of the teacher in the primary grades, depends, as Manicom shows upon the preparation children have had in competences relevant to their functioning in the classroom. If, for example, children have learned to return the same colored brush to the paint pot rather than replacing it in any pot and so eventually reducing all the colors to the same general state of mud, then the teacher can more easily make use of painting in the classroom. The character of mothering is thus a condition of the teacher's work, and the overall character of the classroom presupposes the general character of mothering prevalent in the area served by the school.[23]

In the classroom setting, we can now also begin to see how, for example, the structuring of the classroom into three groups for the purpose of reading instruction and the relation between this and the teacher's "expectations" (described by Rist)[24] can be understood as part of a work organization in which the teacher confronts as the conditions of her classroom work the effects of varying mothering practices and their material conditions, as well as whatever differentials of ability and level of development might exist among children.

But we are not yet satisfied. To have begun to recover the character of the work and work organization is only the first step. The next is to explore how that work process is embedded in the social relations of the extended social and economic process. To do this, we work with a procedure we have come to call "making a design." The design provides a preliminary sketch of the relevant relations, that is, those implicated in the everyday experience that is our point d'appui. The design describes as an area for investigation the relations implicated in and organizing the everyday world. It is a means of extending the analysis from the level of the everyday analyzed as a work process to the expanded social relations in which that work process is embedded. It shifts the scope of inquiry to refer back to an earlier instance, from the little girl who buys candy at the store to the social relations in and through which that is a possible act. A design provides a proximate map, that is, a map of the immediately relevant set of relations. It is constructed to be specifically open "at the other end," where it is tied into the extended relations of the political economy. We can then make use of it, as the work of inquiry fills it out, in spelling out the implications of change and movement in the political economy for the local experience of women in the work of mothering and teaching.

The design embeds the work of mothering in a complex of relations that organizes its social and material character. These relations are sketched in figure 4.1. It is intended only to suggest how the relations might be analyzed and not intended to supply a theoretical model. Specifically also, it reproduces the "focused" character of the

Figure 4.1

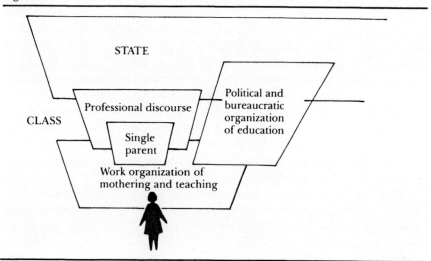

approach which begins from a particular standpoint, a particular point d'appui, and structures the representation of other relations from this perspective. It strives also to capture the coordinative interpenetration of different levels of social organization by the professional discourse. In the design, "single parent" is a constituent of a discourse, naming a form of family that is defective in terms of the complementarity of the work organization of mothering and schooling. The effective form is one in which the man heads the household and earns a salary or wage, thus enabling his wife's labor to be exclusively available for the tasks of housewifery and mothering.

Such actual work processes must be situated in their material conditions. Taking that step directs us to differences in the way in which the complementary relation of mothering and schooling works in different class contexts and as part of the social organization of class. Among the middle classes, privileged access to occupations with the possibilities of career advancement has come to substitute for inheritance in ensuring the transgenerational continuities of class. A family organization making it possible for mothers to invest considerable time and skills in the "development" of children in relation to education is an essential part of this process. Their skills too have been generally acquired through prior investment (both state and private) in advanced training, giving them access to the psychological and child developmental knowledge facilitating the coordination of mothering and school. The career process and the accumulation of personal wealth ensure the material conditions, the settings, equipment and other means, as well as the choice of school in which teachers can function on the assumption that in general mothering in the school's catchment area will enable the middle-class classroom to function as such.

By contrast, the working-class mother is likely to have less available time. She will not be able to substitute paid domestic service for her own labor and, to a lesser extent, for labor embodied in commodities. She is more likely to have to take paid employment. Her mothering skills, particularly those specifically articulated to systematic knowledge of child development, will represent a lower level of educational investment (both state and private). These are effects not so much for the individual child as for the conditions under which classroom work is organized. The working-class neighborhood creates different conditions for the work organization of the classroom as a whole and hence for the local schooling process.[25]

The dependence of the classroom as a work setting on mothering is managed through a variety of organized contacts, interviews with parents, participation of mothers in school activities, Parent-Teacher Associations, and the like. These contacts also mediate the interests of parents in the outcomes of schooling for their children. We expect that these are organized differently as part of the different ways in which the mothering-schooling relation works in different class contexts. Of general significance is the ideological process originating in professional discourse as the conceptual medium in which this relation is rendered accountable. Middle- and working-class mothers participate differently in this process. Middle-class mothers in general have learned the ideological practices coordinating home-school relations. They know how to analyze their experience and what is happening with the child in the classroom, using the same concepts in general as those used by teachers. The institutional ideology provides, to a degree at least, a lingua franca in which the work in the two spheres is coordinated. Further, the middle-class mother is oriented toward experts on child development through her training and "keeps up" with advances in child-development thinking through reading what experts have to say in women's magazines or paperback books. Hence our design includes the ideological processes of sociological and psychological discourse as a constituent of its organization. We do not know for sure, but our suspicion is that working-class women do not participate in these social relations in the same way.

Viewing mothering as a work process articulated to the work process of schooling enables us to locate the relations to be investigated in exploring the local problem of the "single parent." The family she heads is a rump. The man is not there to remove from her the burden of earning a living, which deprives her of the time and energy needed to work in relation to the school. The "single parent," as Griffith shows,[26] identifies the family that is improperly formed and by inference therefore cannot come through properly in the complementary practices of mothering on which the work organization of the classroom depends. This category "single parent" names, from the perspective of the institutional process and hence in terms of its relevance to the school, a particular type of defect in the conditions of effective classroom work organization. The category provides an interpretive procedure that presupposes the defect regardless of a mother's actual practices. A child's problems in the classroom setting are attributed to this "background" effect. Mothers participating in the ideological discourse know how to analyze their own experience, to examine it for its essential defects, and to reflect on them with fear and anxiety.

Recognizing the classroom as a work organization provides a different basis of investigation than viewing the classroom, say, in terms of the teacher's expectations,[27] or in terms of interpersonal interaction or role structures. Such frames render the resource bases of the classroom work organization unobservable as well as concealing how those work processes are regulated and coordinated with others. The classroom is embedded in a hierarchy of adminisitrative and political processes. The teacher works within certain definite resource conditions under definite forms of scrutiny from the school administration. Her work or its products are exposed in various ways to her colleagues. Her year's work in the elementary classroom becomes a working condition of next year's teachers of the same students. The principal and vice-principal plan and administer within administrative policies set by the school board, the Ministry of Education, and parental pressures, and supervise in various ways what teachers do in the classroom. The teacher works within budgetary constraints determining the numbers of children she has in her class, the materials and space available, the specialized skills she can draw on, the time she has for preparation. Time in particular is the key, and the allocation of time is central in the work of the teacher. Such decisions as dividing a reading class into three groups are rule-of-thumb solutions to practical experience of what will best combine the multiple pressures, limitations, standards, supervisory practices of the principal, and classroom resources. In these ways the general policies and budgetary constraints of the administrative hierarchy of the educating state are directly implicated in the classroom work organization.

The intervention of the state at different levels, that is, both the central and local forms of the state (including therefore municipal government, school boards, etc.), sustains and maintains the social relations that reproduce class through the educational process. The articulation of the work processes of mothering and schooling is not a "natural" or merely "contingent" effect. The state is implicated through zoning laws in the creation of residential enclaves tied to income levels. These function as catchment areas for schools, ensuring relatively homogeneous mothering practices and in particular securing to those of higher income levels the conditions for middle-class classroom practices. This residential organization of class is complemented by the taxation practices of the local state, enabling the wealthier communities which generate more educational revenue to reserve it at least in part to enrich schools serving their own community (this is now changing). Middle-class influence in the educational system has been exercised through locally elected school boards as well as through its participation in local state bureaucracies. Furthermore, communities elect boards of trustees representing a largely middle-class section of the community—business and professional people, middle-class housewives, and the like. Although their power is increasingly limited by a centralized bureaucracy representing interests more closely identified with the interests of the corporate sector of the economy, they are still effective in representing the local interests of the middle class in the educational process. The increasingly centralized administrative apparatus regulates resources, standards, curriculum, and so forth. In complex ways these various levels of the state enable the expression of different interests of dominant classes in the educational process.

The effectiveness of the established schooling process in reproducing class relations is ensured by limitations on resources, preventing the teacher working under given conditions of class size and other resources from expanding her participation in developing the child by complementing time and resources unavailable in the home (as has been done in the United States in such programs as Operation Headstart). Effectiveness is ensured also by the development of programs or systems of streaming which compound the differentials initiated at the elementary levels by allowing the effects of resource-poor mothering to be intensified by resource-poor early schooling. It is in processes such as these that we would find the actualities of social relations behind Coleman's finding that "schools bring little influence to bear on a child's achievement that is independent of his background and general social context."[28]

This fashion of exploring the everyday work experience of mothers and teachers enables us to identify in a preliminary way a social relation articulating the two work processes and to enter that relation into a more general set of social relations of class and state. The investigation of these enables us to display the determinations of the actual everyday worlds implicated in this process. Thus we could find or generate differing bases of experience, of middle- and working-class mothers, of "single parents" and two-parent families, of teachers situated in differing class contexts of their work in the classroom, and explicate the peculiarities of the situation of the child who is both object of this work process and participant in it. This latter standpoint has the potentiality of adding important dimensions to our understanding of the relations of children to those who are responsible for their development in the context of actual power relations, the actual organization of work processes, and the peculiar ways in which mothers become responsible in the home for representing the claims and constraints of the educational institution. It is a method of analysis enabling us also to discern the effects of changing economic conditions, not only in terms of cutbacks in educational funding but also in the ways in which the effects of economic crisis on families, and particularly on working-class families, change the resource conditions of the work of mothering and hence the conditions of the teacher's work in the classroom.[29] We can also begin to understand the shifting bases of relations and to see where concealed bases of common interest and concern among women may lie.

V Beginning from Where We Are and Discovering the Institutional Organization of Power

In taking up the everyday world as problematic and developing institutional ethnography as a method of inquiry, we are, of course, attempting to map an actual terrain. The enterprise is one closer to explication than explanation, exploring actual social relations as these arise in the articulation of work processes and work organization in one setting to those of others. There is order, though order as such and the accomplishment of order are not the problematic of a sociology for women. Order arises in and is accomplished by the actual practices of actual individuals, including their practices of reasoning, interpreting, rendering what has happened accountable. The generalizable properties of social relations in the institutional mode are accomplished in people's actual practices. The relation between ideology and the actualities it glosses and makes accountable is continually worked up and maintained, on the one hand, by practices aiming at and intending the institutional description, including those that enforce such practices, and on the other by the development of innovative interpretive forms within the ruling apparatus (and generally by those participating in professional and academic discourses) that extend or rehabilitate interpretive schemata as the changing character of events or the widening scope of control requires. I emphasize that it is not ideological schemata themselves that constitute the institutional mode, it is rather the relation between the ideological and actual practices or events. The terrain to be explored and explicated by the institutional ethnography is one of work processes and other practical activities as these are rendered accountable within the ideological schemata of the institution. The latter are not merely in thought but are also practical activities and in some contexts work processes, organized in relations of textual communication.

In taking up an exploration from the experience of one individual we have already found a general relation, that of a single parent to the school, as a phase of a larger organization of the work of mothering in relation to the educational process. The experience of an individual proposes, or can propose, a problematic directing our inquiry to a set of social relations. Exploring those social relations requires that we understand them as generating various actual experiences, or rather as generating the everyday bases of actual experiences, in characteristic ways. A grasp of a set of interlinked institutional relations will explicate the generalizing relations determining its characteristic and diverse bases of experience. The notion of such bases of experience (in the everyday world) has empirical force in women's experience of consciousness-raising as a method by which, in coming together and talking about our lives, we could elucidate the common grounds of our oppression. Such a common basis of experience emerges in the situation of the "single parent" in relation to the school (where "single parent" recognizes the ideological constituent as integral to the social organization of that experience). The explication of institutional relations brings to light not only common bases of experience but also bases of experience that are not in common but are grounded in the same set of social relations. An institutional ethnography thus explicates social relations generating characteristic bases of experience in an institutional process.

It does so, of course, in terms of the subject's relevances as these arise from the lived actualities of her everyday world. It does not begin in an abstract space with relevances determined by notions such as the cumulation of a body of scientific knowledge. Institutional processes do not form a system that can be represented in its totality. Work processes that do not enter into its "accounting" practices, but are necessary to those that do, are often those that articulate a given institutional process to other social relations. Institutional ethnography then must avoid remaining within the conceptual boundaries defining the institutional domain.

Inquiry of this kind builds in an open-ended character. It is like the making of the piece of a quilt that remains to be attached to other pieces in the creation of a whole pattern. We begin from where we are. The ethnographic process of inquiry is one of exploring further into those social, political, and economic processes that organize and determine the actual bases of experience of those whose side we have taken. Taking sides, beginning from some position with some concern, does not destroy the "scientific" character of the enterprise. Detachment is not a condition of science. Indeed, in sociology there is no possibility of detachment. We must begin from some position in the world. The method recommended here is one that frankly begins from somewhere. The specification of that somewhere and the explication of the relations to which it is articulated, including the ideological discourse, are the aim of inquiry.

The discovery of an objectively existing social process is thus, through its capacity to generate bases of experience, seen *from such bases of experience*. The aim is to disclose the social process from within as it is lived.

Ideally an institutional ethnography is not a solitary pursuit or a single fieldwork enterprise. Grappling with the actualities of extensive social relations is best taken up by inquiries opening up a number of different windows, disclosing a number of different viewpoints from which the workings of a whole (though "open-ended") complex of relational processes come into view. Other work, beyond this volume, enables us to build a picture of how these relational processes work. The researches of Griffith on the "single parent," of Manicom on the dependence of the classroom on mothering, of Noble on the acquisition of skills in "developing" the child, and of Jackson in exploring the implications of economic crisis for the conditions of teaching and hence for classroom teachers give us means of building an increasingly comprehensive grasp of the processes involved.[30] Viewing this collective project as institutional ethnography allows us to specify what was formerly sketchy, to identify areas where more work is needed, and to develop a more exacting knowledge of the social relations determining women's everyday worlds. We increase thus our capacity as sociologists to disclose to women involved in the educational process how matters come about as they do in their experience and to provide methods of making their working experience accountable to themselves and other women rather than to the ruling apparatus of which institutions are part.

Notes

1. Many of the earlier critics have been cited in chapter 2.
2. Helen Roberts, ed., *Doing Feminist Research* (London: Routledge and Kegan Paul, 1981); Liz Stanley and Sue Wise, *Breaking Out: Feminist Consciousness and Feminist Research* (London: Routledge and Kegan Paul, 1983); Angela McRobbie, "The politics of feminist research: Between talk, text and action," *Feminist Review*, no. 12 (1982): 46–57.
3. Dorothy E. Smith, "Women's perspective as a radical critique of sociology," and chaps. 2 and 3 of this book.
4. The more tender and civic-minded of my readers may like to know that two things have changed in my life since I wrote this. One is that I no longer have a dog of my own. I do, however, sometimes dog-sit my two sons' dogs. The second is that we now have "poop 'n' scoop" laws in Toronto, so I have learned to overcome my rural-bred tendencies to let the shit lie where it falls.
5. Barney Glaser and Anselm L. Strauss, *The Discovery of Grounded Theory: Strategies for Qualitative Research* (Chicago: Aldine Press, 1967).
6. Karl Marx, *Capital: A Critique of Political Economy* (New York: Random House, 1977).
7. Nona Glazer, "Housework (review essay)," *Signs* 1 (1976): 905–22.
8. Dorothy E. Smith, "The statistics on mental illness: What they will not tell us about women and why," in D. E. Smith and Sarah David, eds., *Women Look at Psychiatry* (Vancouver: Press Gang, 1975), p. 97.
9. Cf. Don H. Zimmerman, "Fact as a practical accomplishment," in Roy Turner, ed., *Ethnomethodology* (Harmondsworth, England: Penguin Books, 1974), pp. 128–43.
10. Alison Griffith, "Ideology, education and single parent families: The normative ordering of families through schooling," Ph.D. dissertation, Department of Education, University of Toronto, 1984; Ann Manicom, "The reproduction of class: The relations between two work processes," paper presented at a symposium on The Political Economy of Gender in Education, Ontario Institute for Studies in Education, 1981; Joey Noble, "Developing the child," typescript, Department of Sociology, University of Toronto, 1982.
11. Harold Garfinkel, *Studies in Ethnomethodology* (Englewood Cliffs, N.J.: Prentice-Hall, 1967).
12. D. L. Wieder, *Language and Social Reality: The Case of Telling the Convict Code* (The Hague: Mouton, 1974).

13. Dorothy E. Smith, "No one commits suicide: Textual analyses of ideological practices," *Human Studies* 6 (1983): 309–59.
14. See Garfinkel, *Studies in Ethnomethodology.*
15. Dorothy E. Smith, "Textually-mediated social organization," *International Social Science Journal* 36, no. 1 (1984): 59–75.
16. Gerald de Montigny, "The social organization of social workers' practice: A Marxist analysis," M.A. thesis, Department of Education, University of Toronto, 1980.
17. Ray C. Rist, *The Urban School: A Factory of Failure* (Cambridge, Mass.: MIT Press, 1973).
18. See, for example, Noble, "Developing the child."
19. Maurice Craft, "Family, class and education: Changing perspectives," in Maurice Craft, ed., *Family, Class and Education: A Reader* (London: Longman, 1970), p. 7.
20. For example, the Power of Women Collective published a journal taking this position. Their "This Is Housework" section (in *Power of Women* 1, no. 3 [January 1975]: 7–10) typifies this view. Shopping, including the specific conditions of shopping, emotional support for husband, sexual availability, are all aspects of "housework." They are "work."
21. Griffith, "Ideology, education and single parent families."
22. Noble, "Developing the child."
23. Manicom, "The reproduction of class."
24. Rist, *Urban School.*
25. Manicom, "The reproduction of class."
26. Griffith, "Ideology, education and single parent families."
27. This is Rist's explanation in *Urban School.*
28. James S. Coleman, with Ernest Q. Campbell, Carol J. Hobson, James McPartland, Alexander M. Mood, Frederic D. Weinfeld, and Robert L. York, *Equality of Educational Opportunity* (Washington, D.C.: Department of Health, Education and Welfare, 1966), p. 325.
29. Nancy Jackson, "Stress on schools + stress on families = distress for children," Canadian Teachers' Federation, Ottawa, 1982.
30. Griffith, "Ideology, education and single parent families;" Manicom, "The reproduction of class;" Noble "Developing the child;" Jackson "Stress on schools."

5

Researching the Everyday World as Problematic

I Standpoint as a Research Practice

This chapter focuses on the translation of the concept of the everyday world as problematic into a research practice. How do we design a research procedure that will give practical force to the proposal to explicate the social relations implicit in the work organization of women's everyday lives?

In 1984 Alison Griffith and I started on a research project focused on the work that mothers do in relation to their children's schooling. Although this research is not complete at the time of this writing, it forced us to think through how to realize an inquiry beginning with the standpoint of actual women and exploring through them the relations organizing the everyday world as the matrix of their experience. The problem and its particular solution are analogous to those by which fresco painters solved the problems of representing the different temporal moments of a story in the singular space of the wall.[1] The problem is to produce in the two-dimensional space framed as a wall a world of action and movement in time. The boundaries of the wall or its decorations frame a space of a totally different order, which has depth, extension, and temporality incoordinate with the ongoing world of actual activities to which the wall on which it appears is material context. We have placed on our depiction this further constraint—that it incorporate the analogue of a "natural" standpoint in which the depth and structure of the depiction are organized from a standpoint in the world.

The analogy with the fresco paintings, whose devices Gombrich analyzes, has its limitations, of course, because it confines us strictly to a world of illusion. We want rather to create a textual analysis that will instruct our everyday knowledge of how the world works. But Gombrich stresses the "artfulness" of the effects of fresco painting in solving in various ways the problems resulting from the conjunction of narrative intention with particular pictoral site. We seek an analogous artfulness, analogous conventions, in constructing a view into the workings of social relations from the standpoint of particular women. We wanted to begin from particular experiences of a work process and to explore the relations in which they are embedded from just that position. Somehow therefore strategies had to be developed that would preserve the movement from particular experiences to an expanded view of a landscape viewed from just that site with which we began. A major problem was that of building "perspective" into the procedure of inquiry so that the resulting analysis would have the proper relations of "depth."

Our point of entry was women's experience of the work they did in relation to their children's schooling. We would begin by asking women to talk to us about this work. The resulting accounts would provide a wealth of descriptive material about particular women's local practices. There is nothing new sociologically about this procedure. While feminism has brought new sensitivities and a new scrupulousness to open-ended interviewing, it is our uses of material that have been distinctive. And here we are trying something different again. Standard sociological analysis uses some method of coding and interpreting such accounts to order the interview materials in relation to the relevances of the sociological and/or feminist discourses. These enable the interviews to be sorted into topics typical of the study population. In such a process, the standpoint of the women themselves is suppressed. The standpoint becomes that of the discourse reflecting upon properties of the study population. Characteristics of the study population become the object of the knower's gaze.

We sought a method that would preserve throughout the standpoint of the women we interviewed. To do so we worked with a sequence of stages in the research. We were concerned to locate women's work practices in the actual relations by which they are organized and

which they organize. This meant talking to women first. Women's accounts of the work they did in relation to their children's schooling
would then be examined for the ways in which they were articulated to
the social organization of the school.[2] That scrutiny would establish the
questions and issues for the second stage of research, interviewing
teachers and administrators in the schools. Our strategy would move
from particular experiences to their embedding in the generalizing social organization of the school. It would preserve a perspective in which
we could look out from where we are, from where our respondents
are, onto the larger landscape organizing and containing their daily
practices.

The method of thinking we are using makes use of the concept of
social relation.[3] This sense of social relations understands people's activities as coordinated in actual temporally concerted sequences or
courses of action. In and through these the work of a multiplicity of
people known and unknown to one another is coordinated. Rather
than an account of the division of labor as a fixed allocation of functions in people-sized hunks, the concept of social relation analyzes it as
an ongoing concerting of courses of action in which what people do is
already organized as it takes up from what precedes and projects its
organization into what follows.

In situating women's working experience as mothers, we see them
at work at a point of juncture between the actualities of the economy
on which their households depend and the social organization of the
school. While we meant to make schooling our major focus, we also
wanted to situate our respondents' accounts of their work in its real
conditions. The work that mothers do organizes a sequence in which,
traditionally, the wage or salary is transformed into the practical organization of subsistence, the caring for and the social development of
children, which is articulated to the work of the school.

We can envisage it something like figure 5.1.

While we could not undertake to explore both "ends" of the relation in equal detail, it was clear that in exploring women's work as
mothers in these contexts, we were exploring the social relations of
class. As we have written elsewhere:

> It is in . . . these social courses of action that we find class, not as a factor or
> aggregate of abstracted individuals, but as relations which in the main repro-
> duce for children the same occupational levels as that of their parents. . . . Class
> appears not as something external, but as a way of understanding the conditions
> and constraints of mothers' work and the character of their efforts and struggles
> as moments in the social relations of class conceived as extended social courses
> of action in which people are both implicated and active.[4]

Figure 5.1

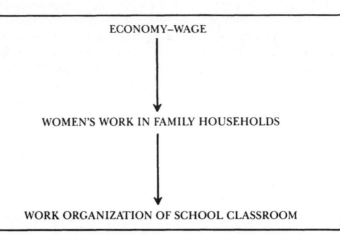

While we could not make the "wage" end of the relation a major focus, we wanted to avoid an artificial boundary to our investigation. We wanted to be able to preserve our sense of the lived actualities of women's lives as being embedded in a more extensive complex of relations than that which we would actually investigate. Therefore we chose to talk to women whose children attended one of two schools located in districts with a markedly different socioeconomic base. One is predominantly a working-class school; the other predominantly middle class; the husbands of these women are employed in a mixture of professional and managerial occupations and skilled trades. We interviewed only mothers with children in primary grades because we wanted to focus on grade levels at which mothers are likely to be most actively at work and to simplify the range of school settings we would explore. We interviewed six mothers in each school district.

Constructing perspective as a methodological procedure involved a step-by-step process. The first phase of our inquiry would engage women with children going to a given local school. The interviews were in-depth. We provided the overall topic, its conceptualization as "work," and the general framework of the interview (we started off after some general information by asking the women we talked to to take us through a "school day"). The second stage of inquiry would require an analysis of these interviews to explicate a problematic to be specified as interview topics for the teachers and school administrators of the schools attended by our respondents' children. Our application for funding was in some state of embarrassment here. We could not know the specific character of the problematic of the everyday until we had explored the everyday. We could not say what the topics of the school interviews would be because they would be developed out of our analysis of the first interviews. The third stage, a move to the administrative level of the school board, was equally undefined, for that part of the investigation would also follow from the first-stage analysis and the organization that became visible at the level of the school. It was this stage-by-stage procedure of building inquiry on the basis of the women's accounts that would establish them as the standpoint from which aspects of school and school administrative organization would be brought into view. Using this procedure, we would go then from a specifically located and characterized experience to an exploration of the relations by which that experience is organized and in which it is embedded. The movement of research is from a woman's account of her everyday experience to exploring *from that perspective* the generalizing and generalized relations in which each individual's everyday world is embedded. That is how a standpoint giving a "perspective" on the world was constructed in this study.

II The Conceptual Shift

This "perspectival" structure was not always easy to hold in place. It was all too easy to slip back into a more or less standard "outsider's" standpoint—if not exactly an Archimedian position. In presenting one of the papers based upon our work, I had noticed, as a result of questions, a peculiar conceptual shift that I could not quite nail down, though it was clearly inept. There seemed to be a conceptual confusion in our project that had gone undetected at earlier stages. I seemed to have to shift modes when I went from presenting our analysis of how mothers coordinate the uncoordinated to our proposals for defining the problematic that would guide our inquiry into the school.

The problem we now encountered was already implicit in the original formulation of institutional ethnography (see chap. 4). Part of the difficulty arose because the institutional ethnography was originally conceived not as a single research enterprise but as an enterprise that more than one might take up, exploring the institutional process (as there defined) from more than one window upon it. Alison Griffith's interest and mine in exploring the work of mothering in relation to schooling was complemented by the work of others, notably by Ann Manicom's investigation into the work of the teacher in the classroom and the ways in which that work depended upon the prior work of mothers. The curriculum, viewed as a production plan,[5] must be implemented in the school under very various conditions created by the very various populations of children. A big part of such differences could be viewed as arising from differences in the amount and type of work done by mothers in the home. The typical work practices of mothers in a given school district could be seen then as consequential for how the school functions in general. This contrasts with the discourse on family and school achievement which examines, among other topics, mothering practices in relation to the performances of individual children.

Our thinking at first had followed a similar direction. We had thought of approaching the schools in terms of how our informants' mothering practices entered into the work of the teachers in our two schools as the conditions of their classroom practices. And those classroom practices of course were "prescribed" by the curriculum, resources, and so forth established by the school board. And so we would have located a key point of juncture between the particularized and, indeed,[6] particularizing work of mothers and the fully generalized and generalizing organization of education through the board and the teaching profession.[7]

To our discomfort, we began to find that thinking in this way created issues of sampling. They arose not as a mechanical issue of sociological sampling methodologies and quantitative analyses; rather we were now talking about "populations" of children in the school setting. If teachers' work in the classroom is shaped by characteristics of the population of children and the latter is shaped by typical mothering practices, then there is a question of how the mothers we talked to could be treated as representing that population.

Changes in the character of a local population can in very sudden ways confront a school with entirely new situations for which its established procedures are inadequate. The schooling process is deeply embedded in the family and (we would argue) in the parenting practices (and in the all too commonly invisible conditions of those practices) that characterize the population of a given area. *From the standpoint of the school,* issues of population and sampling do not arise merely as questions of good sociological method; they are entailed by the nature of the problem once it has become defined as the issue of how the work of parenting (and the varying conditions of that work) is consequential for the work of the school. Questions of population and sample arise as issues of generalizing statements to a population.

But here, of course, we run into the conceptual slippage built into our research proposal. For in posing as the central problematic of the relationship of mothers' work to their children's schooling, the kinds of conditions their work creates for the work of classroom teachers, *we had shifted over imperceptibly from the standpoint of the mothers to that of the school.* In effect we had inadvertently imported into an inquiry that had begun from the standpoint of mothers, the standpoint of school organization. When we look *at* the school *from* the standpoint of women, we do not require a sample; we are not trying to generalize from a small number to the characteristics of a larger population. Rather, we are trying to explore how the institutional practices of the school penetrate and organize the experience of different individual women as mothers. We want to explore this phenomenon from a base in that experience, and we want to "hold" our perspective by moving from the experience of the women we interviewed to the complementary organization of the school.

III *How Then to Proceed?*

First we interviewed the individual women in their homes. We met with six women in each school district.[8] In this process we jointly constructed an account of the work they do as mothers in relation to their children's schooling. These interviews were framed by our enterprise, our interests, and not by theirs. They were structured by the conception of mothering as "work." The methods of interviewing we used were otherwise open-ended. Some of the interviews were very long. Though the general topic and the overall structure that was there to be returned to were managed by the interviewer, informants could explore their situation and experience in fully open-ended ways. This freedom is important because how informants tell the story of their work is essential to the analysis that defines the problematic of the second stage.

We asked the women to describe the work they did in relation to their children's schooling. Our primary structuring device was to run through a day with them.[9] They spoke very fully and freely and for the most part very concretely. They controlled the ways in which their accounts were sequenced, the temporal juxtapositions and continuities, their narrative method. The terms they used were theirs and not ours. We had certain topics we wanted to cover, but we were not held to specific questions. The interviews were tape-recorded and transcribed in full, both questions and answers. The editorial function of the tape recorder has reduced the totality of the interview process to the verbal sequences defining the interview as such.[10] These are the verbal sequences available to our analysis, and we are at this point mostly interested in what the informants have to say about their everyday experience as mothers of schoolchildren.

The simple notion of the everyday world as problematic is that social relations external to it are present in its organization. How then are their traces to be found in the ways that people speak of their everyday lives in the course of interviews of this kind. We do not expect them to speak of social organization and social relations. The methodological assumptions of the approach we are using are that the social organization and relations of the ongoing concerting of our daily activities are continually expressed in the ordinary ways in which we speak of them, at least when we speak of them concretely. How people speak of the forms of life in which they are implicated is determined by those forms of life. Wittgenstein opposed the philosophical practice of lifting terms out of their original home and their actual uses in order to explore their essence.[11] I am taking the further step of arguing that the way terms are used in their original context, including their syntactic arrangements, is "controlled" or "governed" by its social organization (in the sense discussed in sec. 4 of chap. 3) and that the same social organization is present as an ordering procedure in how people tell others about that original setting.

As interviewers we persuade people to talk about the everyday worlds in which they are active. The terms, vocabulary, and syntactic forms derive from those forms of life and express (and indeed it may be said, accomplish) their typicality. It is not so much a matter of a vocabulary specific to a social region. Rather the social organization of our daily practices governs our choice of syntactic forms and terms when we speak of them. An ordinary example from our interviewing procedure was the unthinking way in which we relied on the concept of the school day to organize women's accounts of their work. The women we spoke to had no problem with this idea and we did not give it much thought as such in our first uses of it. We took for granted, as they did, how the notion of "the school day" structured our talk. We both (interviewers and respondents) knew very well how to construct questions and responses in terms of the relevances that notion provided. We "naturally" talked of "getting the kids off to school," of lunchtimes, after-school, and so forth. The ways we (Alison Griffith and I and those we interviewed) referenced the school day in our talk was governed by our tacit knowledge, as practitioners, of that social organization. It would be hard for someone to speak unmethodically in referencing social organization of which she is a competent practitioner.

We speak from the known-in-practice ongoing concerting of actual activities. We speak knowing how rather than knowing that. We do not, of course, except in rare instances, speak *of* that social organization. We speak *methodically*. When we first encounter a new social organizational setting, we typically find that there is a problem of speech. It is like this: while we may be sure that we understand everything that is said, we are not at all sure that we will be able to speak correctly; we are not sure that the appropriate terms, names, titles, and so forth will fall into place or—what is perhaps even more important—that we will know how to assemble these in the appropriate ways. But what are these appropriate forms? They are seldom as distinct as matters of protocol, of different official language uses. They are commonly the difference between how those speak who are ongoing practitioners of a world and who know how to use its language in situ as part of its ongoing concerting and how those speak who are as yet feeling their way into the properties of its everyday practices. The language of the setting observes the relations of its social organization. Its proper uses indeed preserve them. In the interview situation, the original setting is not operative, but registers as an underlying determinant of how the informant talks of the setting because it is the only way in which it makes sense to talk.[12] Given that we do not disrupt the process by the procedures we use, open-ended interviewing should therefore yield stretches of talk that "express" the social organization and relations of the setting.

In proceeding from our base in interviews with mothers to the second stage of our inquiry in the schools, our focus on the interviews is on relations that are in various ways referenced in them but are not fully contained in the local historical settings of mothering work and therefore not explicitly available in them. Our interest is in the social relations in which the work that mothers do in relation to their children's schooling is embedded. Their ongoing practical knowledge of the concerting of their activities with those of others is expressed in how they speak about those activities. How they speak of, as well as what they have to tell us about, how they work in relation to their children's schooling is organized by the social relations and organization that enter into, complement, and determine the social organization of their work. This is where we find the problematic in terms of which our questions for the school are addressed. It is precisely in their practical knowledge of relations known only in part that the more extended relations in which their work is embedded will appear. Our problematic, as those questions that will organize how our inquiry proceeds at the next stage, depends upon an analysis of the social organization and relations implicit in how informants talk from their experience of their work as mothers.

IV Exploring the Problematic of Mothers' Talk

We are constrained by our commitment to ensure that the women we spoke to speak again in what we write without our reinterpretation of what they had to say. We have not coded; we have not sought to identify common themes. Of course a shared thematic structure was provided by our interview procedure. Of course there were recurrent topics and situations, but we were not interested in collecting these or talking about how they were distributed in a sample. The group of women we talked to were not a sample. They were those who provided the outlook on the world from which we began, and if there were common themes and topics—including those supplied by our interview procedures—they were there as expressions of individuals' participation in the generalized organization of the relations of schooling. For example, to explore with each respondent the organization of the "school day" is a "topic" that "reflects" in the interview context an actual legally enforced organization of public education. So rather than inserting into our analysis of the interviews the relevances of the sociological discourse, we are interpreting them as expressions of their part in the local coordination of an institutional process.

Since our interest is primarily in explicating aspects of social organization at a level that directs attention to the school for its complement, no attempt has been made to develop a highly technical analysis of the narratives. When we are exploring social relations or social organization, we are exploring the ways in which the ongoing activities of actual individuals are concerted or in which actual individuals concert their ongoing activities, and hence the way their activities are *social*.[13] In the analysis here, we are working with the assumption that our informants' narrative of events displays their active involvement in the practical concerting of social relations *from their standpoint,* and that social organization of mothers' practices is implicated in the socially organized practices of the school.

I have selected three passages for examination here. Each describes the work of parents in relation to schoolwork done by their children in the home. Our concern is to explicate the social organization of the transaction between home and school from the standpoint of the women who participate in it as mothers. In focusing on social organization we are focusing on the concerting, the coordination, of activities and courses of action as an actual ongoing process.

Parents, and mothers in particular, are involved in managing their children in ways that will sustain or advance their performance in the school setting and on its terms. We find in our interviews many descriptions of mothers working actively with their children as "ancillary teachers" or managing their children's schoolwork in the home. Some of these courses of action were initiated by the school, others by the mothers themselves. Mothers, and in some instances both parents, routinely monitored their children's schoolwork and general performance in school by checking over the work they brought home as well as by spending time encouraging them to talk about what happened at school. We have described elsewhere a "monitoring-repair" sequence starting with a mother deciding that work her child has brought home from school is not up to standard in some way and proceeding to initiate some course of study with the child to remedy it.[14] The narratives we will focus on in this chapter are all sequences originating in the school rather than sequences initiated by the mothers themselves. The home end of these sequences, that aspect managed by mothers, is then part of a course of action that arises in the school setting and loops back into it.

Jamie's homework

In response to a question from the interviewer about whether Ms. Damien keeps track of how her children are doing at school, she responds:

> Well, see, [Jamie]'s only in grade three, so he really doesn't have much in the way of homework or anything. Um . . . not really. I don't know. Friday he had homework. And he did, I thought he had done it all and then on Monday morning at quarter to nine he said, "Oh, I forgot to finish my homework." I said, "well!" He said, "Well, I'll just leave it here." Which I goofed on. I should have said, "No, take it back to school. You can tell the teacher you'll do it tonight if you have to," but I said, "Oh, fine, get out! Go!" And I thought later, I shouldn't have done that, because now anytime he doesn't finish his homework he's gonna feel, or maybe I'm just picking up on that, that he can just forget it and pretend that he didn't remember to bring his books, which is not a good idea, either. So today he never finished it last night. He did some at lunchtime yesterday, but he didn't do it last night, and this morning I said, "Take them back. If the teacher says anything, tell him that you'll do it tonight, but . . ." He didn't say anything at lunchtime, so . . .

Homework as a concept can be seen as interpreting and organizing a social course of action originating in the school and looping back into it as its accountable destination. Ms. Damien's narrative preserves for the interview the local sequencing of her part in the home "loop" that accomplished Jamie's homework of last weekend. Friday Jamie had homework. The interviewer, you, and I do not have to ask what that is. We know he has brought home from school a set task that he has to complete by a given day. The task has to be done in home time, but geared to school time.

A central feature coordinating this sequence is the strongly scheduled and ineluctable character given to school time. There is no flexibility. Getting off to school is not postponed to make time for Jamie to finish his work. It is the "next school day" that marks the deadline for terminating the task. It is the schedule of the school day that marks the "home time" slots into which Jamie's task has to be inserted—the weekend, the lunch hour, and the like.

Ms. Damien uses lunchtime as a home-time slot in which the school task can be fitted. But there was too much to do, and even though she gave him some help (reported later in the interview) by reading the questions and helping him with the spelling, he went back to school again without finishing it. He did not finish it later that day. Next morning she insisted that he take his work back to the school—"and this morning I said, 'Take them back. If the teacher says anything, tell him that you'll do it tonight.'"

Though it seems she has been monitoring Jamie's homework (she knew he had brought work home; she thought he had finished it over the weekend), she does not become actively involved in managing the sequence until Jamie tells her he has forgotten to finish the task. Elsewhere in the interview, she reports that she had told her three school-age sons at the beginning of the school year that they were to be responsible for their homework. She does not get involved until Jamie discloses that he has failed to dovetail completing the task with the next school day as the deadline. Her active management of the sequence gives priority to getting the homework back to school on time rather than to completing it. Her narrative preserves her coordinative practices as part of "homework" as a social course of action focusing particularly on the production of the accountability to the school of the task to be done at home.

She is uneasy, feels she "goofed," about having allowed Jamie to make use of forgetting to finish as an excuse. Transferring responsibility to Jamie for his own homework is not a matter that has been concluded by formally notifying him at the beginning of the school year that such a transfer has been made. Somehow he is still answerable to her; she is the person he tells that he has not finished and who lets him go to school without taking his homework; she is the person (presumably) he might make excuses to; she is the person he might see as getting him out of his accountability to the school for the work he brings home. Notice, by the way, that she describes herself as "helping" Jamie with his homework, not as doing his homework with him. The character of the homework and its product as "his" is preserved.

So Jamie and his work are sent back to school, reinserted into the ongoing work organization of the classroom. The timing and the character of the work in relation to the classroom work and Jamie's part in it are a product of his and his mother's management of the "homework" sequence. Her managerial practices sustain the constitution of the product as *his* work. Though she helped him by reading and spelling out the words for him (as we are told in another passage), she does not *do* his homework. The work he takes back to school is accomplished as his work. His distinctive individual presence in the context of the school classroom is his; it bears but does not betray his mother's backstage management.

Jamie's reading

In another part of the interview with Ms. Damien, there is an interchange between the interviewer and Ms. Damien about the teacher's prescription that Jamie read twenty minutes a day.

> *Jamie's supposed to read 20 minutes a day, which is sometimes very hard to do.*
>
> *Q. So what do you mean? "Jamie's supposed to read twenty minutes a day?"*
>
> *Because of the fact that his reading is sort of below . . .*
>
> *Q. This came from the teacher?*
>
> *Yeah. So he said that he should be reading twenty minutes a day.*
>
> *Q. When did the teacher tell you this? At the . . .*
>
> *No, it was in a . . . when he brought his homework home one time. He writes the homework . . . the teacher had written what he had for homework. And one of them was twenty minutes a day for reading. I didn't even realize he was supposed to do that until I saw the note there. So . . . so I've been trying.*

What Ms. Damien says is fragmented, yet interviewer and reader have no difficulty in filling in with a background knowledge of the terms and modes of communication between parent and teacher. Ms. Damien for example does not actually complete the sentence that we take to be saying that Jamie's reading is below standard. But we "know" that is what she is saying. And though the actual nature of communication between teacher and parent is left quite ambiguous (Was the teacher's note instructing Jamie to read twenty minutes a day directed to Jamie or to Jamie's parents?), both Ms. Damien and the interviewer understand that the instructions are for Ms. Damien and her husband (and in practice it is Ms. Damien who carries them out). Ms. Damien's practices of monitoring the work Jamie brings home from school are taken for granted by the teacher who has used it as a means of communicating with Jamie's parents.

Here there is no specific task brought home from school for completion within a definite space of time. What is at issue is something more indeterminate—the child's performance at school evaluated in relation to a norm established for the class vis-à-vis which Jamie's performance is below standard. The problem is brought into the home to be resolved through work done by the child at home. While it is the child who will do the work, it is clearly the parent's responsibility to see that the work is done. There is a peculiarity here. When does a child's learning become the business of "the home" rather than the school? Under what conditions and in respect to what kinds of tasks does the school properly transfer the management of repairing a child's defective performance to the home?

Amy's French dictée

A third instance—different in some crucial ways—begins not with a note from the teacher, which Ms. Damien has clearly treated as a note to her, but with what appears to have been a comment on Amy's work, intended for Amy, which her mother, Ms. Elroyd, takes up as an issue between her and the teacher. Amy is in a French immersion program.[15]

> *Actually the teacher, when we were having this little problem in the fall, with the French dictée, and we had this one night of tears and trauma and the whole bit, and she brought her book home, they started out with four words and the teacher had written a note saying that Amy had not studied hard enough, and I really took that very personally because she's always been such a conscientious girl, she's a, she tries so hard. She's such a hard worker, type of thing. We didn't even know what this was. She came home with this little pink book with these four French words all wrong and the note was Amy didn't study hard enough. She hadn't told us anything about it, we had no idea. So I didn't know what to do, so actually my husband was upset too, so we wrote a little note, saying we're very sorry, but we don't even know what this is, we're not aware of what this is,*

we didn't know she hadn't studied, if she has to study we're more than happy to go over these words with her because she was very upset. The teacher phoned us the next night after school and explained it all and so on. From then on, granted it took her a while, she was still getting lots wrong until Christmas; it's funny, after Christmas she just clicked. She very rarely has a mistake now. We have to work though, but she wants to, that's the one thing we do every week, Sunday night, do dictée. That's interesting, because I have to give her the words, and she says, Mommy that's not how you pronounce that word, that's awful.

Here the sequence begins when Amy brings home "the little pink book with these four French words all wrong" and that note saying that "Amy didn't study hard enough." Ms. Elroyd "took that very personally because she's always been such a conscientious girl, she's a, she tries so hard. She's such a hard worker, type of thing."

Ms. Elroyd's response to the teacher, the note she and her husband write, suggests that Amy's studying is accomplished both by Amy and her parents, particularly Amy's mother. The teacher should have let the parents know if Amy was supposed to be studying, rather than finding fault with her for not doing what she had not been told to do: "So we wrote a little note, saying we're very sorry, but we don't even know what this is, we're not aware of what this is, we didn't know she hadn't studied, if she has to study we're more than happy to go over these words with her because she was very upset."

The teacher calls next evening and explains it all. So Amy's parents set up a regular plan of work to help Amy with her dictée. Indeed they go beyond this: "My husband and I are struggling with our high school French, dug out all our old textbooks, the very good English/French dictionary and so on. We struggle with it. She'll come home now and all the instructions are in French and she says 'Mommy, help me!' what are you going to do?" They confront the problem that they do not have enough knowledge of French to help their daughter properly. And they know what the "concerned parent" is expected to do: "We are getting little blurbs [from the school] 'the next course in French for parents.' If you are a concerned parent you should be trotting out there and doing that."

Clearly this school is actively promoting a commitment beyond that of merely supervising the child's performance of school tasks at home; it is proposing to parents that they might take a course that would better qualify them to do supplementary teaching at home. Ms. Elroyd's use of the term "concerned parent" shows that she knows what to do to appear within the discourse of the school as a member of that category. She formulates a course of action as an attribute of the category. Taking that course of action, "trotting out there and doing that," would warrant their classification as concerned parents. Or as instances of the type "concerned parent." Here the course of action warranting membership in the category involves parents doing work to improve their capacity to act as supplementary teachers. Does being a concerned parent contribute to their child's standing in school, over and above the ways in which their work contributes to Amy's performance in dictée?

V   The Complementary Organization of the School

At this stage of our research, it is only possible to sketch some of those aspects of the social organization of the work of the school that complement and indeed organize these episodes. Below I have made use of an interview with one third-grade teacher, Ms. Faye. Her account makes visible the ongoing social organization of work in the school in which the child is active. It is in the child's relation to this course of action that these school-initiated sequences in the home arise. In two of the instances, Jamie's reading and Amy's studying, reference is made explicitly or implicitly to some set of standards against which the child's work has been found deficient. Jamie's reading is "sort of below"; Amy has not been studying hard enough. And while Jamie's homework is not initiated with a specific message for the parents and is not a routine expectation, that too is occasioned in some way by the ongoing organization of classwork. It is in these contexts that their deficiencies are constituted as such.

In the context of that work organization and integral to it are practices of impersonal evaluation documenting the child's relative status in the class, in the school, and in some instances relative to an anonymous population defining standards for a grade level and so forth. In the primary grades, teachers may introduce evaluation in gentle and playful forms (for example, as stamps devised by the teacher, representing "kisses" for work completed and correct, and "happy faces" for work corrected), but they are nonetheless the child's apprenticeship to a documentation of the value of her work relative to that of others in the class and in the school. The school classroom as a work setting is organized around the production by the child of work enabling the teacher to evaluate her progress and status in the overall course of work established for the class for a given year.

In exploring aspects of the work organization of the classroom in these respects, we depended upon the experience of women who had worked in elementary schools as teachers. We drew on Ann Manicom's analysis of the role of the curriculum in organizing classroom work,[16] which draws on her own knowledge as a teacher, as a teacher of teachers, as well as on her ongoing research with classroom teachers in elementary schools. We also talked at length with Rosonna Tite, an elementary teacher in the Ph.D. program in our department about her own experience and how it dovetailed with what we had learned from mothers. Ann Manicom's experience is in Nova Scotia and Rosonna Tite's in a different city in Ontario than the one in which we did our work. But while the particulars might differ, we are exploring a generalized system of procedures that within a given province is specifically designed to standardize educational practices and standards. And while there are differences from province to province, the same forms of standardizing are at work. Thus Manicom and Tite helped us locate generalized curriculum procedures as an important feature of the generalizing organization of classroom work.

The curriculum sets definite objectives for each grade level. It therefore organizes the internal articulation of school classrooms from year to year. Curriculum objectives set at the provincial level and specified by the board have to be given practical determination in the context of the actual group of children that the teacher will work with. Here is how one teacher, Ms. Faye, describes the process. At the beginning of the year she sets her plans.

> *Well, for instance about the reading. I set our/my long-range plans where I would like to be generally [by the end of the school year] and then I take each particular group and with my top reading group I set goals for that top reading group that I hope I could achieve, and middle reading group and bottom reading group. Usually the most modification [over the year] has to take place with the bottom reading group because often you get children who have lost a lot more than you have anticipated over the summer and so those are the places where you do make changes.*

The teacher's professionally developed skills translate the bare bones of the curriculum into actual classroom practices, the actual course of learning that she develops for the class and, in the course of the year with an actual group of children, works through. In setting goals and carrying them out the teacher works in the context of the particular set of children she finds, with given and limited resources of materials and time. These are the "ingredients" of the classroom as an actual work organization in a particular year. It is in the context of this work organization that a child's performance becomes observable as needing home-time work and the involvement of a parent.

The progress of the class, of different groups within the class, and of individual children is regularly evaluated: "Each week I give a comprehension test for everybody, whatever the group. The bottom group sticks to quite a structured program and at the end of each unit in reading there is a group test that I give." She also tests regularly for particular reading skills: "And I try to write down on my mark book what particular skill it is that I've tested that time so I can see if someone is having trouble with sequencing or whatever." This is both an evaluation of the individual child's progress and feedback to the teacher directing her to where some additional teaching is needed by a particular child. But time is a limited resource,[17] and in this process particular children will emerge as not keeping within the range of individual variations that the teacher can handle. It is at these points that a message may go home to the parent. Documentary practices such as these provide the teacher with an ongoing map of where the children in the class are relative to one another in the context of the ongoing progress of the class relative to her design for the year. Decisions to transfer remedial work to the home, either as take-home work to be done under parental supervision (at elementary grades) or as specific instructions to the parent, are made in this context.

It is also in the context of the planned progression built into the curriculum that problems of parent-initiated "repairs" can arise. Teachers also develop methods of coordinating and managing the involvement of mothers in their children's school performance. Here is Ms. Faye's account of one such problem:

> [*Sometimes a child will*] *come home with a few errors, sometimes* [*parents*] *will jump the gun and the kids have come back and said to me, "My Mom's making me do math every night because I had four wrong on that last sheet" and really they don't need to do math at all. . . . It happened this year* [*with a little girl*]. *I explained to her that she was getting more mistakes now that her mom was helping her and she really didn't need the help and if, you know, if she wanted to do extra work I could give her a book. Her mom was making up the questions for her and I could give her a book and her mom would like that, you know, the questions wouldn't be as difficult as mom was making.*

Ms. Faye also evaluates the whole group in terms of her year's objectives for vocabulary. She does this

> *to make sure that they do have that vocabulary.* [*A parent volunteer*] *is in the classroom right now, as a matter of fact. And so I broke the vocabulary down into fifteen sections and she tests everybody. Now some children have finished the fifteen sheets long before this and other kids are still plodding along, but, ah, at the end of the year I can say that everyone has covered a part of the program.*

At the end of the school year, the children in the class are all tested using provincewide tests that evaluate their reading level against provincial norms for their grade.

The continual evaluation and documentation of children's work go two ways: into the ongoing feedback enabling the teacher to see where she is in relationship to the curriculum objectives and how she has mapped them out over the year, and into the documentation of the individual child's "performance" in the school as an accumulation of test scores or graded work books. The child's activities in the classroom become accountable as performances as the teacher observes and records those observations; the teacher uses definite procedures to evaluate the child on her progress on a particular segment of the curriculum; the ongoing work of the classroom also includes definite evaluative procedures, such as spelling tests, French dictation, tests of grade level in reading, "performances" produced in specific teaching contexts such as reading aloud in class, and so forth. Such practices, in addition to more explicit class-wide testing situations, provide for a continual monitoring of both class and individual child and produce for the individual child her documented standing in the school.[18]

In these practices, the child is being inserted into a generalized system of documenting her performance *as an individual.* The individual performance of the child is an organizational product of schooling. The child is inducted in the primary grades into the impersonal documented practices of evaluation that will organize the course she follows in school and finally into the credentialed world subtended by the documentary practices of the school. In Ms. Elroyd's narrative we can see the juncture of the individual's experience of the impersonal evaluation of Amy's standing relative to some standard or norm of what is taken to be studying enough in the class. Amy was very upset. Ms. Faye, a third-grade teacher, prefers to make a telephone call rather than write messages to parents for the child to take home: "sometimes the child is upset, especially if they, at the first of the year, when they're not sure as to what you're going to do or what you're like or . . . and then they don't read writing . . . they think that maybe they've been bad or whatever." The child moves back and forth between the home setting in which she is embedded in particularizing relationships and the school setting in which she is being inducted into a standardized curriculum and impersonal procedures that evaluate and constitute her "performance" (as a matter of record).

The child's "performance" is constituted in the documentary practices of the school. This locates a key to the power of the school over child and parents. The child's documentary standing within the school shapes the child's future within the school system and eventually in the labor market. Part of Ms. Elroyd's response to the note suggesting Amy should study harder is that it misrepresents Amy's character as someone who is not conscientious and works hard. It is not just a problem of Amy falling behind in learning the spelling of French words, but a reputational problem as well. The school's documentary accomplishment of the child's performance, individuating the child in the context of generalizing standards, would seem to be a key to the power of the school over child and parents.

But home and parents, and mothers in particular, are also invisibly at work in the production of the child's documented school performance. As we have seen, they monitor their children's work. All mothers we have talked to report scrutinizing the work their children bring home from school. Some fathers are also interested. Ms. Faye talks about the uses of the report card by parents to check out whether there are areas in which they could give extra help. Teachers and parents take for granted that parents will do the kind of work described by Ms. Damien and Ms. Elroyd in the earlier narratives. But it is work done at home under varying conditions. Elsewhere we have written about how the exigencies of shift work for one mother disorganize the completion of the sequence of monitoring the child's work, finding a problem, and working with the child to improve her performance in the relevant area.[19] In the instances we have focused on here, there are also great differences in the conditions under which Ms. Damien and Ms. Elroyd support their children's school performance, for while Amy is an only child, Jamie has four brothers, one of them an infant, and Ms. Damien talks about the problems of getting twenty minutes reading time with Jamie when the other children have to be dealt with. Such differences as these are communicated to the school setting only in their consequences for the child's school performance. There is an invisible transaction between the invisible conditions of women's work as mothers in the home and the ongoing documentary accomplishment of the child's performance at school.

Here then we can begin to see the context of the "concerned parent" conception of which Amy's parents are so conscious. From the point of view of the school, the support that parents give is a resource relevant to the school's capacity to realize its objectives.[20] This relationship has a fully developed ideological ground that is part of the professional consciousness of teachers, the currency of their professional talk about the relationship of children's background and their "performance" in school. It also has its correlate in the discourse of mothering, which defines mothers' role in relation to their children's schooling.[21]

And here there seems to be a difference between Ms. Damien and Ms. Elroyd. For Ms. Elroyd works with a discursive procedure that apparently equates "Amy studying" with herself and/or her husband managing that process, and she and her husband are prepared to do a considerable amount of work around Amy's school performance. Ms. Damien, on the other hand, has verbally at least transferred responsibility for homework to Jamie and is concerned in part at least in this episode to make that transfer stick.

VI The Third Stage

These are preliminary explications of the social organization of schoolwork complementing the mothers' narratives. They direct us toward further investigation beyond the particular school to the bureaucratic and administrative structure in which each school is embedded and the part the school plays in the overall ecology of education in a given context.

We could imagine an entirely different situation than this in which the school would assume complete responsibility for the "production" of the child's performance. Parents would hold that it is the school's business to teach their children and that they have no part in it. They would expect the school to do remedial work with the child if she or he is falling behind. If Amy is not studying hard enough, it is because the school is not supervising her studies properly. If Jamie needs an additional twenty minutes reading a day, it is the business of the school to provide this. The reliance upon mothers to supplement the work of the school transfers the contingencies of her work to the child's documented performance in the school. We asked Ms. Faye what difference cutting her class numbers in half would make to her work. She said that the difference would be "mainly because of the amount of individual attention that you give the child. My goodness, that's the key, isn't it? . . . If you can get right there when someone has a difficulty and you can iron it out right then, it certainly makes things far easier for the child."

Given a different deployment of resources, much of the work of picking up on an individual child's slippage in terms of the overall objectives for the class could be done by the teacher. Thus a child's "performing" below grade level does not of itself point to calling on parents to supplement the work of the school. The transfer to the home of certain forms of educational tasks means that the teacher has decided *not* to do them. This is not a decision that the teacher makes anew on every occasion, nor is it a decision that is made out of context in terms of ideals of teaching practice and the like. It is rather a decision that must be made in the context of the actual conditions of the class, its size, the amount of additional time the teacher has to give to the child who is "behind," the professionally or locally established norms about when it is appropriate to pass "problems" located in the classroom into the home for repair, including, of course, what types of problems parents may be viewed as competent to undertake. It is a question of the practical organization of the classroom, incorporating the curriculum as a kind of production schedule.

The concrete plan for realizing the curriculum for a given grade level and its realization as a practical matter over the school year are carried out with a given group of children, in a given budgetary context, and under given school policies. A given school interprets the curriculum in particular local contexts, with a particular group of teachers, with particular numbers of children, with ratios of children to teacher that are set by the board and that determine what personnel resources are available to the principal, and with a particular collection of children coming from particular families.[22] Decisions about allocating teachers to children, allocating children to classes, creating different kinds of mixtures, setting curriculum objectives for the year for a given class, coordinating the products of the classes of one year, and so forth are made at school level. The production process in terms of levels of documented performance of children ties the school as a whole into the secondary schools it routinely "feeds."

VII Conclusion

Of course this is only a preliminary sketch. It is intended to demonstrate an analytic design in which we move from the experience of women at work as mothers in relation to children's schooling to an explication of the school organization and the administrative relations of the state of which that school organization is a local agent. The aim of analysis has been to disclose a social organization implied but not spoken of in the original narratives, a social organization that is presupposed but not explicit. This strategy has constructed a perspective on school organization, taking as its base what the women we spoke to knew of and told us about, namely, their own work. The procedure we worked with took two women's narratives of their child's bringing work home from school. Our investigation sketched, in a preliminary way, the socially organized work of the classroom in which such initiatives on the part of the teacher arose. The homework process loops through the home, is somehow managed there, and returns to school to be inserted into the classroom work process as part of what becomes the child's documented performance. The explication of this piece of a social relation opens up for further exploration aspects of its determinations in the administration of education by the school board. So we move from the particular experience and the particular relationships in which women are active to the organization of schooling that, among other matters, at the elementary level is in the business of producing differences among children articulated to the secondary division of educational labor and hence eventually to their credentialed status on the labor market.

I could be talking about, in a sense I am talking about, the way in which a traditional division of labor between women and men in the home has been foundational to the development of the North American educational system, the way in which the division has been built into the system as its working "assumption." Insofar as fathers are now in some places playing an increasing role in this work, their role takes over or represents a new division of a role already established for the family and vested earlier in women. That the schools make these assumptions has made it practically and emotionally difficult for women with small children to choose to lead their lives differently. Bringing up children and working with children to articulate their lives to the standard expectations of the schooling process, and particularly of middle-class schooling, are demanding. These operations draw on kinds of time that are not easily defined; they draw on kinds of time not easily plotted into the schedules of paid employment. They have presupposed and still, I think, presuppose the availability of women's labor in the home. Whether women's labor in the home is done by women or not—and regardless of important shifts made by some men in participating in domestic labor, the evidence is that overall the changes are minimal—it always has the character of being expendable without monetary cost. The expendability of women's labor without cost to the school system has been a major support to the level of functioning of schools—again particularly of middle-class schools. If this work is not done by women it has to be done by someone. If it is not done or is not done at the same level, then labor is withdrawn from the school and the school cannot function at the same level. Teachers cannot teach the way they have learned to value themselves and each other for. Changes in the neighborhood, the introduction in a middle-class area of housing for lower-income families, have consequences for how the school will function. Every teacher of experience is aware of these dependences.

This method of inquiry explores relations of ruling from within the working experience of women as subjects. It opens up from within the experience of those who do this work in family-household contexts the relations that frame, organize, and determine their everyday practices and cares. At no point do we lose sight of women as active in these relations. At no point do we reduce them to effects of social processes. The particularities of their experiences, their styles of work, their actual conditions are preserved. They are not reduced to types or variables. Aspects of their accounts have here been addressed as they disclose the absence of their complement in the organization of the schools their children go to. Schools are organized professionally and bureaucratically. The particular school is organized as part of a system of schools within a school board and provincially. Its teachers are trained and certified members of a profession. Viewing these relations from the standpoint of women indicates lines of stress and disjuncture. For parents, it is the child who is at stake, and the child's education is what they work for. In the school, the child is individuated within an impersonal system, governed by professional and bureaucratic organization, informed by an ideology of child development regulating, humanizing, and giving coherence to practices of schooling that individuate the product, the graded child. At the elementary school level, it is in practice generally women teachers who articulate, many brilliantly and with extraordinary care, the particular child to the generalizing system of education. The intersection of these two sets of interests and concerns in the social organization of women's work in the home is integral to our educational system. This has been and remains a major moral constraint on women with small children. When we look at studies that show us that women still do the biggest part of the work in the home, even when they also work outside, we should not think just in terms of men's resistance to taking over "their share" of the housework and parenting. The educational system exercises a huge leverage over parents through their care of children, and over mothers in particular. In the last fifty or seventy years, mothers have been inculcated with an understanding of themselves and their responsibilities that is all encompassing vis-à-vis their children's fate in schools. We have learned a totalizing responsibility for what happens to our children in the school context. It is an ideology, a discourse, that mobilizes our work and care, that takes no account of the realities of the conditions of that work and care (that we work full time, are single parents, etc.), that takes no account of the way in which resources are allocated within the bureaucratic processes of school governance and within the policy processes articulating educational policy to the interests of capital, that takes no account therefore of differences in the workings of the schools. This is a major site for anguish and anxiety, as Griffith and I can testify. Such strategies of opening up the relations within which women's work as mothers is embedded create possibilities of exploring further the differences in racial and class experience of women in such contexts and of grasping the organization of these oppressions in ways that expand our general knowledge of how these relations are organized and how they work.

Notes

1. E. H. Gombrich, *Means and Ends: Reflections on the History of Fresco Painting* (London: Thames and Hudson, 1976).
2. Note that we were not focused at all upon the school achievement of the individual child, and the teachers and administrators of the school did not know which family of which child was involved in our study.
3. For expansion of Marx's conception of social relation, see Dorothy E. Smith, "On sociological description: A method from Marx," in *Human Studies* 4 (1981): 313–37.
4. Alison I. Griffith and Dorothy E. Smith, "Coordinating the uncoordinated: How mothers manage the school day," paper presented at the American Sociological Association, Washington, D.C., August 1985.
5. Ann Manicom proposes this interpretation in her Ph.D. dissertation in process, in the Department of Sociology in Education, Ontario Institute for Studies in Education.
6. See Marj Devault, "Talking and listening from women's standpoint: Feminist strategies for analyzing interview data," paper prepared for the Annual Meeting of the Society for the Study of Symbolic Interaction, New York, 1986.
7. It is this juncture that is, of course, of special interest in the exploration of class.
8. In fact we had more interviews than these because we started originally in a different city, but were eventually denied permission to interview in the schools there by the school board and had to begin all over again elsewhere.
9. Here, of course, at the very center of our methods, was a typifying procedure built into the very substance of the interviews. I am not sure

what to do about this, if anything. But I want to distinguish it from the subsequent introduction of codes or typologies to handle the varieties of topics and their treatment that are characteristically produced in open-ended interviews. The typification of the day is an interesting device and one to be explored further. It clearly operated to allow respondents to collect a range of instances and bring them within one frame. For our purposes it was not essential to discriminate an actual from a typical day. Indeed it was the range of instances that was more to our purpose.

10. There is an ordinary editing process which is controlled by switching the tape recorder on and off during the meeting in which the interview takes place. The talk that went on before the interview started and after it ended is omitted. If, during the interview, someone comes to the door, a child interrupts, or the telephone rings, the interviewer may turn the tape recorder off. These recordable passages of talk which were part of the original encounter have already been edited out.

11. Ludwig Wittgenstein, *Philosophical Investigations* (New York: Macmillan, 1953), p. 48e.

12. This relationship between how an informant talks and how her talk makes sense (to her) conforms to the documentary method of interpretation, where the sense of talk depends' upon a background knowledge of the setting in which talk goes on and of which it is part. The developing talk both produces and is read in terms of the setting it develops. See Harold Garfinkel on the documentary method of interpretation in *Studies in Ethnomethodology*, chapter 3.

13. For as George Herbert Mead emphasizes, the socially oriented actions of individuals are formed and have as their distinctive character an articulation to the foregoing actions of another or others and a projection of the other's or others' response.

14. Alison Griffith and Dorothy E. Smith, "The monitoring-repair sequence: Mother's work for school," paper presented at the Women and the Invisible Economy Conference, Institut Simone de Beauvoir, Montreal, February 1985.

15. Canada has two official languages, French and English. French immersion schooling programs have been developed in the public school system and are popular with parents who want to give their children opportunities for jobs in or in relation to the public service in Canada.

16. Ann Manicom, Ph.D. dissertation in progress, Department of Sociology in Education, Ontario Institute for Studies in Education.

17. See again Manicom's discussion in her dissertation-in-progress.

18. See James Heap's analysis of how children's reading "performances" are accomplished in classroom contexts. James Heap, "What counts as reading: Limits to certainty in assessment," *Curriculum Inquiry* 10, no. 3 (1980): 265–92; and idem, "Discourse in the production of classroom knowledge: Reading lessons," *Curriculum Inquiry* 15, no. 3 (1985): 245–79.

19. Griffith and Smith, "The monitoring-repair sequence."

20. This is also the viewpoint from which arises an interest in how a given sample might represent a population of parents.

21. See Alison Griffith and Dorothy E. Smith, "Constructing cultural knowledge: Mothering as discourse," paper presented at the Women and Education Conference, University of British Columbia, Vancouver, B.C., June 1986.
22. See Nancy Jackson, "Stress on schools + stress on families = distress for children," Canadian Teachers' Federation, Ottawa, 1982.

PART FOUR

Textual Politics

I think of the enterprise that is laid out here as a journey.[1] It begins with the most general formulation of the barriers to our speaking and being heard as women, the barriers to the creation of a knowledge, an art, a literature, a politics, for ourselves. It begins with addressing the conditions of a public discourse among women. In part 2 we moved from this general critique to the special problems of the forms of consciousness of our society which sociology creates and then to a consideration of how to pose questions differently, and how to think and write a sociology from the standpoint of women. In part 3, on research strategies, we got down to more immediately practical questions of how to do research as an inquiry from the standpoint of women. In this final part, we turn again to more general issues of the textual discourses in which our consciousness of society and of our struggles as women is formed. But we do not come full circle. If you have been reading these papers in the order of the chapters of the book, you have come to a place that was not yet made at the beginning. The last chapter returns us to the world outside the text, the world of a women's movement, the scope of which has been transformed in the ten years or so between the first and last of these chapters. The texts of this journey had and have their context. They were worked out as part of a political as well as a discursive enterprise. They addressed political as well as discursive problems. This last chapter, "Beyond Methodology: Institutionalization and its Subversion," returns us to the political dimensions and implications of our textual practices. When we do so, other problems and questions come into view than those we addressed or could address at the outset of this journey. Questions are raised about our susceptibility to capture by the relations and apparatuses of ruling or to the replication of those forms in our own textual practices. Though the practice of a sociology for women offers a discourse organizing different relations among subjects than those created by the relations of ruling, we should not delude ourselves that a critique vested exclusively in texts has political force as such. This is a problem as much for the work presented here as for any other.

Note

1. For the part title I have taken the term "textual politics" from the title of Toril Moi, *Sexual/Textual Politics: Feminist Literary Theory* (London and New York: Methuen, 1985), though I have used the term to shift away from the sense of textual as solely the written to textual as mediating social relations.

6

Beyond Methodology:
Institutionalization and its Subversion

I Discourse as Practices

When we write letters, we have no problem seeing the text as a way of relating to another or others. I have suggested in chapter 2 that sociological texts characteristically relate us to others and even to ourselves as objects. From there we have gone on to work out methods of thinking and writing texts that will relate us to each other in ways that preserve the presence of subjects in the text as knowers. In part 3, research strategies were proposed that gave practical embodiment to these theoretical proposals. Here I want to take up consciously the problems and questions of how our political discourses and texts organize relations among us.

Our major political discovery is expressed in the equation the personal *is* the political. This equation locates an oppression invading our most intimate relationships, the immediate particularities of our lives, the power relations between persons. We have seen that intimate and personal experiences of oppression are anchored in and sustained by a patriarchal organization of ruling. Our political vision has denied, for the first time, the distinction between the powers of the public and the private domains. The method of thinking and writing sociology that I have put forward here has intended the *systematic* development of a consciousness that traces these relations from this standpoint, the standpoint of she who stands at the beginning of her acts of consciousness.

We have sought in these pages the methods of thinking and inquiry that will construct a knowledge of society and social relations from women's standpoint. Note that we have sought to do more than opening the social scientific discourse to women's voices and concerns. We have gone after something more radical—a sociology, a social science, an inquiry into a totality of social relations beginning from a site outside and prior to textual discourses. Women's standpoint has been explored here as specifically subversive of the standpoint of a knowledge of ourselves and our society vested in the relations of ruling.

Throughout we have emphasized the organization of power in texts and the relations of ruling mediated by texts. Texts are the medium of a knowledge that is a property of organization rather than of individual.[1] The consciousness of who we are, of our social relations, which standard sociological methods of thinking produce, participates in a standpoint within the relations of ruling, creating a knowledge apt for ruling. By contrast, we have insisted on a knowledge that assumes we are part of the world that we explore and make visible; we have seen that the knowledge we create becomes part of that world as a constituent of whatever relations it is articulated to; we have seen that our understanding can be turned to an examination of our own practices, our own relations, indeed that it "naturally" incorporates such reflections; we have sought to make a sociology that will extend and expand people's everyday knowledge of how things work.

This feminist sociology aims to display the actual, ongoing coordering of practical activities in and through which we daily and nightly bring our world into being. When I use the term "practical" I do not mean "practical" as contrasted with what is of the mind, impractical, merely ideal. I think of "mind" also as actual, temporally ordered practices, and the atemporal modes in which we think we think and in which we write our thought as specifically textual practices. The notions of practices and actual bear no special theoretical weight. By practices I do not mean a new and special class of actions. I mean rather to direct our gaze toward the ongoing coordering of activities that brings our world into being, toward how, to use the ethnomethodological term, it is "accomplished." The emphasis is on the "how," and the notion of practices is intended to capture the ongoing of our doing of what we, generally, know how to do. And when I use the terms "actual," or "actuality," I mean to direct our gaze outside the text to that world in which the text also exists as it is brought into being as a material form in the hands of the reader who is reading somewhere. Such a gaze is not easy to bring off. It is hard to learn to see what we so much take for granted as we do what we know so very well how to do. But seeing this way has the capacity to write a sociology that shifts outside the relations of ruling to a stance from which the relations and powers of the world we live become visible from the sites of people's actual experience.

In considering the textual politics of a consciousness of society, the same method applies. The abstractions that ordinarily limit our thinking are substructed to find the actual practices of actual people which they both express and conceal. We can see this method as a particular way of addressing the contexts in which we write and speak. For example, de Beauvoir has written of immanence as characteristic of women and transcendence as characteristic of men.[2] Under what conditions of the social organization of daily and nightly life does it make sense to write or speak of immanence and transcendence as gendered? What gender division of labor is the background that we take for granted in eking out the sense of such abstractions? The relations of ruling have a strongly gendered character. Power of various kinds has come to mean for men the entry into an economic world of rational calculation and management or into a technical and scientific world of the expansion of systematic knowledges. It has meant the deployment of skills informed by such systematic knowledges. It has meant the application of systematically rational modes of theorizing and inquiry in a wide variety of settings, bringing politics, literature, art, and warfare under their dominion. These expansions of men's powers in the elaboration and expansion of the relations of ruling in this mode were built first on women's exclusion from the extralocal organization of market relations. But men's commitment to the daily practices of the relations of ruling also required that they be wrapped and cushioned against an encounter with their bodies. If their bodies had needs—to eat, to have sex—these must be met without the delays, hesitations, and obstructions that would require them to work at meeting needs, to do some thinking, to take some time out to overcome obstructions. Men's daily environment had to be brought into line with the practices of an existence out of this world. And I am not just talking about mathematicians or historians, I am talking about stockbrokers, managers, and advertising copywriters. There has been and still is an interdependence here between the capacity of men to exist and work in extralocal relations and women's practical production of the conditions of such an existence and such work.[3] Such are the actual practices underlying the abstractions of transcendence and immanence, of the "universality" of men versus the "particularity" of women.

So when we speak of a sociology for women, we must recognize that we have not yet moved to address the organization of actual relations that such a conception might direct us to, let alone the relations within which it finds its contemporary and actual practice. To do so we must look at the social character of discourse rather differently than we usually do. The notion of discourse used here derives from Foucault.[4] But because we are talking sociology, not philosophy, we want to address discourse as a conversation mediated by texts that is not a matter of statements alone but of actual ongoing practices and sites of practices, the material forms of texts (journals, reviews, books, conferences, classrooms, laboratories, etc.), the methods of producing texts, the reputational and status structures, the organization of powers intersecting with other relations of ruling in state agencies, universities, professional organizations, and the like. Attention to discourse as socially organized does not discard or invalidate the statements, conventions, and knowledges that its texts bear. Rather texts are understood as embedded in and organizing relations among subjects active in the discourse. We are talking then about actual people entering into actual relations with one another. Sociology as a form of consciousness ceases to be an abstract fluid entity that somehow leaks into people's minds and can be seen as ongoing and actively produced and maintained in relations mediated by texts. Institutional forms of discourse create relations between subjects appearing as a body of knowledge existing in its own right. These externalized forms of consciousness are specific forms of social relations, accomplished in determinate socially organized practices.

II The Problem of Institutional Capture

In the work I have done around a sociology for women, I began with the actual problems of doing research for women. I worked with a group of other women to establish a research center for women. Our conception was to invert the standard relationship whereby women (and men) became resources for and objects of knowledge available in the universities and the discourses of the academy and the profession. We wanted to make knowledge and skills available to women. We undertook a variety of enterprises; we worked with women in single-industry towns in researching their own needs and situation and

helped them organize first a conference to bring together their thinking and then a much larger and politically oriented conference to make
a statement of their common needs and concerns. We arranged a series
of workshops between women's groups in the city we worked in and
women working in the various, largely state-funded organizations concerned with immigrants. We wrote broadsheets disclosing how government policies and changes in policies were directly affecting women.
We helped native women organize a workshop for native women. All
these enterprises were buttressed by research and depended upon research being well done. We did not already *know* what women's concerns would be. It was our business to help women investigate and discover them. We insisted on a method that examined women's local
spaces and that women themselves could learn from one another directly. But we also insisted on an analysis that anchored those experiences in the political, economic, and social processes that shaped them.
Women's experiences and concerns in their everyday lives were not independent of determinations in relations beyond them. It was our business also to give them a handle on these. That meant, of course, a more
specialized work of research and reflection that complemented and
conversed with the research women did in their local communities. Part
of our problem was that we did not, in spite of our training, know how
to work in this way. While we had skills, such as the ethnographic skills
of an anthropologist, we found that the methods of social science did
not produce material that would orient toward the women themselves
as subjects. The methods we knew would only do the kind of job we
were trying to get away from; they would only turn women into objects
and produce their lives in abstractions. These were methods that had
their uses when we had to write briefs, when we had to write within the
conventions of the relations of ruling, to struggle on that terrain.
Which of course we had to do. But we did not have a method that
worked the other way, that explicated how the society worked for those
implicated in it, to whom its workings were otherwise invisible. As they
were, of course, for all of us.

The enterprise of making a "sociology for women" came out of that
experience. It attempted to rethink the epistemology of sociology so
that we could have a sociology that would write its texts the other way
round. That is what I have tried to work through. It is a strategy that
takes as central that women should speak from themselves and their
experience and that the communities of their oppression are to be discovered in a discourse that can expand their grasp of their experience
and the power of their speech by disclosing the relations organizing
their oppression. Such a sociology presupposes a constant process of

discovery from within, from differing bases and matrices of consciousness. It aims at the making of a discourse that is always being rediscovered and remade from a standpoint that is always beyond, outside, discourse, always pressing on discourse for a means to speak, explore, find, know, map, organize, struggle. And I emphasize the making of a sociology, not merely of particular applications to particular problems, because the sociology we have inherits the conceptual and research methods of its site in the circles of men's ruling and "looks" at the world from the standpoint of the relations of ruling. Not from below, from underneath, from outside. Not from the standpoint of a lived actuality, an actual subject.

But a research center organized in such a way could not survive for a very simple reason. It could not get funding. We tried in various ways. When I left the city in which that center was founded, a group of us tried to form, within the Ontario Institute for Studies in Education, a Wollstonecraft Research Group dedicated similarly to work for women in education. That too foundered on the same rock. Enterprises with the orientation toward what we called "preorganizational" work, work that enabled women to grasp the power contexts of their lives and situations, were not the kinds of enterprises that the state or other agencies of ruling would fund. The devious ways in which earlier our intentions could be disguised were thwarted increasingly by a state that became increasingly adept at designing its funding conditions so that the voluntary organizations of the women's movement worked in a subcontractual relationship to government. A detailed examination of this process in the case of an immigrant women's employment support and advocacy group shows how the funding procedures shaped the functions of the organization so that the advocacy dimension of its commitment fell away and it came to operate as an extension of government rationalizing of the market for immigrant women's labor.[5]

Though the particulars differ, they are the same relations of ruling that had captured the issue of the beating of women by their spouses or partners of which Patricia Morgan has written. She describes the expansion of the state's "social problems apparatus" since the 1960s, identifying the state practices that incorporate the issues of a political movement into what I have called the relations of ruling. Bureaucratization fragments issues of class opposition, converting political into social demands. Issues and interests are incorporated into the institutionalized forms of electoral constituencies, interest and pressure groups, and the like. Professionalization uses knowledge to restructure "collective noncapitalist forms of organization" into hierarchical strata, detaching them from the movements they originate in and connecting them to the relations of ruling. Professionalization also individuates the collective construction of issues and problems.[6] This was Catherine Russell's experience when she went to the conference on family violence and found herself making the transition from the professional stance, impersonal, external, to taking up a standpoint among the oppressed.[7] The organization of professional knowledge is more than a guarantee of standards, more than a monopoly of knowledge and skill, it is a monopolization of control within a dominant class. It ensures that bases of organization do not arise out of the discovery of personal troubles; it ensures that personal troubles become no more than public issues framed and contained within the public media, and that they do not become the bases of political organization uncontrolled by the institutional structures of state and relations of ruling.

Looking back over the last fifty years, we can see that these practices of control within a dominant class were developed in relation to the working class. Institutionally differentiated spheres were developed as professional and or bureaucratic forms that managed different aspects of the issues and problems arising for people as a total experience of living. Housing comes under one jurisdiction; public health another; mental illness yet another; issues of wages and working conditions are incorporated into elaborated structures in which class struggle is displaced onto struggles within legal and bureaucratic contexts; women's domestic situation is parceled out into issues of housing, mental illness, poverty, welfare, child abuse, and neglect. If class is less visible today as a basis of struggle, it is in part at least because the institutional organization of ruling has dispersed class over a range of institutional sites.[8] The way we conceptualize class as the third party in a pluralistic political pantheon of gender, race, and class takes this dispersion of the sites of class for granted. It is the discursive expression of what can be reassembled as a distillation of relations that have become invisible other than as differences in socioeconomic level. But the living is always actual and always total experience.

I have continued to find it difficult to write about class from the standpoint of women and in ways that will display for us dimensions of the practical assumptions and conditions of our texts and discourses. The terminology of class has been used in political contexts to invalidate the speaker. To call someone a "bourgeois feminist," for example, was to introduce a rule depriving the voice of the woman so named of all authority. This is a trivial usage that depletes the capacity of the concept to do more vital and important work for us. We need to translate the power it has for working-class women to name the oppressive relations which are immediately their lived experience into a corresponding analytic capacity that would explicate the relations governing all our lives. As a member of the tripartite "gender, race, and class," the concept of class does useful critical and political work within the women's movement. As used in this way, the concept of class lacks the analytic power we need to grasp the substructure of those fractures in our capacity to say "we," meaning "we women," that are too deep to be papered over. In our work as feminists within or on the margins of the institutional forms of society, we experience constraints, barriers, and betrayals that bound and transform our political projects and their accomplishments. In various ways, the institutional forms confine the boldness of our thinking, the adventures of our knowledge, the formation of a feminist social consciousness, the redistribution of resources to organize the unorganized, and the full completion of the enterprise of liberation. Here too is class; class is a feature of the institutional process, structuring and constraining our struggles for liberation; class is part of our political experience, but as yet we do not know how to specify and analyze its dimensions.

Our active participation in the institutional orders sustaining the development of knowledge and thinking by women for women ties us into this order of relations. We find, whether we want it or not, that somehow the practices of our art come to take on the distinctive character that they do as we participate in relations that are not fully within the scope of our knowledge and certainly not fully within the scope of our control. We find, whether we like it or not, that our relationships with those who are the "subjects" of our research are always ambiguous. In the contexts of our work, we are going to take what we have learned from them and make use of it in contexts in which they do not speak; this remains despite the care we take to return what we write to them, to check for accuracy and faithfulness with them. We are still not doing this work for them; we still have funding obligations to meet, reports to write that are part of them, academic papers to produce that are also part of our funding obligations (particularly if we are ever to be funded another time around).

We are also responsible to the institution within which we work. The school phase of Alison Griffith's and my research on mothering and schooling requires the permission of school boards. Their permission is given partly on the reputation of our institute. If we should use our knowledge of the school system to do "preorganizational" work with the mothers and fathers of schoolchildren in the districts we studied, taking up some of the issues our explications might raise for parents, we would be in trouble not just with the leadership of the institute but with other researchers who also depend on the reputation of the institute and its researchers. In our home city, Toronto, when for a time a progressive left-wing caucus was in control of the school board, parents were helped to organize to represent their *collective* interests. Our research could serve organizations of this kind. But such organization was immediately done away with when a caucus more to the right was mobilized and was successful in winning a majority on the board. Educational research in the schools has to have the permission of the board. It has to be framed and organized in terms of the methods and practices of institutionalized educational discourse and hence takes up an "administrative" or professional educators standpoint. It does not examine the schools from the standpoint of parents, let alone mothers.

These are some of the constraints. Others arise as the reputation of the professional herself is vested in her standing as author within discourse. Her standing there depends upon how her work is read and taken up by others. Her standing in the academic setting she works in, her capacity to get grants to do research, and so forth depend to a large degree upon her standing in professional discourses external to her work setting. Her individual standing in her profession contributes to the overall standing of the institution of which she is a member. These relations interlock and support each other. Awareness of and responsibility to them are what makes a professional. Awareness of and responsibility to them contain one's work as a researcher within the relations of ruling. Research into how schooling depends and is imposed upon mothers could be used to contribute directly to the collective strength of parents vis-à-vis the school system. But such bold contravention of professional constraints would be a one-time-only operation. It would risk the beachhead in the institutions of ruling established by women for women in the area researched. An educational system is in the business of producing differentiation; it produces inequalities of race, class, and gender in the normal (though not the official) course of doing its business; an organization of parents knowledgeable about how educational inequalities are produced would be threatening; education, like other institutions functioning nondemocratically in democratic society, depends on ignorance. The professional and administrative structures as well as the practices of professional and academic discourse interlock to prevent knowledge leaking out to form the social consciousness of those who do not participate in the relations of ruling.

III   The Accommodation of the Discourse of Women to the Relations of Ruling

Among women, we have created, perhaps for the first time in history, a public discourse. We established media independent of the institutionalized media of the relations of ruling, and we have also invaded, however, marginally, the relations of ruling themselves. We hold sites for women's studies in universities and community colleges; we have made substantive inroads in some disciplines at least; we have become a recognizable political constituency and active as political agents. At the same time our discourses have become organized by the relations of ruling, observing their characteristic procedures and contouring themselves to their fractures and breaks. Teresa di Lauretis in her introduction to a collection of papers exploring "the relation of feminist politics to critical studies," located them at "a time when the women's movement is being both integrated and quietly suffocated within the institutions, when the feminist critique is partially accommodated within some academic disciplines and emarginated otherwise, when feminism is nudged into the pockets of the economy with one hand, and of the intelligentisa with the other."[9]

Though we have created a public discourse among women that is in the present historical context a major new achievement, it has not been without the costs of an accommodation to the ruling apparatus. The emergence of the ruling apparatus organizes social consciousness in new ways. They are forms of consciousness that are properties of organization and relations rather than of individuals. In formal organizations, systems of information collection and storage constitute an organizational knowledge; decision processes, analyses, evaluation, and judgment can be vested in procedures and formulas in which "subjectivity" intervenes in a purely technical manner; or reasoning, judgment, and decision making are practices of highly trained minds that know how to reason, judge, and decide within the parameters of the organization and the realities its information processing systems create. The great textually mediated discourses of science, social science, and the humanities in their different ways have also come to form systems of knowledge that are properties of discourse rather than of individuals. When Annette Kolodny describes how she learned as a Jew and a woman to read Milton, she is describing the ways in which she appropriated the competences of the discourse of literature to which as a graduate student she was a neophyte practitioner.[10] The construction of the canon creates a body of "literature" as contrasted with other kinds of writing, as well as methods of interpretation that constitute a

mode of discursive consciousness over and above the individual subjects who learn, practice, reproduce, and extend its forms.

In sociology, an important dimension of the construction has been
the conventions that have eliminated "bias," seeking to create a consciousness of society independent of the ways in which particular individuals are situated in the world, and to construct, as I have shown
elsewhere, an objective knowledge that, appearing to view the world
from no place, in fact operates from the standpoint of the patriarchal
relations of ruling. The importance of "theory" to feminists has been,
it seems, the importance of creating the terms that will "run" discourse
from a standpoint independent of that of particular individuals speaking to one another. The "structural" metaphor captures precisely this
development of a discursive process, the statements of which are its
properties rather than expressions of subjects.[11] The conventions, the
statements, the phenomenal universe of objects, and the methods of
discourse make up the textual dimension of a social organization that
constitutes a social consciousness independent of particular actual individuals. To participate in such discourse, we take on its methods of
speaking and writing texts. We stand outside the world in which we live
and in which that discourse, its texts, and its statements are brought
into being.

We find in our political struggles, as well as in our intellectual and
cultural struggles, that we move and have to move onto this terrain. As
we evolve a discourse among women, it crystallizes the issues and concerns of those of us who got there first and have defined the types of
statements, the relevances, the phenomenal universe, and the conventions that give it a social form independent of the particular individuals
who are active in it. The entities we have fashioned—abortion, rape,
pornography, violence against women, sexual harassment—define the
consciousness of the women's movement. C. Wright Mills argued that
the political purpose of sociology should be the transformation of private troubles into public issues. In being converted into public issues,
private troubles are given new and determinate forms in the context of
public media. The relevances they incorporate are those of the women
who were in on their making. Issues become externalized. Their character is negotiated in institutional contexts. Their formulations are already accommodated to legal, administrative, and professional niches.
As women's issues occupy the terrain of ruling, even though only its
margins, they conform to its boundaries, and the breaks and fissures
that underlie it. If the discourse of women is a discourse of white
women, it is in large part because it has become organized in institutional contexts that have excluded black women and native women as

a routine accomplishment of how they work. In chapter 1, I described an educational system that excluded women from positions of power and influence as a routine feature of its functioning. The same or similar effects exclude black women, native women, women of other than the dominant classes.

As women's discourse becomes institutionalized, it is built upon exclusions that it has not produced but takes for granted. As its objects and issues are given fixity and become the world in common known in the texts of women's public discourse, these exclusions structure that discourse actively but invisibly.

> the category human has no meaning
> when spoken in white.[12]

The relevances crystallized in the discourse of white women may overlap with but are not the same as the relevances of black women. Curious hybridizations mark these underlying fractures. For example, black women have wanted the abortion issue to be linked to the issue of the use of sterilization in white policies of genocide. The issues crystallizing in the women's movements of societies very different from ours are also very different. The array of issues establishes a standpoint external to us, organizing our texts, organizing the relevances of our thinking. In our theoretical and political texts, they become presences and agents subordinating the speaking of women's actualities. Women's experience thus interpreted is abstracted from the local contexts of its actual political and social connectedness, becoming an instance of the textual entity. Interpreting the torture of women political prisoners in Latin America, for example, as an instance of violence against women detaches it from the contexts of political struggle and organization against an oppression common to women and men, from women's part in resistance to military dictatorship, from the tortures of men political prisoners that are also sexual.[13]

IV Subverting Institutionalization

The sociology I have wanted to create is meant to subvert this process of institutionalizing both feminism and Marxism. It proposes discourse organized differently, where knowledge does not become a body of knowledge, where issues are not crystallized, where the conventions and relevances of discourse do not assume an independent authority over against its speakers and readers. It would have the capability of continually opening up a different experience of the world, as women who have not yet spoken now speak. Each speaker from a new site discloses a new problematic for inquiry. It is in this continually opening up that the sociology I have wanted has its home and sense. But the possibility of its expanding as a consciousness of society from the standpoint of women, the possibility of going beyond particular cases to exploring the relations of ruling and the relations of capital and their internal articulations from the standpoint of women, depends, as I have tried to show in chapter 4, on discovering from within the expanded relations that contain, organize, and provide the dynamic interconnections linking our one-sided knowledge of our own existence into a larger knowledge of a historical process in which we are active and to which we are captive.

That larger knowledge of a historical process has Marx as its primary theorizer and original methodologist. Feminists have made a sustained attack on Marx, for the most part, displaying an extraordinarily superficial knowledge of Marx's lifetime of thinking and research. But I do not want to engage with those criticisms here. In part, they are justified, but for the most they are beside the point. The power of Marx's theory and analysis is in its capacity to explicate the dynamic of capitalist relations and forces that are continually at work in the ongoing transformations of our everyday lives. Structuralism has attempted to rewrite Marxism as a theoretical procrustean bed to which the actualities of our experience are to be brutally tailored. But this is at odds with Marx's own work, which never separates itself from the everyday realities in which the relations it explores are realized and which indeed bring them into being. The volumes of *Capital,* volume 1 in particular, are continually enriched with accounts of the everyday lives organized by the relations it explores. As Marx and Engels write of class in *The Communist Manifesto,* they address the world in which their readers exist *in class.* The pamphlet enters directly the struggle it analyzes and incites. Class is addressed not as a theoretical object for the investigation and contemplation of intellectuals, but as a fundamental organization of the relations in which peoples' lives are caught up. Marx's later analysis of the social forces and relations of capitalism as objective relations begins from actual subjects. It specifies and explores the relational forms in which their presence and activity are obscured. It has the capacity to display the inner relations *driving* the processes of change and the character and direction of change that we live and to display the shifting bases of power. It contributes an explication and analysis of actual relations in which we are active as subjects.

The Marxism of the nineteenth century knew no separation between discourse and class struggle. Marx was not part of an academic establishment. The relations of ruling now so extensively and comprehensively organized were only then appearing. A critique of political economy explored and developed theories that were situated directly in and contributed to one side or the other of an ongoing class struggle. But the discourses of our time are situated quite differently. As they are institutionalized, they are incorporated into relations of ruling containing them within the boundaries coordinating social processes with capital accumulation and articulating them to the division of the labor of ruling. This process has special implications for a sociology, for as we have seen it becomes an alienated mode of knowing society and of social relations expressing the standpoint of the ruling of one class, one gender, and one race, expressing them in the universalized modes of an objectified representation fitted precisely to the objectified and objectifying forms of ruling. Such sociological texts subordinate us to the relevances and themes and methods of knowing of the relations of ruling. In developing a sociology from the standpoint of women, we are also seeking to reconstruct the relations of social consciousness among its participants.

A method of inquiry, however, as a reorganization of the relations of discourse does not stand on its own. It is necessarily articulated to the relations organizing its actual ongoing existence as actual practices. I see the limitations of what we might be able to write when it is unconnected to relations tying its relevance to consciousnesses subjugated by those very relations of ruling within which we work. Those connections have to be such that women can speak to us and through us to others as subjects; those connections have to be such that we who are doing the technical work of research and explication are responsible in what we write to those for whom we write; we have to do our work in such a way that it continually addresses, speaks of, and explicates the world that is known directly and practically outside the text and including the text. Though we might be able to write a method of inquiry and a method of writing texts that will construct a knowledge of society from the standpoint of outsiders to the relations of ruling, we deceive ourselves if we think that the critical moment is complete in finding new methods of writing sociological texts. Methodological strategies, such as those proposed here, do not transform in and of themselves. They make, or should make, texts that will work differently in coordering discursive relations, hence the relations forming political consciousness and organization. But they do not work magic. Such strategies themselves become merely academic if they are contained within the relations of academic discourse, even a feminist discourse. Methods such as those I have put forward must also be anchored in relations connecting them with women who do not participate in the relations of ruling and the discourses that interpenetrate them. The critical force of these methods is contained and "institutionalized" if they are not articulated to relations creating linkages outside and beyond the ruling apparatus, giving voice to women's experience, opening up to women's gaze the forms and relations determining women's lives, and enlarging women's powers and capacities to organize in struggle against the oppression of women.

Notes

1. Dorothy E. Smith, "The social construction of documentary reality," *Sociological Inquiry* 44, no. 4 (1974): 257–68.
2. Simone de Beauvoir, *The Second Sex* (New York: Bantam Books, 1961).
3. It is true, as Barbara Ehrenreich has shown us, that some men at least were already moving away from this dependence, finding that they could exist in this mode without the support of women, a possibility sustained by technological innovations in domesticity and also, I suspect, by the technical changes in birth control that made sex available to men on an as-you-please basis with women they did not have to pay or marry. But the division between genders and their relative sites in the relations of ruling still bear the commitments of their history. Barbara Ehrenreich, *The Hearts of Men: American Dreams and the Flight from Commitment* (Garden City, N.Y.: Doubleday/Anchor Press, 1983).
4. See in particular Michel Foucault, *The Archaeology of Knowledge* (London: Tavistock Publications, 1972).
5. Roxana Ng, "Immigrant women and the state: A study in the social organization of knowledge," Ph.D. dissertation, Department of Education, University of Toronto, 1984 (to be published in 1987 by Garamond Press, Toronto, Canada).
6. Patricia Morgan, "From battered wife to program client: The state's shaping of social problems," *Kapitalistate* 9 (1981): 17–39.
7. See chap. 2 in this volume.
8. Morgan, in "From battered wife to program client," shares this view.
9. Quoted by Teresa de Lauretis (one of the organizers of the conference) in "Feminist studies/critical studies: Issues, terms, and contexts," in T. de Lauretis, ed., *Feminist Studies: Critical Studies* (Bloomington: Indiana University Press, 1986), pp. 1–19.
10. Annette Kolodny, "Dancing through the minefield: Some observations on the theory, practice, and politics of a feminist literary criticism," in Dale Spender, ed., *Man's Studies Modified: The Impact of Feminism on the Academic Disciplines* (Oxford: Pergamon Press, 1981).
11. Foucault, *Archaeology of Knowledge*.

12. Himani Bannerji, 'Apart-hate,' in Himani Bannerji, *doing time: poems* (Toronto: Sister Vision, 1987).

13. The reference here is to a paper by Ximena Bunster, "The military state of torturer," discussed by Pauline Bart in a review of books on violence against women, "Unexceptional violence," *Women's Review of Books* 4, no. 3 (December 1986): 11–13. Bunster's paper appears in Kathleen Barry, Charlotte Bunch, and Shirley Castley, eds., *International Feminism: Networking against Female Sexual Slavery* (New York: International Women's Tribune Center, 1984).

References

Althusser, Louis. "Ideology and ideological state apparatuses." In *Lenin and Philosophy and Other Essays*, pp. 127–86. New York: Monthly Review Press, 1971.

Antrobus, Judith. "In the final analysis" (review of Hannah Lerman, *A Mote in Freud's Eye: From Psychoanalysis to the Psychology of Women* [New York: Springer, 1986]). *Women's Review of Books* 4, no. 5, February 1987.

Aries, Philippe. *Centuries of Childhood*. Harmondsworth, England: Penguin Books, 1975.

Bannerji, Himani. *doing time: poems*. Toronto: Sister Vision, 1987.

Barrett, Michele. *Women's Oppression Today: Problems in Marxist-Feminist Analysis*. London: Virago, 1980.

Bart, Pauline. "Sexism in social science: From the iron cage to the gilded cage—The perils of Pauline." *Journal of Marriage and Family* 33 (November 1971): 734–45.

———. "Unexceptional violence." *The Women's Review of Books* 4, no. 3, December 1986.

Bem, Sandra L., and Daryl J. Bem. "Training the woman to know her place: The power of a nonconscious ideology." In Michele Hoffnung Garskof, *The Roles Women Play*. Belmont, Calif.: Brooks/Cole Publishing, 1971.

Berle, Adolphe, and Gardiner C. Means. *The Modern Corporation and Private Property*. New York: Harcourt, Brace and World, 1968.

Bernard, Jessie. *Academic Women*. New York: New American Library, 1964.

———. "My four revolutions: An autobiographical history of the ASA." In Joan Huber, ed., *Changing Women in a Changing Society*. Chicago: University of Chicago Press, 1973.

———. *The Sex Game*, New York: Atheneum, 1972.

Bernikow, Louise. *The World Split Open: Four Centuries of Women Poets in England and America, 1552–1950*. New York: Vintage Books, 1974.

Berson, Ginny. "Slumming It in the Middle Class." In Charlotte Bunch and Nancy Myron, eds., *Class and Feminism: A Collection of Essays from THE FURIES*, pp. 56–62. Baltimore: Diana Press, 1974.

Beynon, Huw. *Working For Ford*. Harmondsworth, England: Penguin Books, 1973.

Bierstedt, Robert. "Sociology and general education." In Charles H. Page, ed., *Sociology and Contemporary Education*. New York: Random House, 1966.

Bostock, Anya. Talk on the British Broadcasting Corporation Third Programme. Published in *The Listener*, August 1972.

Boston Women's Health Collective. *Our Bodies, Our Selves*. New York: Simon and Schuster, 1973.

Bunster, Ximena. "The military state as torturer." In Kathleen Barry, Charlotte Bunch, and Shirley Castley, eds., *International Feminism: Networking against Female Sexual Slavery*. New York: International Women's Tribune Center, 1984.

Burstyn, Varda, and Dorothy E. Smith. *Women, Class, Family and State*. Toronto: Garamond Press, 1985.

Canadian Teachers' Federation Status of Women. *The Declining Majority*. Ottawa: Canadian Teachers' Federation, 1978.

Carlson, Rae. "Understanding women: Implications for personality theory and research." *Journal of Social Issues* 28, no. 2 (1972): 17–32.

Carter, Sandy. "Class conflict: The human dimension." In Pat Walker, ed., *Between Labor and Capital: The Professional-Managerial Class*, pp. 97–119, Montreal: Black Rose Books, 1978.

Caudill, William. *The Psychiatric Hospital as a Small Society*. Cambridge, Mass.: Harvard University Press, 1958.

Chandler, Alfred D., Jr. *Strategy and Structure: Chapters in the History of American Industrial Enterprise*. New York: Doubleday, 1966.

Chesler, Phyllis. "Patient and patriarch: Women in the psychotherapeutic relationship." In Vivian Gornick and Barbara Moran, eds., *Women in Sexist Society: Studies in Power and Powerlessness*, pp. 362–92. New York: Signet Books, 1972.

———. *Women and Madness*. New York: Doubleday, 1972.

Chicago, Judy. *Through the Flower*. New York, Doubleday, 1975.

Cicourel, Aaron V. *The Social Organization of Juvenile Justice*. New York: John Wiley, 1968.

Coleman, James S., with Ernest Q. Campbell, Carol J. Hobson, James McPartland, Alexander M. Mood, Frederic D. Weinfeld, and Robert L. York. *Equality of Educational Opportunity*. Washington, D.C.: Department of Health, Education and Welfare, 1966.

Coulson, Margaret, Branka Magas, and Hilary Wainwright. "The housewife and her labour under capitalism: A critique." *New Left Review*, no. 89, January–February 1975, pp. 59–71.

Craft, Maurice. "Family, class and education: Changing perspectives." In Maurice Craft, ed., *Family, Class and Education: A Reader*. London: Longman, 1970.

———, ed., *Family, Class and Education: A Reader*. London: Longman, 1970.

Daly, Mary. *Beyond God the Father: Towards a Philosophy of Women's Liberation*. Boston: Beacon Press, 1973.

Daniels, Arlene Kaplan. "Feminist perspectives in sociological research." In Marcia Millman and Rosabeth Kanter, eds., *Another Voice: Feminist Perspectives on Social Life and Social Science*. Garden City, N.Y.: Doubleday, 1975.

David, Sara J. "Becoming a non-sexist therapist." In Dorothy E. Smith and Sara J. David, eds., *Women Look at Psychiatry*. Vancouver, Canada: Press Gang, 1975.

Davis, Angela Y. *Women, Race and Class*. New York: Random House, 1981.

de Beauvoir, Simone. *The Second Sex*. New York: Bantam Books, 1961.

de Lauretis, Teresa. "Feminist studies/critical studies: Issues, terms, and contexts." In de Lauretis, ed., *Feminist Studies: Critical Studies*. Bloomington: Indiana University Press, 1986.

de Montigny, Gerald. "The social organization of social workers' practice: A Marxist analysis." M.A. thesis. Department of Education: University of Toronto, 1980.

des Jacques, Smache. "Women in the French Revolution: The thirteenth brumaire of Olympe de Gouges, with notes on French amazon battalions." In Ann Forfreedom, ed., *Women Out of History: A Herstory*. Culver City, Calif: Peace Press, 1972.

Devault, Marjorie. "Talking and listening from women's standpoint: Feminist strategies for analyzing interview data." Paper prepared for the annual meeting of the Society for the Study of Symbolic Interaction, New York, 1986.

Didion, Joan. *Play It As It Lays.* New York: Bantam Books, 1971.

Dixon, Marlene. "Women's liberation: Opening chapter two." *Canadian Dimension* 10, June 1975.

Donnison, Jean. *Midwives and Medical Men: A History of Inter-professional Rivalries and Women's Rights.* London: Heinemann, 1977.

Ehrenreich, Barbara. *The Hearts of Men: American Dreams and the Flight from Commitment.* Garden City: Doubleday/Anchor, 1983.

Ehrenreich, Barbara, and Deidre English. "Complaints and disorders: The sexual politics of sickness." *Glass Mountain Pamphlet,* No. 2, New York: Feminist Press, 1973.

Eisenstein, Zillah R. "Developing a Theory of Capitalist Patriarchy." In Zillah R. Eisenstein, ed., *Capitalist Patriarchy and the Case for Socialist Feminism,* pp. 5–40, New York: Monthly Review Press, 1979.

Ellman, Mary. *Thinking about Women.* New York: Harcourt Brace Jovanovich, 1968.

Etzioni, Amitai. *The Active Society: A Theory of Societal and Political Process.* New York: Free Press, 1968.

Fidell, L. S. "Empirical verification of sex discrimination in hiring practices in psychology." *American Psychologist* 25, no. 12 (1970): 1094–97.

Flax, Jane. "Political philosophy and the patriarchal unconscious: A psychoanalytic perspective on epistemology and metaphysics." In Sandra Harding and Merrill B. Hintikka, eds., *Discovering Reality: Feminist Perspectives on Epistemology, Metaphysics, Methodology, and Philosophy of Science,* pp. 245–81. Dordrecht, Holland: D. Reidel Publishing Co., 1983.

Fleming, Suzie. "All women are housewives." In *The Activists: a Student Journal of Politics and Opinion* 15, nos 1–2 (1975): 27–33.

Foucault, Michel. *The Archaeology of Knowledge.* London: Tavistock Publications, 1974.

Fox, Margaret. "Women's speaking justified, proved, and allowed by the Scriptures, all such as speak by the Spirit and Power of the Lord Jesus." In *A Brief Collection of Remarkable Passages and Occurrences.* London, J. Sowle: 1710.

Freeman, Jo. "The social construction of the second sex." In Michele Hoffnung Garskof, ed., *The Roles Women Play: Readings towards Women's Liberation,* pp. 123–41. Belmont, Calif.: Brooks/Cole Publishing, 1971.

Freire, Paulo. *Cultural Action for Freedom.* Harmondsworth, England: Penguin Books, 1972.

Friedan, Betty. *The Feminine Mystique.* New York: W. W. Norton, 1963.

Gardiner, Jean. "The role of domestic labour." *New Left Review,* no. 89 (January–February, 1975): 47–59.

Garfinkel, Harold. *Studies in Ethnomethodology.* Englewood Cliffs, N.J.: Prentice-Hall, 1967.

———. 'What is ethnomethodology?' In Roy Turner, ed., *Ethnomethodology.* Harmondsworth, England: Penguin Books, 1974.

Garfinkel, Harold, Michael Lynch, and Edward Livingstone. "The work of a discovering science construed with materials from the optically discovered pulsar." *Philosophy of the Social Sciences* 11 (1981): 131–58.

Garskof, Michele Hoffnung, ed. *The Roles Women Play.* Belmont, Calif.: Brooks/Cole Publishing, 1971.

Gilbert, Celia. *Queen of Darkness.* New York: Viking Press, 1977.

Glaser, Barney, and Anselm L. Strauss. *The Discovery of Grounded Theory: Strategies for Qualitative Research.* Chicago: Aldine Press, 1967.

Goffman, Erving. *The Presentation of Self in Everyday Life.* New York: Doubleday/Anchor, 1959.

Goldberg, Philip. "Are women prejudiced against women?" *Transaction,* April 1969, pp. 28–30.

Gombrich, E. H. *Means and Ends: Reflections on the History of Fresco Painting.* London: Thames and Hudson, 1976.

Greenspan, Miriam. *A New Approach to Women and Therapy: Why Current Therapies Fail Women—And What Women and Therapists Can Do about It!* New York: McGraw-Hill, 1983.

Griffith, Alison I. "Feminist counselling: A perspective." In Dorothy E. Smith and Sara J. David, eds., *Women Look at Psychiatry*. Vancouver, Canada: Press Gang, 1975.

———. "Ideology, education and single parent families: The normative ordering of families through schooling." Ph.D. dissertation. Department of Education: University of Toronto, 1984.

Griffith, Alison I., and Dorothy E. Smith. "Coordinating the uncoordinated: How mothers manage the school day." Paper presented at the meetings of the American Sociological Association, Washington, D.C., August 1985.

———. "Constructing cultural knowledge: mothering as discourse." Paper presented at the Women and Education Conference, University of British Columbia, 1986.

———. "The monitoring-repair sequence: Mother's work for school." Paper presented at the Women and the Invisible Economy Conference, Institut Simone de Beauvoir, Montreal, February 1985.

Harding, Sandra. *The Science Question in Feminism*. Ithaca: Cornell University Press, 1986.

———. "Why has the sex/gender system become visible only now?" In Sandra Harding and Merrill Hintikka, eds., *Discovering Reality: Feminist Perspectives on Epistemology, Metaphysics, Methodology, and Philosophy of Science*, pp. 311–24. Dordrecht, Holland: D. Reidel Publishing, 1983.

Harré, Rom, and Paul F. Second. *The Explanation of Social Behavior*. Oxford: Basil Blackwell, 1972.

Hartsock, Nancy. "The feminist standpoint: Developing the ground for a specifically feminist historical materialism." In Sandra Harding and Merrill B. Hintikka, eds., *Discovering Reality: Feminist Perspectives on Epistemology, Metaphysics, Methodology, and Philosophy of Science*, pp. 283–310. Dordrecht, Holland: D. Reidel Publishing Co., 1983.

Heap, James. "Discourse in the production of classroom knowledge: Reading lessons." *Curriculum Inquiry* 15, no. 3 (1985): 245–79.

———. "What counts as reading: Limits to certainty in assessment." *Curriculum Inquiry* 10, no. 3 (1980): 265–92.

Hegel, Georg Wilhelm Friedrich. *The Phenomenology of Mind*. Trans. A. V. Miller. Oxford: Oxford University Press, 1977.

Hochschild, Arlie Russell. "The sociology of feeling and emotion: Selected possibilities." In Marcia Millman and Rosabeth Moss Kanter, eds., *Another Voice: Feminist Perspectives on Social Life*. Garden City, N.Y.: Doubleday, 1975.

Jackson, Nancy S. "Describing news: Towards an alternative account." M.A. thesis, Department of Anthropology and Sociology, University of British Columbia, July 1977.

———. "Stress on schools + stress on families = distress for children." Canadian Teachers' Federation, Ottawa, 1982.

Jaggar, Alison. *Feminist Politics and Human Nature*. Totowa, N.J.: Rowman and Allanheld; and Brighton, England: The Harvester Press, 1983.

Jardine, Alice A. *Gynesis: Configurations of Woman and Modernity*. Ithaca: Cornell University Press, 1985.

Jencks, Christopher, with Marshall Smith, Henry Acland, Mary Jo Bane, David Cohen, Herbert Gintis, Barbara Heyns, and Stephan Michelson. *Inequality: A Reassessment of the Effect of Family and Schooling in America*. New York: Basic Books, 1972.

Juhasz, Suzanne. *Naked and Fiery Forms: Modern American Poetry by Women, A New Tradition*. New York: Harper Colophon, 1976.

Kahn, J., and J. Nurstein. *Unwillingly to School*, pp. 13–15. London: Pergamon Press, 1964.

Kanter, Rosabeth Moss. *Men and Women of the Corporation*. New York: Basic Books, 1977.

Kimball, Meredith. "Women, sex role stereotypes, and mental health: Catch 22." In Dorothy E. Smith and Sara David, eds., *Women Look at Psychiatry*, Vancouver, Canada: Press Gang, 1975.

King, Elinor. "How the psychiatric profession views women." In Dorothy E. Smith and Sara David, eds., *Women Look at Psychiatry*. Vancouver, Canada: Press Gang, 1975.

Kolodny, Annette. "Dancing through the minefield: Some observations on the theory, practice, and politics of a feminist literary criticism." In Dale Spender, ed., *Man's Studies Modified: The Impact of Feminism on the Academic Disciplines*. Oxford: Pergamon Press, 1981.

Komisar, Lucy. "The image of women in advertising." In Vivian Gornick and Barbara Moran, eds., *Women in Sexist Society: Studies in Power and Powerlessness*, pp. 304–17. New York: Signet Books, 1972.

Kosik, Karel. *Dialectics of the Concrete: A Study of Problems of Man and World*. Boston Studies in the Philosophy of Science, 52. Dordrecht, Holland: D. Reidel Publishing, 1976.

Laing, R. D. *The Divided Self: A Study of Sanity and Madness*. Chicago: Quadrangle Books, 1960.

Lefebvre, Henri. *Everyday Life in the Modern World*. London: Allen Lane, 1971.

Lerner, Gerda. "New approaches to the study of women in American history." In Bernice A. Carroll, ed., *Liberating Women's History*. Urbana: University of Illinois Press, 1976.

———. "Placing women in history." In Bernice A. Carroll, ed., *Liberating Women's History*. Urbana: University of Illinois Press, 1976.

Lessing, Doris. "The old chief Mshu Langa." In *The Black Madonna*. St. Albans, England: Granada Publishing, 1966.

Liebow, Elliot. *Tally's Corner: A Study of Negro Streetcorner Men*. Boston: Little, Brown, 1976.

Lippard, Lucy R. *From the Center: Feminist Essays on Women's Art*. New York: E. P. Dutton, 1973.

McCormack, Thelma. "Towards a non-sexist perspective on social and political change." In Marcia Millman and Rosabeth Moss Kanter, eds., *Feminist Perspectives on Social Life and Social Sciences*. Garden City, N.Y.: Doubleday/Anchor, 1975.

MacDonald, Madeleine. "Schooling and the reproduction of class and gender relations." In Roger Dale, Geoff Esland, Ross Fergusson, and Madeleine MacDonald, eds., *Education and the State, vol. 2, Politics, Patriarchy and Practice*, pp. 167–77. Basingstoke, England: Falmer Press, 1981.

MacDonald, Rita, and Dorothy E. Smith. "A feminist therapy session." In Dorothy E. Smith and Sara J. David, eds., *Women Look at Psychiatry*. Vancouver, Canada: Press Gang, 1975.

McRobbie, Angela. "The politics of feminist research: Between talk, text and action." *Feminist Review*, no. 12 (1982): 46–57.

Manicom, Ann. "The reproduction of class: The relations between two work processes." Paper presented at the Symposium on the Political Economy of Gender in Education, Ontario Institute for Studies in Education, 1981.

Mannheim, Karl. *Ideology and Utopia*. New York: Doubleday/Anchor, 1965.

Martin, Jane Roland. *Reclaiming a Conversation: The Ideal of the Educated Woman*. New Haven: Yale University Press, 1985.

Marx, Karl. *Capital: A Critical Analysis of Capitalistic Production*. Vol. 1. Moscow: Foreign Languages Publishing House, 1954.

———. *Capital: A Theory of Political Economy* Vol. I, New York: Vintage Books, 1977.

———. *Grundrisse: Foundations of the Critique of Political Economy*. New York: Random House, 1976.

Marx, Karl, and Frederick Engels. *Feuerbach: Opposition of the Materialist and Idealist Outlooks*. The first part of *The German Ideology*, published in accordance with the text and arrangement of the original manuscript. London: Lawrence & Wishart, 1973.

———. *The German Ideology, Part I*. New York: International Publishers, 1970.

Meissner, Martin, with Elizabeth W. Humphreys, Scott M. Meis, and William J. Scheu. "No exit for wives: Sexual division of labor and the cumulation of household demands." *Canadian Review of Sociology and Anthropology* 12 (1975).

Millett, Kate. *Sexual Politics*. New York: Avon, 1971.

Millman, Marcia, and Rosabeth Moss Kanter, eds. *Feminist Perspectives on Social Life and Social Sciences*. Garden City, N.Y.: Doubleday/Anchor, 1975.

Mitchell, Juliet. *Woman's Estate*. Harmondsworth, England: Penguin Books, 1972.

Mitchell, Juliet, and Ann Oakley, eds. *The Rights and Wrongs of Women*. Harmondsworth, England: Penguin Books, 1976.

Moi, Toril. *Sexual/Textual Politics: Feminist Literary Theory*. London and New York: Methuen, 1985.

Morgan, Patricia. "From battered wife to program client: The state's shaping of social problems." *Kapitalistate* 9 (1981): 17–39.

Ng, Roxana. "Immigrant women and the state: A study in the social organization of knowledge." Ph.D. dissertation. Department of Education, University of Toronto, 1984. To be published in 1987 by Garamond Press, Toronto, Canada.

Noble, Joey. "Developing the child." Typescript. Department of Sociology, University of Toronto, 1982.

Oakley, Ann. *Sociology of Housework*. London: Martin Robertson, 1974.

———. "Wise woman and medicine man: Changes in the management of childbirth." In Juliet Mitchell and Ann Oakley, eds., *The Rights and Wrongs of Women*. Harmondsworth, England: Penguin Books, 1976.

Oates, Joyce Carol. *Them*. New York: Fawcett Publications, 1970.

Olsen, Tillie. "One out of twelve: Women who are writers in our century." In Tillie Olsen, *Silences*, pp. 22–46. New York: Delacorte Press/Seymour Lawrence, 1978.

Osen, Lynn M. *Women in Mathematics*. Cambridge, Mass.: MIT Press, 1974.

Parsons, Talcott. *The Structure of Social Action*. Vol. 1, New York: Free Press, 1968.

Power of Women Collective. "This is housework." *Power of Women* 1, no. 3 (January 1975): 7–10.

Rich, Adrienne. *Poems: Selected and New, 1950–1974*. New York: W. W. Norton, 1975.

Richardson, Dorothy. *Pilgrimage*. London: Virago, 1979.

Rist, Ray C. *The Urban School: A Factory of Failure*. Cambridge, Mass.: MIT Press, 1973.

Roberts, Helen, ed. *Doing Feminist Research*. London: Routledge and Kegan Paul, 1981.

Rowbotham, Sheila. *Women, Resistance and Revolution*. Harmondsworth, England: Penguin Books, 1973.

———. *Women's Consciousness, Man's World*. Harmondsworth, England: Penguin Books, 1973.

Ruether, Rosemary R. *Religion and Sexism: Images of Women in the Jewish and Christian Traditions*. New York: Harper & Row, 1974.

Russell, Elizabeth. Letter. In *Kinesis* 5, February 1977.

Ryan, Alan. *The Philosophy of the Social Sciences*. Oxford: Oxford University Press, 1970.

Said, Edward W. *Orientalism*. New York: Vintage Books, 1979.

Schechter, Susan. *Women and Male Violence: The Visions and Struggles of the Battered Women's Movement*. Boston: South End Press, 1982.

Scheff, Thomas J. *Being Mentally Ill: A Sociological Theory*. Chicago: Aldine Press, 1962.

Schegloff, Emmanuel, and Harvey Sacks. "Opening-up closings." In Roy Turner, ed., *Ethnomethodology*, pp. 197–215. Harmondsworth, England: Penguin, 1974.

Schutz, Alfred. "Commonsense and scientific interpetations of human action." In *Collected Papers*, 1:3–47. The Hague: Martinus Nijhoff, 1962.

———. "On multiple realities." In *Collected Papers*, vol. 1. The Hague: Martinus Nijhoff, 1962.

———. *Reflections on the Problem of Relevance*. Ed. Richard Zaner. New Haven: Yale University Press, 1970.

Seccombe, Wally. "The housewife and her labour under capitalism." *New Left Review*, no. 83, January–February 1974.

Seidenberg, Robert. *Corporate Wives, Corporate Casualties*. Garden City, N.Y., Doubleday/Anchor, 1975.

Sherif, Carolyn Woods. "Bias in psychology." In Julia A. Sherman and Evelyn Torton Beck, eds., *The Prism of Sex: Essays in the Sociology of Knowledge*, pp. 93–133. Madison: University of Wisconsin Press, 1979.

Sloan, Albert. *My Years with General Motors*. New York: Doubleday, 1964.

Smith, Dorothy E. "The ideological practice of sociology." *Catalyst* 8 (1974): 39–54.

———. "The intersubjective structuring of time." *Analytic Sociology* 1, no. 2 (1977).

————. "No one commits suicide: Textual analyses of ideological practices." *Human Studies* 6 (1983): 309–59.

————. "On sociological description: A method from Marx." *Human Studies* 4 (1981): 313–37.

————. "The social construction of documentary reality." *Social Inquiry* 44, no. 4 (1974): 257–68.

————. "Some implications for a sociology for women." In Nona Glazer and Helen Y. Waehrer, eds., *Woman in a Man-made World*, pp. 15–39. Chicago: Rand McNally, 1976.

————. "The statistics on mental illness: What they will not tell us about women and why." In Dorothy E. Smith and Sarah J. David, eds., *Women Look at Psychiatry*. Vancouver, Canada: Press Gang, 1975.

————. "Textually mediated social organization." *International Social Science Journal* 36, no. 1 (1984): 59–75.

————. "Women and psychiatry." In Dorothy E. Smith and Sara J. David, eds., *Women Look at Psychiatry*," pp. 1–19. Vancouver, Canada: Press Gang, 1975.

Smith, Dorothy E., Jane Haddad, and Yoko Ueda. "Teaching as an internally segregated profession: Women and men teachers in the public schools of Ontario." Typescript, Department of Sociology in Education, Ontario Institute for Studies in Education, Toronto, Canada, 1986.

Stanley, Liz, and Sue Wise. *Breaking Out: Feminist Consciousness and Feminist Research.* London: Routledge and Kegan Paul, 1983.

Statistics Canada. *Educational Staff of Community Colleges and Vocational Schools.* Cat. 81–241, Ottawa: Minister of Supply and Services, September 1985.

————. *Educational Staff of Public Schools.* Cat. 81–202, Ottawa: Minister of Supply and Services, February 1982.

————. *Teachers in Universities 1983–84.* Cat. 81–254, Ottawa: Minister of Supply and Services, January 1986.

Strodtbeck, F. I., and R. D. Mann. "Sex role differentiation in jury deliberations." *Sociometry* 19 (March 1956) 3–11.

Szasz, Thomas, ed. *The Age of Madness: The History of Involuntary Hospitalization Presented in Selected Texts.* Garden City, N.Y.: Doubleday/Anchor, 1973.

Thrupp, Sylvia L. *The Merchant Class of Mediaeval London 1300–1500.* Ann Arbor: University of Michigan Press, 1962.

Tonnies, Ferdinand. *Community and Association.* London: Routledge and Kegan Paul, 1955.

Turner, Roy. "Introduction." In R. Turner, ed., *Ethnomethodology.* Harmondsworth, England: Penguin, 1974.

Vickers, Jill McCalla, and June Adam. *But Can You Type? Canadian Universities and the Status of Women.* Toronto: Clarke Irwin/Canadian Association of University Teachers, 1977.

Vonnegut, Kurt. *Slaughterhouse Five, or The Children's Crusade: A Duty-Dance with Death.* New York: Delacorte Press, 1969.

Walsh, Mary Roth. *Doctors Wanted, No Women Need Apply: Sexual Barriers in the Medical Profession, 1835–1975.* New Haven: Yale University Press, 1977.

Weber, Max. *Economy and Society.* Eds. Guenther Roth and Claus Wittich. New York: Bedminster Press, 1968.

Weisstein, Naomi. "Psychology constructs the female, or the fantasy life of the male psychologist." In Michele Hoffnung Garskof, ed., *The Roles Women Play.* Belmont, Calif.: Brooks/Cole Publishing, 1971.

West, Candace. "Sexism and conversation: Everything you always wanted to know about Sachs (but were afraid to ask)." M.A. thesis. Department of Sociology, University of California, Santa Barbara, Calif.

Wieder, D. L. *Language and Social Reality: The Case of Telling the Convict Code.* The Hague: Mouton, 1974.

Winant, Terry. "The feminist standpoint: A matter of language." In *Hypatia: A journal of feminist philosophy* 2, no. 1 (Winter 1987): 123–48.

Wittgenstein, Ludwig. *Philosophical Investigations.* New York: Macmillan, 1953.

Wollstonecraft, Mary. *A Vindication of the Rights of Women.* New York: W. W. Norton, 1967.

Wolpe, AnnMarie. "Education and the sexual division of labour." In Annette Kuhn and AnnMarie Wolpe, eds., *Feminism and Materialism.* London: Routledge and Kegan Paul, 1978.

Women's Bureau. *Women in the Labour Force: Facts and Figures, 1973.* Ottawa: Labour Canada, 1974.

Wright, Eric Olin. *Class, Crisis and the State.* London: Verso, 1974.

Zimmerman, Don H., and Melvin Pollner. "The everyday world as phenomenon." In Jack Douglas, ed., *Understanding Everyday Life: Towards the Reconstruction of Sociological Knowledge.* London: Routledge and Kegan Paul, 1971.

Index